Upon a Clay Tablet
The Definitive Guide to Healing with Homeostatic Clay
Volume I

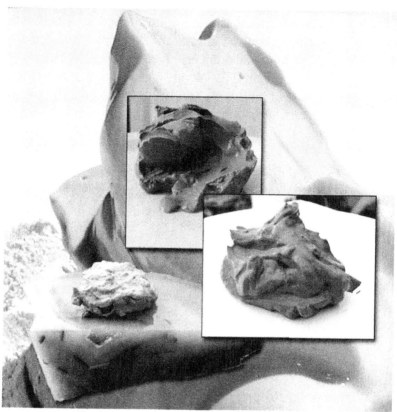

Hydrated Therapeutic Healing Clays
(**courtesy of** www.greenclays.com)

Upon a pale horse death rode to reclaim what had been spun
And upon a clay tablet life rose to birth what had begun.

And who could say for truth or dare?
What held and drove the beating hoofs of the mare?
And who could say in honest words?
What light has shown through clay's crystal orchards?

Who but God himself and mystics born?
But God speaks not and mystics simply sit and churn...
Which only leaves the clay tablet upon which life rose
Beneath the pale horse death rode.

This book presents information based upon the research and personal experiences of the author and contributors. It is not intended to be a substitute for professional healthcare. Neither the publisher nor the author can be held responsible for any adverse effects or consequences resulting from the use of any of the information provided by this book. They also cannot be held responsible for any errors or omissions in the book.

ISBN 978-0-615-32937-6

This book has been printed in the United States, and has been published by

AV Websites Marketing Group, LLC.
9504 Chanticleer Court
Las Vegas, NV 89129
Contact: Jason@eytonsearth.org

Copyright 2009 by Jason R. Eaton

All rights reserved. No part of this book may be reproduced in any form or by any means without the prior written consent of the author, except brief quotes used in reviews.

Ancient clay tablet cover picture © JeanLee - Fotolia.com
Cover Art and Photography done by Jason R. Eaton – Eytonsearth.org

First Trade Printing, November, 2009

Second Trade Printing, February 2010

For those who seek answers
by asking better questions

For those who seek solace
holding fast to and in the center of life's storms

For those who seek a more natural way
A truer, both older and newer way

For those who seek the greater power
of water, earth and sunshine

For those who wish to begin to leave
disease far behind

May this work lead you
One step closer
To the place you most need to go…

TABLE OF CONTENTS

A PERSONAL INTRODUCTION — - 1 -

BOOK I PART A: CLAY THERAPY STORIES — - 4 -

Introduction — - 4 -
- The Faith of Annie May — - 7 -
  - Author's Note — - 25 -
- Peggy Sue Knew — - 26 -
  - Author's Note — - 34 -
- No Shade between Heaven and Hell — - 36 -
- The Singing Chef and the Sorrowed Finger — - 53 -
- The Tribe of the Sacred Clays — - 60 -
  - Author's Note — - 76 -
- Never Look Back — - 78 -
- Sally's Shattered Brow — - 84 -

BOOK 1 PART B: CORRESPONDENCES — - 89 -

- Introduction — - 90 -
- Far Infrared TDP Mineral Lamps, Qi Gong, and Clay — - 96 -
- Not all Water is Created Equal — - 101 -
- Clay Baths Cause Severe Reaction — - 115 -
- Mysterious Splinters in Austin Texas — - 119 -
- Clay Facial Masque: Itching Skin — - 120 -
- Aluminum Content in Clay — - 122 -
- People Splashing Around in Clay Baths — - 125 -
- Dog Drinks Clay for Skin Cancer — - 130 -
- Clay for Skin Use: Strange Reaction — - 131 -
- Jungle Rot, Clay Induced Illness & Experimentation — - 134 -
- Hydrating Clay with the Right Water — - 136 -

BOOK II PART A: CLAY THERAPEUTICS — - 141 -

Introduction — - 142 -

Cano Graham, the Crystal Cross and the Clay Disciples — - 144 -
- The Crystal Cross — - 144 -
- End Game — - 164 -

Ray Pendergraft, the Big Horn Mountains & Pascalite — - 167 -
- Introduction — - 167 -
- Life Mud — - 170 -

Table of Contents

Pascalite	- 172 -
Neal Bosshardt & Utah's Redmond Clay	**- 176 -**
External Use of Redmond Clay	- 179 -
Ankle Infection Healed	- 179 -
A Very Painful Torch Burn	- 180 -
Road Rash from a Bike Crash	- 181 -
Internal Use of Redmond Clay	- 181 -
Internal Use of Redmond Clay	- 182 -
Terramin: California Desert Earth Red Clay	**- 184 -**
Introduction	- 184 -
Neva Jensen, NASA and "The Source"	- 186 -
The Source	- 186 -
Neva Jensen: Hydro-thermally Produced Living Clay	- 188 -
NASA and Terramin	- 191 -
Author's Note	- 193 -
From India with Love: Gandhi, Anjou & Pascal	**- 195 -**
Introduction	- 195 -
Clay Cures, Nature's Miracle for a New Age	- 197 -
Mahatma Gandhi: Nature Curist	- 199 -
The Accounting of Anjou Musafir	- 201 -
The Accounting of Pascal Chazot	- 205 -
Pascal's Clays	- 207 -
Pascal's Clay Therapy	- 208 -
The Treatment for Asthma	- 209 -
The Treatment for Cancer	- 209 -
The Treatment for a Coma	- 209 -
The Treatment for a Common Cold	- 210 -
The Treatment for Diabetes	- 210 -
The Treatment for Poor Eyesight	- 210 -
Author's Note	- 210 -
Raymond Dextreit: Naturopathic Earth Cures	**- 211 -**
Author's Note	- 211 -
Raymond Dextreit, Earth Therapist	- 213 -
Raymond Dextreit on Using Clay Internally	- 218 -
Raymond Dextreit on Using Clay Externally	- 220 -
Other Clay Therapeutic Adepts Independent Researchers and Clay Practitioners	**- 225 -**
Line de Courssou & Thierry Brunet	- 225 -
Victor Earl Irons & Sodium Bentonite	- 229 -
G. Michael King and the Sacred Clays of Oregon	- 231 -
Siberian Healing Clays	- 233 -

Table of Contents

RESOURCES — - 235 -

Purchasing Therapeutic Clay — - 235 -

For Further Research — - 238 -

For Further Reading Sources and Recommendations — - 238 -

CREDITS AND ACKNOWLEDGMENTS — - 240 -

BOOK II PART B: SCIENCE AND RESEARCH — - 242 -

Introduction — - 243 -
On Which Clays to Use — - 244 -

Oligodynamic Silver & Smectite Time Kill Study — - 246 -

Hydrated Bentonite Studies: Dr. Howard E. Lind — - 252 -
- EXPERIMENT I — - 252 -
- RESULTS — - 253 -
- EXPERIMENT II — - 254 -
- RESULTS — - 254 -
- EXPERIMENT III — - 256 -
- RESULTS — - 257 -
- COMMENTS — - 258 -

Pascalite Article — - 260 -

REDMOND CLAY: A HIGH AFFINITY SORBENT OF AFLATOXIN B, AND CHOLERA TOXIN — - 268 -
- LIST OF TABLES — - 269 -
- ABSTRACT — - 270 -
- INTRODUCTION — - 271 -
- Affinity of Redmond Clay — - 277 -
  - MATERIALS AND METHODS — - 277 -
  - RESULTS — - 279 -
  - DISCUSSION — - 280 -
  - CONCLUSION — - 281 -
  - APPENDIX A — - 284 -
  - APPENDIX B — - 285 -
  - PATHOpHYSIOLOGY OF DIARRHEA — - 288 -
  - SECRETORY DIARRHEA — - 289 -
  - APPENDIX C — - 290 -
  - BIOCHEMICAL ASSAY OF SODIUM BENTONITE — - 291 -
  - BIBLIOGRPAHY — - 296 -

Table of Contents

Terramin NASA Study by Dr. Benjamin Ershoff, Ph.D. — 301 —
    FOREWARD — 302 —
    Introduction — 302 —
    Experimental: Procedure and results — 304 —
    Discussion — 328 —
    Summary — 330 —
    REFERENCES — 331 —

AFTERWARD — 335 —

Introduction to Volume I

A Personal Introduction

I have come to believe that if any individual has an *honest* desire, that they will henceforth attract an *open-minded* unity (relationship) for the *willing* expression of that desire. And what will the result of that attraction be? Ultimately, it will be the ability to *express* that desire *freely* in this moment (*the now*) with a profound *love* (sacred appreciation) of, with, and for *life*, emanating from a place of profound *serenity*.

The first caveat is that this honest desire must exist within what some of us call the realm or sphere of potentiality. Thus, I distinguish between a healthy and wonderful *fantasy* which fulfills imagination and subconscious stress release (I am going to visit the nearest star system in this lifetime!), and a *desire* which is a nature (or God) given impulse to fulfill a destiny in harmony with the highest good of the individual, and the world which the individual was born into (I am going to develop the nuclear star drive that will power the first generation of star-faring space craft).

The second caveat is that this involves an actual *process* that is usually quite painful at times. Growing is difficult. Change is hard. The ability to let go is truly a *gift* of the spirit.

The third and final caveat is that the individual must first learn about real individual values, real principles and real goals. You can't buy that in a store, and you can't learn that by reading any book. Reflecting on life experience is the best teacher, in this case: Achieving a depth perception on the value of living one's life.

I have been successful at achieving most of the personal goals in my life thus far… but never right away. My success is completely due to the fact that I have failed so often, and that I have learned to love what failing has had to teach me. I suppose that makes me both a dismal failure and a success story.

This four book project has been the most difficult thing I've ever attempted. There is so much that I feel that individuals *need* to see and experience, for their individual empowerment and for the *grace* that can be embraced through living within and for a reality with cherished value. And honestly? I'm not qualified to do it.

That has been my excuse for a long time when people asked me "So Jason, we want to see a book about clay, when are you going to write it?" Well, I'm going to write it when I am finally qualified to write the book; when I've done the scientific studies, when I've unraveled all of the mysteries, when I've talked in depth with everyone who knows about clay; about science; about healing; about truth; about writing; about books… about life.

I finally figured out that I would be ready to write the book about ten seconds after I took my last breath. That would be about two years and ten seconds too late, give or take a year.

Right, then: Ok. My English degree from Oxford University will just have to wait a few decades.

The title of this work wrote itself. It absolutely *had* to be called *"Upon a Clay Tablet"*. Not only does the title symbolize the ancient origin of clay therapy, but it is indicative *of the origin of life itself.* Yes, the author believes that *life itself evolved from early contact with clay*. The very cell walls that make up all complex organisms were very likely patterned after hydrated clay molecules; it is as if clay itself was responsible for engineering the complex cell that is the basis for all organic life as we currently understand it. Nobel prize winning scientist Graham Cairns-Smith was the first formally trained scientist to hypothesize and explore clay's role in the evolution of biological life, but noted personalities down through ages, including the famous seer Nostradamus, were clearly aware of the importance of special clays.

In Volume One, book 1 Part A, I attempt to whet your appetite for clay with some very profound stories. If the stories do not absolutely ring with the purest kind of truth, than I have failed at my duty.

In Volume One, book 1 Part B, I attempt to give you insight into both processes and engagements… real people communicating with each other sharing common values, interests, and goals. If you do not hunger for community or at least marvel at the ability to question and explore potential, than I have failed at my duty.

In book two, I attempt to overwhelm you with very amazing people who all have a near-religious belief in clay therapy, who all come from different walks of life to present to you personal and collective experience about the marvels of therapeutic clays. Book two is comprised of a mob of clay disciples that will lynch you if you don't learn to use clay for your health. It is also a book that is designed to keep this author honest. Meticulous detail was shown to the masters of the craft, prior to my publishing my own rendition in books three and four.

Books three and four are currently in process. The last two books are very ambitious dissertations combined with a natural medicine handbook, coupled with a scientific treatise on the therapeutic clay sciences. In book three, I attempt to combine traditional (real) medicine with metaphysics and complementary medicine in an actual handbook for study with a focus on alternative therapies.

I made the decision to try to help connect the unseen world with the seen world (the mind with the body) because doing so can add so much value to an individual's experience with healing and natural medicine. Ultimately, I have been unsuccessful at eliminating metaphysical thought from clay therapy. I personally find developing a depth perception into any subject matter to be deeply rewarding.

There is still much work to be done in the field of pelotherapy and natural medicine. We, as a civilization, have lost so much of the ancient wisdom that once guided our human race. Yet we have also come so far in understanding the world which we all have inherited. I believe that both worlds, the ancient world and the modern world, can be perfectly balanced and achieve a state of equilibrium to the benefit of all mankind, and for all life on our tiny little globe we call Earth.

The secret, I've always believed, lies in the individual and that individual's relationship with the self, with society, and with the greater purposes that each individual was born to discover and explore in this lifetime. The key to unlocking that secret involves setting the individual free from the slavery of selfishness... both selfishness of self and the selfishness of a world that often appears to have gone clinically insane.

Healing clay therapy, along with a metaphysical, holistic approach to life, has the ability to bring back the mystery, awe, and the beauty of nature. Becoming one with the processes of natural health can empower individuals on a very profound level.

Studying clay therapy and natural medicine is one way that individuals can gain back the personal power that we as people so often wrongly give to others. In a modern world that is so lacking in intimate caring, so devoid of profoundly sensitive moments, so neglectful of true spiritual community, clay therapy and natural medicine can help bring people back together in a caring and authentic community.

I give all of this knowledge, experience, and information freely to you. It now belongs to you, and it is your job to take care of it!

The time for real, effective, nurturing and natural medicine has come.

Book I Part A: Clay Therapy Stories

Introduction

Everyone likes a great story. Storytelling is one of the most important art forms in human history. Society itself, one might argue, at one time was held together, inspired, and shown a true value only by virtue of story telling.

As an art form, storytelling has largely fallen by the wayside in this new world, swept aside by less inspiring social networking customs fueled by the ever starving digital information age. Gone are the campfire gatherings, where the elders sat and spun yarns to a captive audience held in place by the moonlight, where mothers and fathers, grandparents and siblings joined together to bridge the gap between generations. Gone are the fireside chats that passed jewels of wisdom down from one weary throat to the eager ears that were captivated by the voice just as much as the tale woven ever so boldly.

Storytelling as a necessary teaching and survival strategy for a civilized world has been lost; lost in a way that almost reminds me of how clay therapy itself was once lost to the modern world. Not lost out of disinterest, but because a more powerful, intoxicating and addictive poison was introduced into the world.

Out of the eons that preceded the technological age, modern civilization rose in frenzy, and demolished anything not made in its own image. The collective superego of humanity quickly began to cause a starvation which only it fed, but fed without any real nutrition.

We live in this time, a time when it is the fools who become kings; in a place where the comfort of nature has been lost. It is a time when artists have been enslaved by marketing demigods who live to sell illusions. This is a time when the wise speak only to mirrors; a place where nobody wants to learn about truer things, only newer things. It is the time when mankind is demonstrating just how childish mankind really is; and it is a place where nobody of importance is paying much attention.

This modern age of man could not have been stopped. Our growing pains could not and cannot be side-stepped. However, as we progress through these next thousand years, we will no doubt begin to learn how much we have truly lost through the process of our own growing up.

Introduction to Book I Part A

I can speak of such things, as I am a product of this modern age. I was born into it. I worshipped the information technology age as if it were the only god that mattered. Even so, from within my deep loneliness I scoffed at the perpetually rising steel-born and concrete laden cities, and often saw the world of humanity as being all too plastic. I knew I was steel-born and sealed in plastic. I never had a doubt, not from early youth, that I was born into a prison with very illusive walls. Even while I lived my heritage, I searched for and through the smoke and mirrors, to find and then find a way to penetrate the walls that held me captive.

There was one big, important difference stemming from my youth, largely due to the wisdom of my own mother and father. I had an edge that gave me something valuable.

I had stories. I had stories AND they gave me a deep strength and sense of direction that I didn't know other people DIDN'T have. Pure creativity, I knew, could be equal to any perceived notion of reality. My mind remained fluid. My computer might have been powered by the mighty Pentium, but I was powered, deep within my heart, by the stories I read that were much, much truer than the plastic, steel, and concrete world I was inheriting.

I had Ben Bova. Arthur C. Clark. Orson Wells. Roger Zelazny. Glen Cook. Robert Anton Wilson. Stephen R. Donaldson. James Blish. Diane Duane. John Meyers Meyers. Isaac Asimov. David Gerrold. Marion Zimmer Bradley, Vonda McIntyre, Ann McCaffrey, Ursula K. Le Guin and Tannith Lee. And that is just to name a very, very few of the minds and hearts that filled my imagination as a child. They passed their secrets on to me. They held me up. They gave me a center of self. They allowed me to explore my own heart and mind, discover my own creativity and imagination, and something else important: both a true sense of autonomy from the men and women of this world and a true sense of unity with all of humanity. That has been a most precious gift.

This section, powered by stories, has been modeled after two of my greatest story telling, modern literary heroes: Richard Bach (author of Illusions) and Orson Scott Card (author of Ender's Game).

I would never claim to aspire to their storytelling greatness. My desire is to impart each story's true essence and record the details in a pleasing manner. Having achieved this, I will be most satisfied.

Why Orson Scott Card, one might ask? I desire to emulate Orson Scott Card's ability to characterize, and aspire to duplicate his gift of being able to present, and sometimes solve, strange and interesting moral juxtapositions.

And what about Richard Bach? Let's just say I plan to borrow his creative license to power many of these stories. Richard Bach has always had a genius ability to do whatever it takes to present a story in its deserved light: The rules be damned.

I've decided to include this as book one, because I feel that bringing clay therapy to life by chronicling exactly how people have discovered, used, and learned to love clay is more important than the technical aspects of clay. Healing is first and foremost about people. And it is the amazing people that I personally have met that have led me through my own clay "discipleism".

I know that stories, by their very nature, are often more powerful than even the most excellently executed scientific studies. Science is all too often devoid of soul.

It is my hope that by reading and experiencing the following stories, you too will see how my own passion for clay therapy was birthed and why it has become a lifelong dedication. And, just perchance, you might discover that there is a clay disciple hidden and ready to emerge deep within you.

The stories that follow are true. However, they have been fictionalized. Sometimes the names and places have remained the same, sometimes they've been changed. The people are real, although I've taken some great liberties at characterization to try to add a depth perception that I could not possibly possess. However, I would like to make it very clear that the healing stories themselves are absolutely true, and there have been no exaggerations on how clay was used, what the people experienced, and their ultimate reactions.

My promise to the reader is that I shall maintain the accuracy and the integrity of the experiences themselves.

But the story? That, my friends, is mine to tell!

Now then, onward. Let's get started, and take a look at the amazing Faith of Annie May.

The Faith of Annie May

Annie had to lie down. Her leg was hurting very bad. It was swollen. The skin looked like it was going to split open. Sometimes, she couldn't feel anything in her foot. Her left leg was nearly twice the size as her right leg. She could not sleep at night very well, as the pain just gnawed at her. She felt so very sick and alone. So she started to sing:

> "Singing songs in the courtyard
> Rain: Go away!
> Away! To the east or the west, just away!
> This day is for the sweet child's play."

This day is for the sweet child's play... today, Annie sang to herself in her mind. Or had I just been singing out loud? Annie thought to herself.

"I was singing out loud," she whispered. Annie glanced at the window but could not see if it was still raining out. It was dark outside, and the single candle that lit the room did not even allow her to see down the hallway. In fact, as she glanced at the shadows dancing menacingly on the wall, she curled herself up, lying on her side, bending around the candle as if it could protect her; as if it could even lend her a smidgen of warmth.

"One day you will ask me which is more important? My life or yours? I will say mine and you will walk away not knowing that you are my life," Annie said, in a louder voice, not so that anyone else could hear, but so that she herself would *listen*. She spoke the words of Khalil Gibran as if the passage were a Christian prayer. And to Annie, it most certainly was. She repeated the words over and over again until she believed them, felt them, until they exploded through her chest.

"I am God's child." Annie was back to whispering again. "I am not alone. The sun shines in my heart, and the sun is the light of God." She felt better.

These days, Annie had to talk to herself a lot. She would feel darkness creep into her mind, or dread creep into her chest; a heavy, cold darkness. When that happened, the light within her would dim. And when that happened, Annie felt like she *could* go crazy. The light was the only thing she had, and she absolutely could not lose that.

The dark of the room scared her. "I'm so scared," Annie whispered. Then she laughed nervously, realizing that no one in the neighboring houses could actually hear her. Nobody would likely even bat an eye if she screamed at the top of her lungs. *That's just the kind of world it was, these days,* Annie thought. *Maybe when someone else screams, people think that it is themselves doing the screaming. Maybe they think that they are screaming, but only in their head. Maybe everyone is just walking around screaming all the time.*

Still, it was obvious to Annie that she felt guilty. This was her mother's and her sister's house; she didn't belong here, even though they were long gone. *Long gone from the house, long gone from Las Vegas, long gone and good riddance from Annie's life,* she thought. Gone, yes, but not by Annie's choice.

Her sisters had long since convinced her step-mother that Annie was probably deranged and crazy. Never you mind that it was only Annie's poor mother who had a few marbles loose now and again (and couldn't be trusted with anything of importance); it hadn't been too hard for her sisters to slander her, while always eyeing *both* the family's modest estate and her mother's trust fund. Like mother like daughter, they would say.

Her mom may have had one foot in the grave, but once Annie had been completely disowned it sure looked like both her sisters were nudging that other foot toward the edge. And Annie's step-mother? Annie didn't understand her at all.

A tear formed in one of Annie's eyes. She missed her mother, loved her mother; she even loved her sisters and step-mother. She said prayers for all of them every day. Sometimes, though, she would have to talk to herself for awhile before she *felt* the prayers she said for her sisters. *Prayers you can't feel are not prayers at all,* she thought. *And prayers that others hear you say are only sermons, and mostly only self-gratifying.* Annie felt that praying and chanting and singing were private things. She only did them when she was alone, and she actually never really even considered the *idea* of going to a church.

Suddenly Annie burst into tears, sobbing as she remembered her father's funeral.

Her father's warm and compassionate smile could always drive away any storm. True, Annie was... Life-challenged. Challenged, but not because she was a bad person. It was because she was too kind, too caring, too giving, and too trusting. She felt too much.

The whole world, day after day, just seemed to break Annie's heart into tinier and tinier pieces. To build a buffer between her and the selfish world, and to try to come to terms with it, Annie wrote great lyrics (some of them still being sung on the radio today) and wrote beautiful poetry. But most of all, Annie prayed.

If it was the one thing that Annie did have that nobody has been able to take away from her, it was her faith. Her faith: That was a gift that her father gave her. That is the one thing that she and he shared, that nobody else could understand.

Mostly, nobody even noticed. Nobody, that is, except her sisters. Her sisters saw, and her sisters hated Annie for it. Toward the end of their father's life, it was as if they counted the days, even the hours to his death. Tick tock tick tock. Annie understood that her father's death would mean that her sisters' greed would one day be fully realized and rewarded. But what Annie didn't know was that they weren't actually counting down to their father's death. No. They were actually counting down to *her death*.

Yes, her father's gentleness and understanding had powered Annie since childhood. It was as if he reached into her heart, and gave her the light of God. Just... gave it, freely, where it shone out of its own accord, where it was ever-present, no matter what Annie did. Whether she was good or bad even as a teenager, the light would just seem to pour out all on its own. She was always either dearly loved or deeply despised by those who truly stopped to take a look at Annie.

But Annie wasn't strong like her father. She couldn't deal with people the way he could, with that confident, quiet knowing, that firm but fair disposition that his friends and supporters loved. No, the best that Annie could learn was the quiet part, which she quickly learned to be with extreme aptitude. Even that sometimes didn't seem to be enough, so she learned to avert her eyes. She avoided eye contact with everyone but her trusted friends.

Trusted friends. Today, there were none of those. When she moved to Las Vegas, she left everyone she would consider a friend, back home. And she could never return home. Not now.

Here, Annie had nobody. Annie had no place to live. Annie had nobody to talk to. Annie had nobody to listen to. Annie had no money. Annie had no food.

But Annie still had her faith. And even as she felt this ugly darkness within her leg, she just *knew* that everything was going to be ok. She knew it, but she didn't feel it right now. Too many bad memories, too much loneliness clouded her heart.

"'Death most resembles a prophet who is without honor in his own land or a poet who is a stranger among his people.'" Annie knew she was being tested, but she didn't know why. That was what Khalil was for, to remind her. *God works in mystical ways*, Annie thought.

For Annie had been tossed to the street without a second thought, the day after her father's funeral. Her father left everything he built to his wife, Annie's step-mother. That was father's one flaw, his one blindness: He trusted his family, refusing to see even a hint of rottenness in anyone.

"Annie," he had once told her, "You have to give your family what they ask for so that they can make the mistakes they need to in order to learn. The secret is to give it to them in a way that prevents them from hurting themselves with it. And you cannot think in terms of just this lifetime. What do we know about the nature of all of eternity?" he finished.

Still, Annie could not help but feel that somehow all of this was her fault. Her mother's mental illness, her father's disease, her sisters' jealous hatred, her step-mother's disinterest... Annie just knew she had somehow botched *everything* up.

So she left without a fight, without as much as a word of protest. She quickly got a job at a 7-11 in a seedy part of North Town, where the owner saw virtue where Annie felt only shame. It was a hard life, and Annie had no real work skills, but she was thrifty and in a few weeks found a one-bedroom apartment to rent.

Her faith carried her through the days, even as her sorrows weighed on her. She was content to write, to sing, and to mourn her father in the peaceful isolation of her apartment during the evenings after work. She spent her days off at a local meeting hall, where various groups came and met with special speakers or group therapies or even the occasional book reading. Annie liked to sit in the back, in the shadows, and just listen to what people had to say.

A few days after her 36th birthday, her leg started to hurt. She didn't feel well. She didn't go to the doctor because she couldn't afford insurance. She didn't qualify for Medicaid or welfare because she had a job. Never mind that her job didn't pay her enough money to even be able to drive a car, let alone get medical insurance. So she ignored it.

She ignored it until she couldn't stand on her leg for more than an hour at a time. She ignored it until she had to call off work, sick. She ignored it until store owner had to fire her because she was not capable of working. She ignored it until she was back on the streets, with no food or place to sleep.

Then, having nothing else to actually do, she went to the University Medical Center. They ran tests. And more tests. Days passed.

Finally, one of the doctors told her, as if were just a few kind words spoken in passing:

"Annie, you have advancing bone marrow cancer in your leg. Unless you can find a way to get insurance, there is nothing we can do besides palliative care. When you get sicker, just keep coming back."

"I'm going to die?" Annie whimpered.

"Yes, I'm sorry. It's terminal."

The doctors had given up on her, too! Annie thought with a deep sense of despair building within.

Annie wanted to hate the doctor. She wanted to hate her leg. She wanted to chop it off. She wanted cry. To laugh.

But she did nothing besides walk to her mother's—her sisters'--- old abandoned house, and break in, to get away from the cold winds that ate at her soul.

But now, two days later, Annie wanted to see and be around people. She needed to see someone smile, someone laughing. Someone actually living a life worth living. Even someone crying about something worth crying over. *Anything* to get out of her own skin, if even for just a moment.

She made her way to the public meeting hall she loved and grabbed a chair in the corner of the room, trying to ignore the gnawing pain in her leg. She looked around, trying to identify what was going on; a handful of people were chatting amongst themselves. She bent her ear to try to hear what they were talking about...

"... no, I've found that the apple cider vinegar won't last that long, once mixed with the clay and water. It's better to make it fresh. Add the water to the clay first, and let it sit outside and charge in the sunlight," said one of the young gentlemen at the table.

The others muttered some things that she could not hear.

"Right," he said. "Yes. Exactly."

"No, the lemon juice itself won't work for most people who have any actual skin conditions. What I was thinking was that if we could actually liquefy the lemon rind. That it might work. The rind itself is far less acidic than the lemon juice itself; I just haven't taken the time to try it yet, mostly because high quality Aloe Vera works so well and is so easy to use," he said.

But Annie wasn't listening. For the individual turned his head and she recognized him from a talk he had given to a small group of people a few weeks back. She had come in late, and only heard the last thing he had told the group:

"But, it has been my experience, and it is my belief, that nothing else matters other than finding what it is that you love to do, and doing it with everything that you are. I found that the one key, at least for me, is to take an action without thinking too much, and trust that you will be lead to the place you most need to go. If you are failing with all of your heart, then you are doing it right. Fail often and love your learning."

He was still sitting there chatting, but Annie got up and started walking toward him anyway, oblivious to the fact that she was sobbing yet again.

--- --- ---

-

Steve laughed. "No, no, it was Jim Steinman who wrote those words, and it started out like this: 'You can't run away forever, but there's nothing wrong with getting a good head start...' Then, how Steinman approached the chorus is what truly made the lyrics work: 'When you are alone and afraid, and you're completely amazed to find there's nothing anybody can do. Keep on believing...'"

John laughed as well, and took a generous gulp of coal black coffee. "Yes, ok. And I could paint that, very easily! But what I would rather do is to paint a vignette and portray the song at the point where it really stands up on its own. Right here: 'Once upon a time was a backbeat, once upon a time all the chords came to life. And the angels had guitars even before they had wings. If you hold onto a chorus you can get through the night.'"

Steve nodded. "I've always wondered if that verse was Jim's way of acknowledging the true healing power of sound. OM, Steinman style." He grinned, and then shrugged. "Or maybe he just liked the imagery of angels holding electric guitars, and the all mighty drumming in the background, like thunder personified. No, here it is

John: You paint a group of angels with Stratocaster guitars, right? Now, they have clipped wings, so they have to run to try chasing down this young chap. You paint a Zeus like depiction of God, cartoonish so as to not be insulting, put him in the clouds, looking down, and have him pounding on a set of bongo drums. But the young chap is morphed, so you can see him as a child running, then as a teenager running, and then again as an adult, then again, as an old man, who finally looks back over the shoulder and sees the now completely exhausted angels still chasing him. The message itself could go on the guitar straps, quoting from Corinthians I-12 in scripted lettering. Or something like that."

"Right, right. Now that imagery would appeal to the kids in their late teens, perfect. Just brazen enough to be antiauthority and rebellious without stepping over any line. Good! I'll do a story board and see if my client wants to use it as the primary poster." John settled down a bit, pleased.

"Oh, yeah, how did it go with that apple cider vinegar thing? Do you think you can jar it for months at a time?" he asked.

"I don't think so, no. I've found that the apple cider vinegar won't last that long, once mixed with the clay and water. It's better to make it fresh. Add the water to the clay first, and let it sit outside and charge in the sunlight," said Steve. "Then add the apple cider vinegar, and blend it through.

They were just about done here, Steve knew. As they finished up the conversation, he wondered what he should do with the remainder of the night. It was too early to go home, and he was still completely locked into his creative mind. There was no way he could sleep, or even rest. Matt and Lisa were already getting up to leave, and John was now deep into another conversation with Sue; they were heading over to get some more coffee.

Steve turned around to face the door, and was greeted by a woman walking up, tears racing down her cheeks. Steve was stunned to silence. He was so taken aback that his thoughts stopped completely, and he froze in a posture of half-rising up and half sitting down.

"You *have* to help me!" she sobbed.

Steve relaxed a bit, and came back to his senses. He saw that this woman probably needed some change for the bus, or perhaps she needed to get something to eat. She looked rattled and a bit tattered, as if times had been tough as of late.

Steve nodded and smiled, reaching for his wallet. He was about to try to comfort her a bit; he sensed she was a very bright, kind person, and everyone needed a helping hand now and then. He was glad to help. But, she continued speaking before he could act:

"I know you can help me. Please. I just know it! Please, please, please, don't say no!" she implored. Her eyes were bright blue, and deeply penetrating. Steve saw a deep intelligence in her gaze, and something that he didn't understand, something he couldn't pin down.

Steve was right back out of the comfort zone he thought he had rediscovered. Something clearly wasn't right, here. He stood up and faced her.

"Hi, what exactly is the matter? Are you ok? Do you need to sit down?" Steve asked.

The lady didn't speak. Instead, she took off her left shoe, and pulled her pant leg up.

"I'm Annie May. The doctor at the hospital said that I have bone marrow cancer, and that I am going to die. I don't have medical insurance, or any money. I just know that *you* can help me, I don't want to die."

The leg looked terrible. Steve had never seen such a sight before. It looked painful.

"Hi Annie, I'm Steve. Please, sit down. Would you like a cup of hot coffee?" Steve asked.

Annie breathed a deep sigh of relief, and sat down. "Thank you, thank you, and thank you. Thank God. I knew it; I saw it in your eyes. I knew you would help."

Steve went to get them both a fresh cup of coffee, walking over to the refreshments stand on the other side of the room. The walk gave him a chance to try and think. He was shaken up. No, that's not the right word. *I'm scared out of my mind*, he thought to himself. *What the hell am I supposed to do? What do I know about bone marrow cancer?*

The problem was, Steve would never say no to any honest person who asked for his help. Not if he could help, without in turn hurting himself or others. He poured the coffee ever so slowly. He really wanted to walk back and ask Annie why she thought he *could* help her. That might make it easier for Steve to figure out what he was actually expected to do.

But Steve was afraid to ask her. He didn't know why. Annie's very presence seemed to invoke something different, strange, and even a bit eerie. *Perhaps*, Steve thought, *I am afraid of what her answer would be.* Steve knew that when most people looked around, they saw nothing outside of themselves. But Annie was clearly different. Again, he thought about those eyes. It was like when she looked out, she saw more than what was actually there. No, that wasn't quite right, either. It was like she saw everything that everyone else was likely missing.

Steve glanced down, and noticed that he was pouring coffee all over the table. He refocused; cleaned up the mess he'd made, and then headed back toward the table, still thinking.

Steve had purchased a book called, "Our Earth, Our Cure", written by a French naturopath, Raymond Dextreit, a few years back. Steve had long been aware that there were supposed curative properties of prized healing clays, but aside from making custom cosmetic clay blends for skin care, Steve really had no experience with natural medicine or healing; and no real interest in the subject, for that matter. But now, he thought back to the handbook, and considered a few of the unbelievable stories he'd heard from some old timers out who lived way out in the desert.

He rejoined Annie, passing her a cup of coffee. He sipped his own. "So, Annie, have you lived in Las Vegas a long time?" he said, basically because he didn't know what else to say.

Annie poured forth her entire two-year story, as if issuing it forth in one giant breath. Steve was riveted, and couldn't believe what he heard. The story she poured forth was insane, but her eyes clearly demonstrated the truth of the words. Steve was stricken by the tragedy of her family story. *If she wasn't crazy before*, Steve thought to himself, *she should be after all of that. Should I believe the story? How could I not? But then again, does it really matter what I believe?*

The way Annie put it, her life had turned from being full of promise and meaning to useless and dreadful almost over night, once her father died. She wound down her story, and then returned back into real time, as if escaping from the past she had just been bent on sharing.

"And you remind me so much of my father. The minute I saw you, I thought that." Annie said.

A heavy pit dropped from Steve's throat and crashed into the bottom of his stomach. He suddenly felt ill. Never mind that Annie looked to be about forty years old, and Steve was barely twenty-one years old. If it came from anyone else's mouth, Steve would have felt that he was being set up as a mark for one big con; or at the very least, being pandered to. But he didn't get that from Annie. Being compared to her father was deeply disturbing to Steve. He wanted to get up and walk away, and chalk the whole experience up to some crazy lady speaking nonsense. He wanted to tell her that he couldn't even begin to accept any responsibility in helping Annie; that he was the wrong person, not the right one.

But there he sat, still and quiet.

"So, Steve, what do you do?" Annie asked.

"I'm a student," Steve replied, still lost in his own thoughts.

"Oh, you're in college? How nice, what are studying? I went to college for a few years, I really loved it."

"No, no, I'm sorry… What I mean is that I'm a student of life. I study whatever presents itself. Every day is sufficient unto itself, and I consider myself an explorer of life. I'm here to learn the things they won't teach in college or at a university. I hope to, one day after I retire, go back and get a master's degree in either English or philosophy. Or chemistry," Steve mused.

"Right now, I'd much rather spend my time studying what artists are doing, or those people studying metaphysics, or writing music, or creating things. I have a passion for exploring truth, and I want to learn what it means to be truly free, if that's possible, and I want to find a way to express real value in my own life."

Annie listened with an attentive calmness, as if they were just two old friends, chatting over a cup of coffee after a day of hard work.

Steve made a decision just then. He no longer felt like he could ignore the old stories about green clay's ability to heal. Not with Annie sitting right here in front of him. He at least had to take the action, to find out for certain. He saw little harm in trying.

"Annie, I don't know anything about bone marrow cancer. But here is what I do know: There are no solutions in problems, only more problems. What I mean is that you have to rise above any problem in order to begin to seek the solution. Everything contains its own vibration, and by living that vibration, one will only attract more of the same," said Steve. "If you are able to let go of the problem and yourself absolutely, I truly believe that a solution will present itself, if you are willing to act."

"I have to work tomorrow and Friday," Steve said. "But, if you're willing to, I know of a place away from the city where anyone can go to get away from it all. I also know about this natural clay that supposedly has amazing curative powers. I would be willing to take you there, and we can see if this clay actually helps your leg. If you are willing."

Annie, serene as could be, having gone through a transformation of panic, dread and hopelessness into some strange type of calm in the middle of a storm said, "Yes, I would love to go. This is *obviously* the answer to my prayers. I can feel it!"

Steve had never had much use for faith, himself. He had smaller gods like information, knowledge, and learned experience. Wisdom, he felt, was hard-earned. The only prayers that he really knew were creative action and mantras to keep his mind clear and focused.

Only, in this case, Steve had little information. No knowledge at all, nor experience. Steve did believe in a divine, intelligent force in the universe. *Only,* Steve thought, *God is the only thing that can create something from absolutely nothing. What exactly am I to do?*

He decided to let Annie have her faith, and he would simply source the moments as they presented themselves, and hope for the best.

--- --- ---

-

The weather was perfect. Spring was approaching rapidly, and spring was very kind to this otherwise harsh desert. It was almost warm during the daytime. They had arrived at their destination, deep in the far reaches of the Mojave Desert.

"Steve, it is so beautiful out here. If I sit still and hold my breath, it's absolutely silent. It feels so great to get out of the city."

Steve nodded. "When I can, I try to come out here on the weekends. I bring a few books, but more often than not, I enjoy spending the time writing, or just listening to the winds sing in the evening and watching the dust and sands dancing across the landscape."

Surprisingly, when Steve had gone to pick Annie up at her sister's house, she had a friend with her. She introduced her friend as Lucas, and Annie acted as if she'd known Lucas for years. But Steve suspected that *he'd* known Annie longer than Lucas had.

He suspected that after their first meeting, Annie came to her senses and decided it probably wasn't the best idea to allow herself to be taken out into the middle of nowhere by some strange man who talked about burying her leg in earth... At least, not alone. But, on second thought, Lucas didn't look much like a protector to Steve. In fact, it looked to Steve like Lucas might need some protecting himself.

But there was something more going on; he'd seen Lucas around before at the meeting hall. Maybe she'd looked at Lucas, later that first night, and said something like: "Please, please, please, you have to come with me! I know you just have to go with me to the desert!"

Steve didn't want to butt into business that was not his. In fact, Steve really preferred not to know any details at all. Again, pausing to think, Steve thought that maybe he was, yet again, afraid of what the answer might be. What was it really that he was afraid of her saying? Steve suddenly realized the truth. He was afraid she was going to say something like: "Why, Steve, I came with you and I brought Lucas because I *already saw* all three of us out there."

No, Steve didn't really want to know what Annie was thinking. Lucas seemed a tad bit strange, but he was actually quite pleasant, and it was fine to have him along. Besides, anything normal would look out of place on this journey. There was nothing normal about this whole trip. This whole trip was an exercise in craziness. There was no place for thinking at all, on this trip, at least, not logically; trying to apply logic was simply... painful.

The words he and John were talking about a few days ago came to mind: *You can't run away forever, but there's nothing wrong with getting a good head start.* Run now, think later. And don't look back. *Words issued from the fool to the wise man?* Steve wondered.

Lucas chimed in. "There's nothing out here. What's out here? Nothing. Nothing at all. Zilch."

Steve chuckled to himself. "That is what gives this place its value. It is spaces opening into spaces, dominoing into distance; it's the distance that is holding up the mountains in all of their majesty. Everything is blue skies and wide landscapes. If you listen deeply, deeper than the apparent absence of sound, I think you can hear the spirit of the desert itself, ocean born. If you lend your eyes to the landscapes, you can see mirages. They hint to all the vastness of all unplayed and unborn dreams, all untested desires. This is a great place to come and dream your dream, or even to discover a new one. It's also a great place to come to escape from a nightmare."

"Ohhh, wonderful, are you saying you can actually hear the ocean?" Annie asked, enjoying the idea.

"Well," said Steve. "This was once part of an ancient sea, called the Lahontan Sea. It's not so much that I can hear the sound of the ocean, more like I can feel the sound of it."

Annie took in a big breath of air through her nose. "Yes, you can almost, almost smell it."

Lucas said, "There's no people here. Where is everyone? This is great, just great. All those city people running around back home like little ants and here this is, just a few hours away." Lucas acted like he was pleased at having discovered a precious secret; and one he planned on keeping to himself.

Steve nodded. "Yes, people are simply busy attracting what they perpetually project. It is a very human problem."

We all got out of the truck, having parked alongside the road. Steve lead Annie and Lucas to the nearby hillside. It was clear that quite a bit of the hillside had been dug out.

"There are clay deposits all throughout this region. Some of them are good, and some aren't. *This*," Steve picked up a handful of greenish clumped dirt, motioning, "Is some of the better clay which has been used by the locals as long as there have been locals in the area. According to the book I've been studying, some people actually drink clay water. But this is not a clean enough deposit. *That* deposit, the purest one, is located quite a distance from here. But this is the perfect deposit for external use."

Steve realized that Annie and Lucas had no idea what he was talking about. They picked up some "dirt", and simply had puzzled looks on their faces.

Lucas said, "It's like nothing: Dirt. Dirty dirt: Green. What exactly are you going to do with this stuff?" He let the clay pass through his hands like sand pouring through an hourglass. Obviously he couldn't even imagine what *could* be done with it. Steve didn't blame him one bit. Lucas rubbed some of it on his hands, and then examined them closely to see if he could tell if it did anything.

"I'm going to take this plastic garbage can *here*," Steve had grabbed a large plastic garbage can from the back of his truck, trying to sound confident, "and I'm going to fill about one quarter of it full of dry clay, and then hydrate it with the natural water at the well over *there*." Steve pointed somewhere out in the distance.

"Oh," said Lucas. "And then what are you going to do with it?"

"I'm going to put Annie's entire leg in the garbage can filled with wet clay."

"Oh," said Lucas. "And what exactly is that going to *do*?"

"I have absolutely no idea, but I sure expect to find out."

And with that said, Steve packed about 15 pounds of green calcium bentonite clay into the garbage can, drove it over to an artesian well, and filled the entire garbage can to its rim with piping hot geothermally heated water.

--- --- ---

-

Later that Saturday evening, they had all settled in to the cabin that Steve had rented. Steve was waiting for the clay to finish soaking up all of the water. He used his hands to turn the clay, to speed the process up. He actually found himself saying a silent prayer while doing this, which was completely out of character for Steve. *No*, thought Steve, *I'm not praying, I'm begging... Begging the clay to please do something.*

Usually, he could relax up here, far away from the fast paced city from whence he came. But not today. Today he was certain that he was crazy. He couldn't even fathom exactly how clay could do anything for such a condition. He knew what was going to happen with the clay therapy. Exactly nothing. Zero. They were going to make this big mess, waste a day, and then Annie was going to be back to sobbing, in that strange sort of despairing hope that she had first presented to Steve when they met.

Steve wanted to turn and run away. But he was afraid that if he did, he would turn around to find angels chasing him down. Not angels with guitars, but angels with sharp tridents. *This*, Steve thought, *is what insanity must feel like.*

But, it was amazing to see the transformation Annie had undergone having escaped to the desert. She was happy, laughing, thoroughly enjoying herself as if she had no care in the world. But Steve knew that this was most likely simply denial, and that reality would soon come crashing back upon her, and with full force. He could still see the pain lining her eyes, the trouble she had with walking, the tremble in her every step. *This isn't a solution*, Steve thought to himself, *it's a delusion.* He sighed.

Steve did not want to see Annie's smile disappear. He strangely felt that all that mattered was Annie's continued bright smile. Steve realized that it was Annie who had transferred this optimistic, hope-filled disposition to *him*. Her zealousness was intoxicating and contagious.

Perhaps the truth was that *Steve* didn't want to lose this feeling. It was a feeling that literally felt that some divine force was very close, watching over everything. He was definitely feeling a spiritual presence. Steve was quite daunted by the idea, but at the same time strangely comforted.

Finally it was time to try out the clay. An hour or so had passed, and while the clay was not fully hydrated, it was hydrated enough. Steve told Annie it was time.

As Steve prepared the garbage can, he noticed that Annie was crying.

"I'm ready!" she sobbed.

"Annie, what's wrong? What happened?" Steve asked.

"I'm ok," she said. "I'm ready. But... Can you tell me? How badly is this going to hurt?"

Steve relaxed and actually laughed. "Annie, no, this isn't going to hurt at all. In fact, it should feel extremely soothing."

Annie sat down, and both Lucas and Steve helped her insert her foot, and then the leg, into the clay-filled garbage bin. Once her leg was in, Annie let out a big sigh, finally actually believing there would be no additional pain to worry about.

"Ok. Great. Now, we'll want to leave your leg in the clay as long as it is comfortable. At least an hour. Two if possible. If anything feels uncomfortable, we can stop at any time, though, ok?"

With that, Steve decided to go for a walk to watch the sun slowly dive behind the mountains, wishing he could join it.

Two hours passed before Annie elected to remove her leg from the garbage can. Her leg looked light green, with clumps of clay falling from her leg as she removed it. Annie showered, and all three of them examined the leg and the foot with great interest. However, none of them knew what they were supposed to be looking *for*.

There appeared to be no change, so the trio ate dinner, and went to bed.

Morning came much more quickly than Steve expected. When Annie woke in the morning, she came into the kitchen where Steve was drinking his first morning cup of coffee.

"You won't *believe* this, Steve. Last night, I slept and there was no pain. The pain was gone. I actually slept deeply. The pain was gone! It's a miracle!" she exclaimed.

Lucas came in, having heard Annie's report. Again, all three of them examined the leg, which seemed to look just like it had the day before. Steve wondered to himself, *more delusions*?

But Annie didn't even notice Steve's air of skepticism. "It's as if the *darkness* is gone! Gone."

She did one more one-hour clay treatment on her leg that morning before they headed back to the city; they were out of time.

On the drive home, about an hour into the trip, Annie got violently ill. Steve had to pull over to the side of the highway, at the top of Spring Mountain Pass.

Annie threw open the door, and starting vomiting. Over and over again she retched. She was throwing up so badly, it looked like she wasn't able to catch a breath at all, and Steve began to panic.

As irrational as it may have been, Steve thought to himself, *oh my God I've killed her. Why is this happening?*

But as quickly as she started to throw up, she stopped. She got back into the truck after a moment's rest.

"Steve, it felt like all of the toxic poison in my body just *had* to come up, and right *now*! I've never felt anything like it!" Annie said.

Lucas asked, "Are you ok? How do you feel?"

Annie replied, "Oh I'm fine! Just fine!"

Steve almost actually believed it.

Arriving back in town, Steve dropped Annie and Lucas back off at her sister's house.

--- --- ---

-

Steve didn't see Annie or Lucas for a little over two weeks.

He was actually glad. Steve really just wanted to forget the whole experience. He wasn't even sure why, but he felt that the whole foundation of his life had just been obliterated. He felt that nothing was ever going to be the same again if he didn't just keep looking forward. *Yes*, thought Steve, *don't look back, something might really be chasing you.* He could almost hear bongo drums, drumming.

After the first week, Steve settled back into his routine, and nearly managed to forget about the whole experience, most of the time.

Then one day, after finishing up a collaborative art meeting with his associates, Steve saw Annie run through the door.

"It's healed!" she exclaimed. She lifted up her pant leg as if she were showing off a dress, and tossed her shoe off with a quick kick.

Huge pieces of skin were peeling off of her foot. Steve estimated that one piece of dead skin was six inches by four inches long. All of the swelling was gone from both her foot and her leg. Annie actually almost looked like a new person.

It became readily obvious to Steve that the swelling in Annie's foot and leg had cut off circulation to some of the skin on Annie's foot. The skin, peeling off as if Annie was shedding, was covering new, vibrantly pink skin beneath.

She said, "I never felt anymore pain at all the day after you dropped me off. The swelling started to go down in the leg and the foot. Everything felt like it was loosening up. And I got all of the feeling back in the foot!" She danced around.

"Last week," she continued, "Lucas took me back to the hospital. They ran a bunch of tests. We just got the results back."

"The doctor said that there had obviously been a mis-diagnosis, because there was no indication that bone marrow cancer had ever been present!" she beamed triumphantly.

Steve was stunned, and just kept looking at the leg. He really did not believe what he was seeing. It was... simply... not possible.

"It's a miracle, Steve, and you did it! One day, you are going to be so famous, I just know it! God is with you!" she hugged Steve, who was still too shocked to say anything.

Steve had done nothing at all. There was no miracle he created, not in his thoughts or actions.

Steve must have sat and chatted with her for awhile, and then she must have left, but Steve really wasn't paying any attention at all.

No, Steve hadn't done anything at all. But the question was: What *would* he do now? He had a choice to make.

Either he would walk out that door, and pretend nothing really happened, that it was just a crazy dream, a coincidence, a mistake, a placebo effect, or a divine miracle. Or, Steve could actually take a closer look at what had just transpired, and try to understand it, come to terms with it.

Steve, numb to the core, rose from the chair. He walked out the door, telling himself to ignore what had just happened.

But he couldn't ignore it. Not in a million years. He was terrified, as he had a strong grasp of most sciences, and he could not even make up a feasible science fiction explanation as to how wet dirt placed on a leg in that bad a condition would do anything aside from make the leg dirty; maybe cause an infection.

Steve considered himself a rational human being with a few metaphysical leanings. The world did make sense. Always. The sense the world made was rarely very pretty to Steve, but sense it did make. This. This was… something different.

Everything had just changed.

No, Steve couldn't ignore it. He would dig in, and learn every single thing possible about this strange substance known as healing clay. *Every single thing known to man,* Steve silently vowed. *I have a responsibility to determine if this stuff would work again, a responsibility to those who may be needlessly suffering.* Steve was overwhelmed with a heavy sense of urgency.

And that was the day a clay disciple was born… Born from the faith of Annie May.

Author's Note

In the following years, Steve got to know Annie quite well. Annie never had any further problem with her leg. In fact, while she continued to love using clay cosmetically she only ever needed clay one time after that: to heal a sprained finger (the clay took the pain away in less than 15 minutes, and by the next day the swelling was gone).

I have never seen another case reported or example like this one. I've never seen a report of clay therapy curing bone marrow cancer, or failing to cure bone marrow cancer. The best that I can state is that: *Something healed something!*

Therefore, I've included as much pertinent detail as possible in this story. Perhaps Annie's recounting of her past which haunted her so much induced a miracle state of mind. Perhaps simply discovering new friends and escaping from self (and the city / environment) contributed. Perhaps it *was* her faith, and perhaps she did know it right from the start. Perhaps it was divine intervention. Or perhaps it was all of it combined, through the vessel of: Healing Clay.

I know not.

Over the years, I've had plenty of experience with individuals who have had cancer, and have used clay therapy. Clay therapy has always provided support, and made any worse situation better. I have seen clay cure cancer again, and I've received many reports of the same. But, I've also seen it fail to cure cancer.

Therefore, I encourage the reader to study Book III, where I will delve deeply into the topic of why clay may work against cancer, and why it might have failed (when it fails), and what one can do about it to try to ensure the best possible outcome.

This is Annie's exit point from our Book of Stories, but the reader may be interested to note that Lucas just might be back, somewhere in the pages that follow.

Peggy Sue Knew

Peggy Sue Torrez just *knew* her son was up to no good, as usual. He was always hanging around the wrong kind of people. *No, it was him that was the wrong kind of people*, she thought dryly. He was lying all the time, never able to look her in the eyes. *His own mother*, she thought, shaking her head. She was pretty sure he was on drugs. If not on drugs, then he was selling them, killing off the next generation of kids. *That's my son*, she thought. *He was probably a baby killer, or making crack babies.*

She just knew something bad was going to happen with that boy. As usual, she just *knew*.

She knew her knee was hurting real bad today, too. Her doctor just gave her useless drugs that didn't even work, except to upset her stomach, *as usual*. *Antiflam this, antiflam that, whatever*, she thought silently. The doctor was an idiot. He didn't even deserve a medical license out of a Cracker Jacks box.

She was just waiting for the day to come when she could find a way to *sue his ass*. If she couldn't get her knee fixed, then maybe she could get a nice new car from the whole deal. The jerk should try *practicing* medicine on himself, and see how far that got him. *Antiflam hiself for a change*, she thought. She'd like to stick *him* with a Tamiflu shot.

Maybe I'll just trip in his office and break my hip, Peggy Sue thought. Sue his office, sue him, and sue that damn insurance company for making me go there.

The front door to her house banged open.

"Mom, are you awake? Are you here? Mother!" said Michael Torrez, Peggy Sue's son, as he walked through the door.

"I'm in here, Miguel, in the kitchen, stop your screaming already!"

"I wish you would *stop calling me Miguel*, mother. It's Mike, or Michael."

"Your father would be rolling around in his grave hearing you disrespect his and your name like that! Your father was *proud* to be an immigrant."

Walking into the kitchen, Mike lowered his voice a bit. "Mother, dad always called me Mikey, you know that," he said with a sigh. "And I'm *not* an immigrant!"

"Your father was only being nice; because your *father* was such a kind, loving man... to be able to put up with you, he musta had the patience of a saint. God bless and rest his soul."

"Mom, I have a few friends coming over to the house in a bit. I think they can help with your knee."

Mike always had to try very hard to keep his temper in check around his mother. It was not easy. He didn't think he'd ever met anyone as miserable as she was. And her favorite pastime was spreading her misery as far and wide as she possibly could. At times, Mike thought that maybe she had dementia, that it was her age and physical pains that drove her to be so ill-tempered. But the only problem was, she had been this way as long as Mike could remember.

--- --- ---

-

Gene drove up to the little house. Gloria was in the car with him. She was been being strangely quiet; probably as nervous as he was.

He really didn't know what they were doing here. Yesterday, Gloria had introduced him to this guy named Michael because he was interested in therapeutic and spa clays.

Mike had met with Gene and Gloria to show them a sample of about 60 pounds of wet clay. It turns out that the clay was improperly hydrated with water and mixed with cheap olive oil. The stuff would no doubt rapidly turn rancid. He explained to Mike that the clay looked like it might have been Whittaker Bentonite, which was a brand of technical grade sodium bentonite, or something similar, and that it really wasn't healing grade clay. Gene told him that it might work in a pinch, but that he hoped Mike didn't spend too much money on it.

While he was putting his sample back in his truck, Gloria whispered to Gene: "I think this guy is in the New Mexico mafia or something. My friend Lisa told me that he's a friend of her brother's Meth dealer. And Mike himself had mentioned to me that he wanted to start a legitimate business with clays... Maybe open up a spa, or something. I mean, you don't say you need to open a legitimate business if you don't already have an illegal business, right?"

Gene's mouth dropped open. "You think this guy is *what*? Are you *crazy*?" he whispered back in distress. "The New Mexico mafia is actually the Mexican Mafia. The Mexican mafia makes millions of dollars smuggling guns into Mexico from New Mexico and Texas, and smuggling drugs out of Mexico into the States. These people don't play games, Gloria, and they are not like the mobsters on the old TV shows."

"Oh," said Gloria, as if that were beside the point. "But Mike is really, really a nice guy, though, you'll see."

Gene was trying to figure out how *not* to see when Mike returned from his truck.

"Hey, Gene, gracias hombre. Thanks for letting me know about the clay. Listen; what I'd like for you two to do is come over to my ma's house. She's got a bum knee that she is always complaining about. I'd like you to try your clay on the knee, see if it helps at all."

Maybe it was Gene's overactive imagination, but it didn't seem to him like Mike was making a request, but rather, a demand. It was clear that Mike was used to getting his way without much debating.

"Eh ese, come on, I'll pay you guys," he offered, as if sensing Gene's discomfort.

Gene said, "Fine, Mike that would be great, we'd be glad to. And no payment is necessary, we'd just be glad to be able to help." He said that mostly because he wasn't certain of the consequences of saying what he wanted to say: *Hell, no.*

Now, he was sitting in front of Mike's mother's house, getting up his nerve to go knock on the door. Gene got out of his truck, and grabbed a glass five-gallon container filled with pre-hydrated, raw clay.

He and Gloria walked up to the door. Gloria knocked.

Mike answered the door. "Hey! Hola, Gene, Gloria, great of you to come! Thanks for coming! Ma, they're here! Right this way, here, in the kitchen."

Gene and Gloria followed Mike into the kitchen. The house was decorated in an old 1970's style decir, which was actually a bit quaint, and helped to relax Gene's nerves. It looked just like a normal house, in a normal neighborhood.

"Ma, this is Gene and Gloria. Guys, this is my ma," said Mike.

--- --- ---

-

"Peggy Sue Torrez, but you can call me Peggy Sue, everyone else does," she said, reaching her hand out to Gloria.

Gloria dutifully took her hand. "I like your home, Mrs. Torrez," she offered.

"Oh. Well. You know, everything is falling apart. I think the hot water heater is shot, and the swamp cooler fan is obviously going out, it is so loud you know. They can't build anything to last these days, everything's all from China or Taiwan. Everything is simply junk, these days. I sent a letter to the governor, but what can he do he's a democrat for God's sake," Peggy Sue said.

She continued, "I just hope it doesn't rain, because I think the roof is going to start leaking. Still, it suits an old lady alright, but not much to show for 73 years of hard living."

There was an awkward silence for a few moments. Then Gene spoke up.

"Hi Mrs. Torrez, I'm Gene. Can you tell me what is wrong with your leg?"

"It's my knee," corrected Peggy Sue. "And it hurts, that's what's wrong."

Peggy Sue glanced at Gene. *Just more of Mike's wayward friends*, she thought. *Probably pot smoking hippies from California. The boy certainly didn't seem to know that it looks like his hair should have been cut ten years ago. And the girl sure could lose a pound or two.*

"And what has the doctor said about the knee?" asked Gene.

"The doctor told me I'm getting old: It's arthritis, or just 'wear and tear' whatever. It's been bothering me for a few years now. He gave me medications that only served to make the drug companies richer, and me poorer. That is what this country's come to, I'll tell you."

Gene said, "Do you know what to tell the doctor the next time he tells you your knee is bad because of your age? Tell him, 'Doctor, my other knee is the same age as this one, and it's just fine!"

Gloria and Mike laughed. Peggy Sue just sat there.

"That's not original, by the way. I took that from Catherine Ponder's book, 'The Healing Secret of the Ages'," said Gene.

Peggy Sue was not impressed. "Ok, now what do you two want me to do? I don't do drugs if that's what you're thinking!" she cautioned.

Mike rolled his eyes. "Mother! Stop."

"No, no Mrs. Torrez," Gloria said. "We are just going to wrap your knee with a clay poultice, cover it, and let it sit there for an hour or so."

"Where would you be most comfortable sitting?" asked Gene.

"Hmmm. How about out front on the patio? I sometimes like to sit out there and read my magazines." Peggy Sue replied.

"Excellent."

--- --- ---

-

Peggy Sue sat there and just *stewed*. *This was just absolutely absurd*, she thought. Now she just knew these guys were all on drugs; all three of them. *They are just plain whacked out of their minds*, she thought. *That's what kids said these days right, whacked out, all of them.*

But Peggy Sue just held her tongue. She grew up with manners, and you didn't treat guests badly, no matter what kind of trash they were. She counted every second, though, and watched Gloria take this gooey mud and *slap* it directly onto her knee with a *thwack*.

"I don't know," Peggy Sue couldn't help but state. "I can't possibly see how this can do any good." *They are going to give me an infection with that filth on my leg*, Peggy Sue thought quietly. *Flesh eating, and they'll have to take my leg OFF. I'll end up on the Oprah show.*

Peggy Sue just knew that nothing good was going to come of this. "I have to sit here for an hour?" she asked, while Gloria finished wrapping a clean dressing around the leg, securing it with an ace bandage and a few pins.

"Yes," said Gene. "It should go relatively quickly. The clay isn't uncomfortable, is it?"

"It's so heavy," Peggy Sue said. "And it's cold."

"It will start to feel warm before long, don't worry." Gene said, regretting each and every second as it passed with agonizing slowness.

Gene motioned to Mike, who seemed to be interested in everything that was going on with the treatment. "Remember, Mike, that it is important that you cover the entire area to be treated, and then even overlap the area. That means, that if it is an arm, leg, hand, or foot, that you put thick clay all the way around the appendage, not just on one side. Make it as thick as you comfortably can, at least ¾" inch thick."

"Where did you learn this, in college?" asked Peggy Sue with obvious sarcasm. She was in a very bad mood, and wanted to embarrass this crazy guy into admitting he was a flunky.

"Actually, I am currently in college studying computer science and networking," replied Gene.

Computers are the work of the devil, thought Peggy Sue.

"No, Mrs. Torrez, this is an old Native American remedy. Actually, it's not just Native American. Nearly all, if not all, native, indigenous cultures have used healing clays for thousands, even tens of thousands of years, all around the world. The use of therapeutic clays, in fact, almost certainly predates recorded history. People were likely using clays for healing long before complex languages were developed."

Oh, it's an Indian thing. Probably voodoo, too, thought Peggy Sue.

"I heard that the Apache Chief Geronimo would use healing clays in ceremonies when the tribes gathered at the seven sacred hot springs right here in New Mexico. They would use them in sweat lodges and stuff," Mike said.

"Yes, that was up in Truth or Consequences, New Mexico. We go up there occasionally. I've been looking for two local clay sources reported to be there. I found the first source, which is a sodium bentonite. But, sadly, when Lake Butte was created, the whole vein of clay was contaminated and is actually at the bottom of the lake itself. The other source is a pure white clay; I'm assuming it is either a calcium bentonite or a Kaolin," commented Gene.

"But you are correct, Mike. All of the southwestern Native American tribes would actually trade in clays. The indigenous peoples used to have an immense knowledge base on clay use. They knew which clay was perfect for what use. Blue clays used to be highly prized for their rarity, and used to get the best 'trade price'. Evidently, the men knew how to use the clay for ceremonial, cleansing treatments in sweat lodges, and for their spiritual rituals. But it was women who made and mixed clays, and knew how clays were used for general healing, according to my research. Sadly, almost all of that knowledge was lost only a few generations after the European and British settlers took over this part of the North American Continent."

"That's sad," said Mike. "My friend Tommy from Santa Cruz got this rash that wouldn't go away. The doctors gave him creams, and steroids, and ointments, but they did nothing. Then he got this healing clay from a friend. He mixed the powder with a little water until it was like a gel, just like your guys' stuff. He put it on every night, and before long, the rash was completely gone. That's why I got interested in this stuff."

Gene had never lived a longer hour in his life, but the last moment finally melted out of eternity and into oblivion. We were done!

He asked Peggy Sue, "How does your leg feel, Mrs. Torrez?"

She replied, "How am I supposed to know, I've been sitting down for an hour." She thought to herself, *Thank God this is almost done.*

Gene sighed, but under his breath. Gloria removed the dressing, and cleaned the leg, gently and completely.

Peggy Sue thought, *good, that God awful muck is finally gone. What a waste of an hour just to humor my useless son. He should be out looking for a job, not sitting here with these California hippies with their Godless voodoo crap.*

"Ok," Gene cringed. "You can get up now." Gene wanted to close his eyes, and bolt into his truck.

Peggy Sue got up and started walking. "I told you Miguel, that I thought this was going to be a waste of time. I told you that this stuff was going to be absolutely use–"she paused.

"Wait. It doesn't hurt." Peggy Sue gently stepped on her leg a few times, and then stomped once. "This can't be right, it doesn't hurt. Well, I'll be a..."

For just a moment, Peggy Sue was stunned into being an entirely different person. She beamed with amazement, her eyes shown awe and disbelief. For a moment, it really looked Peggy Sue might actually smile.

But that moment passed very quickly.

"This is just plain crazy."

And with that, Peggy Sue trudged forward, as if her knee had never, *even dared* bothered her to begin with.

"Miguel, ask your little friends if they want to stay for dinner. I've got some leftovers in the fridge that we can heat up…"

However, Gene and Gloria were more than done with this experience, and quickly declined the invitation.

As Mike walked them both over to their truck, he said, "Damn. I heard about the power of clays before, but I didn't even think it would work like *that*. That's crazy good stuff. Amazing. Thank you guys so much."

"It's not a problem, Mike, we're glad we could help," said Gene.

"Hey. Listen," Mike said. "Let me talk to some people about this stuff. Make some *phone calls*. Maybe we could do some *business* together."

"Interesting, Mike," Gene said. "You have my number. Give me a call, and maybe we can discuss it."

"All right, great, then! I'll see you guys later!"

And with that, Gene and Gloria went home.

Gene immediately called the telephone company:

"Yes, thank you. I would like to change my telephone number, immediately, to an unlisted number… Yes, as soon as possible. Ok… Ok… Great! Thank you!"

Gene dropped down onto the couch.

Gloria smiled. "See, Gene. I told you Mike was just the nicest guy, looking out for his mother like that!"

Gene stared at her, blankly. "Yes. They are both just sweethearts. Let's put them on our Christmas card list."

Author's Note

"In your life, you meet people. Some you never think about again. Some, you wonder what happened to them. There are some that you wonder if they ever think about you. And then there are some you wish you never had to think about again. But you do. Oh yes, you do!"

-- Author Unknown, but possibly: *"That Guy/Rodeo"*

Gene never knew for sure if Michael was really a part of any organized crime. He was grateful that he never had to actually find out for sure.

Gene was also certain that Peggy Sue's leg wouldn't be bothering her again. He'd seen it on more than one occasion. When an individual has an isolated injury or inflammatory condition, clay therapy was often dramatically effective.

Meaning, when "arthritis" is in one knee, but no other joints; when an ankle has been damaged, but it is *just* the ankle; when it is just one finger and not all of them. In such situations, one can always expect some improvement. In some cases, relief can be achieved with one treatment. In other cases, success takes a few weeks. In one case, only partial relief was experienced, and it took six months; but the condition had previously been degenerative, and so the degeneration *had* been reversed.

Amazingly, it doesn't matter how long the damage has been there. Efficacy is evidently dependent upon the nature and extent of the damage. When the damage is minimal, then there is often this dramatic recovery that seems instantaneous. When the damage is greater, to the cartilage, joints, or bones, recovery can take longer. Either way, Gene realized early on as a clay disciple, recovery also largely depended on the person's ability to heal; it was as if the clay simply directed the natural healing power of the person, and gave it a push, now and again.

The author hypothesizes that Peggy Sue's pain came from an inflamed joint with very little actual joint damage. The inflammation was likely caused by over-acidity in the soft tissues, and or an exaggerated immune system response at the injury site.

Perhaps there were mild imbalances in her calcium, potassium, sodium, and magnesium levels. However, the deficiencies must have been minor and the inflammation was obviously rapidly eliminated by the clay.

The method of action of the clay: It likely induced (as a catalyst) increased circulation at the joint, and assisted in the elimination of any acidic byproducts or toxins that were trapped in the tissues, which could have caused the inflammatory response to begin with.

What absolutely amazed Gene about this particular experience was that the clay worked independent of Peggy Sue's own belief and expectations. In fact, Peggy Sue had Gene convinced that it wasn't going to work. Gene often wondered how anything could work to heal something when an individual had that poor of an attitude.

Gene truly expected Peggy Sue to create a nocebo effect, which is the opposite of a placebo effect. It seems that the clay action is "intelligent" enough to sidestep even the most stubborn situations.

Gene found this to be the case not just once, but time and time again.

Faithless or faithful, the clay just kept performing admirably, and Gene kept learning from the wisdom imparted by the clay.

Gene had a feeling that Mike was not done with clay therapy, and that his journey perhaps was only just beginning. But thankfully, Gene's role in Mike's journey had ended.

No Shade between Heaven and Hell

Charles William Hank the Second took the foot in his left steel-toed boot, and kicked as hard as he could into the raw ground underneath him. Dust flew. The wind greedily whisked the dust up and spat it back in his face. He breathed a bit in and coughed it back out. Then he chuckled.

He would have used his right foot. The problem was that there was a giant hole in the bottom of it. Charles was a tough-as-nails, bona fide redneck from just outside of Casper, Wyoming. But he wasn't tough enough to avoid becoming diabetic from all of those years eating prison slop. And his body wasn't tough enough to beat the slowly growing infection that ate away at his foot, either.

The prison doctor always joked with him: "If yew don't close that those chops of yers right this here minute, I'm jest gonna cut off the entire leg so I don't have to listen to yer whining anymore!"

That was the doc's way of telling me we're doing everything we can do, it's just not working.

Now, Charles just wanted his foot to last long enough to get him to Los Angeles. Charles had seen pictures of his little girl that his wife had sent him, but he'd never met her. *Ex-wife*, he reminded himself. She was a trooper, but a little over a year after Sara was born, she decided to move on. He didn't blame her.

Charles only had about thirty-five dollars to his name. He walked into the Chevron station and asked the lady behind the front counter, "Excuse me, ma'am, where can I get a map of California?"

She reached and grabbed a map from the stack that was displayed on the counter. "Here you are, that will be three dollars thirteen cents, with tax."

Charles paid her, and unfolded the map on the counter, "Can you show me where we are?"

"Sure thing, hon. *Here*. Independence California. Ain't nothin' free 'bout this place, though." She mused as she pointed.

He took a cigarette pack out of his shirt pocket, and picked up a pen sitting on the counter. Using the pack as a ruler, he drew a straight line from Independence to Los Angeles. He circled the town of Baker, as it was the closest town on the major interstate highway leading into Los Angeles.

The store clerk was watching with mild disinterest. "Now, sweetheart, I hope you don't plan on hoofin' it all the way to Baker.

There ain't one ounce of shade on *that* entire stretch of road out there, and ain't nobody gonna pick the likes of you up, neither. No offense, but there ain't no drinkin' water out there neither. And the only thing that black cowboy hat of yours is going to do is to bake your thick skull in the sun like a potato. They don't call this area Death Valley for nothin', you know."

Charles shrugged. "Darlin', I got a place to get to; I got a map to get there and two feet to carry my ass. A man can't ask God for much more than that."

The clerk shrugged back. "Suit yourself, but don't say you weren't warned."

--- --- ---

-

Charles had walked for hours before a truck driver stopped to give him a lift. He thought he'd gotten lucky; that the driver was going straight through to the interstate. But it turned out that the driver was going to Pahrump, just over the Nevada border. He dropped Charles off about three miles (an hour's walk or so) before Shoshone California.

"I have to drop you off here," the driver said. "The sheriff and highway patrol sometimes hang out in Shoshone. I don't want them to see me with a hitch-hiker. You don't want them to see you hitch-hiking either. Not out here. They might just cart you all the way back to the jail in Independence. Make you stay the night, and then you'd have to start all over again. Maybe they'd give you a bus ticket, but not to where you're going, probably Pahrump. It's not that they are mean, it's just that there is only a few of them, and they all got hundreds of miles of very lawless area to patrol. But watch out for the Silver Streak. He's a Cali Highway Patrolman, and if he's in a bad mood, he'll give you a ticket for putting your hat on crooked. You'll know him by the color of his hair."

Charles nodded and chuckled. "Well, thanks a bunch for the lift, then. You drive safe," Charles said, as he got out of the truck.

"Hey there, wait! Don't forget your guitar!"

Charles thanked him, and grabbed the guitar case and strung it over his shoulder.

Now, darkness had claimed the desert. Charles was off the road about ½ of a mile. He was surprised that he'd been able to find plenty of brush and wood for a nice campfire. He was warming up a can of pork and beans. The trucker had given him some frozen water. It had melted, and felt cool and soothing splashing down this throat.

Charles had thought that the desert heat would kill him. He had only walked a maximum of 9 miles before being picked up. The trucker had told him that it was 113 degrees Fahrenheit. He also had told him that tomorrow it was going to be hotter.

The dry heat was like fire on his skin, and his lungs felt like hot coals with every breath. He had felt that his sweat was going to boil. When a breeze finally started blowing, it felt even hotter. Breathing was like sticking one's head into a dry oven. Sand kicked up and felt like tiny knives across his skin.

But the biggest problem was his foot. Steel-toed boots, he realized, was not a very good idea. While putting on his normal clothes had gone a long way to help him restore an actual self-identity, his attire was not designed for this weather, or for his rotting foot.

His foot throbbed. It oozed. It stank.

He'd been off of it for a few hours now, and was able to start to ignore the pain.

As the deeper parts of night approached, the desert cooled. Charles wasn't all that tired. In fact, he really felt good. The wide open spaces of desert poured into his soul. The calm of the night, and the peace it carried made Charles feel like he actually was, in truth, free. Far from home, but free.

He had seen a bunch of references to the old Tonopah & Tidewater Railroad that used to run through these parts. He thought of how much better it would have been to be able to hook an arm around an old boxcar, and just sit and watch the desert roll by; he wondered if travelers of old in these parts didn't do just that.

He grabbed his guitar and started strumming an old Jimmie Rodgers song, *"Waiting for a Train"*:

> "All around the water tank, waiting for a train
> A thousand miles away from home, sleeping in the rain
> I walked up to a brakeman just to give him a line of talk
> He said "If you got money, boy, I'll see that you don't walk
> I haven't got a nickel, not a penny can I show
> "Get off, get off, you railroad bum" and slammed the boxcar door
>
> He put me off in Texas, a state I dearly love
> The wide open spaces all around me, the moon and the stars up above

Nobody seems to want me, or lend me a helping hand
I'm on my way from Frisco, going back to Dixieland
My pocket book is empty and my heart is full of pain
I'm a thousand miles away from home just waiting for a train."

He felt a bit feverish. He wasn't sure if it was just mild heat stroke, or the infection. But, he decided to settle down, at long last, for the night.

--- --- ---

-

Trevor baked in the morning sun. It was about six thirty in the morning, and Trevor had been sitting there, nude, next to the tent, for about an hour and a half. He never grew bored of watching the sunrise.

He gazed across the seemingly endless dry, cracked clay flats. He heard no birds. He heard no machinery. Not even the wind blew this morning, and therefore Trevor held his breath and closed his eyes, listening to absolutely… nothing. He opened his eyes and spent a few moments staring intently at the flats, looking for one of the small spiders crawling around, or trying to see if he could see a scorpion scurrying about before the flats became too hot to walk on.

Nothing. Silence in the air, stillness on the ground. *Absolutely perfect*, Trevor thought to himself.

He threw on a robe, and walked for about three minutes with his eyes closed, not peeking once. Each step he took was deliberate and slow. He listened intently to the rhythmic, crunching beneath his feet as the dry clay cracked and shattered beneath him. He paused, and opened his eyes. *Not bad*, Trevor thought. He was about a forty-second walk from the natural hot springs. He disrobed, and dipped into the water. The heat instantly melted any tension that was left in his muscles, and started traveling to his very bones.

He took a deep breath. "Ahhhh," and closed his eyes.

People thought he was insane, traveling to the far edges of the Death Valley Region, and living out on some clay flats.

Trevor didn't think so. He thought, in a strange way, that he fit right in with everyone he'd met out here. Here, the desert rats were normal and sane, and it was the city folk who were out of their minds.

But that wasn't quite true, either. Even the locals thought Trevor was crazy. They couldn't fathom what, exactly, he was doing.

Trevor spent a lot of time trying to justify to himself what he was doing out here; but never to anybody else. He thought, they just don't understand that you don't have to have a paintbrush or a pen to be an artist, just like you don't have to have a pocket protector and calculator to be a scientist.

There were many reasons Trevor had left the city; cast off the polished shoes and necktie. The most important one to him, was that in order to understand the Mystic Desert (as he called it), he needed to *become* the mystic desert.

He had had a dream many years ago. In the dream, he was lying down, staring up at the blue sky, in the middle of vast clay flats. It was peaceful; serene. Suddenly, clouds rushed in from all directions. The sky grew dark, the air became moist. Rain started pouring down. The desert drank the water in, becoming a giant mud pool that quickly expanded into a shallow sea that spread from horizon to horizon.

Trevor was captivated by the flashing lightening scarring the sky over and over. But even as he was mesmerized, he sank into the Earth, underneath the mud, and *he became the mud flats*. He became the Earth, and the Earth became him.

Then, lightening began striking the Earth, striking *him*, over and over. The POUND of thunder followed the electric strike as it whipped the desert floor with an exploding *snap*. Trevor's entire being seized with each blast, every muscle in his body locking up, his mind freezing, overloaded by the sensory input. His body would relax for one short moment, and then the next strike would snap again.

Trevor screamed. He then opened his eyes, and found himself lying on the floor next to his bed. Everything was quiet. Now, only his heart pounded.

So here he was, still trying to answer the same question he woke up with the night of his dream: Was the desert punishing me, torturing me? Or was the desert trying to wake me, or waken something within me?

He still could not answer that question completely, to this day.

Trevor was done with his morning soak and completely dry within a few short minutes. He took his hand, placed it palm down on the desert floor, trying to feel the raw energy emitted by the clay.

Even the local Paiute natives thought Trevor was crazy. One once told him: "No, don't sleep out there. There are skin walkers out there. That is where bad skin walkers go. It's a place of death not a place for life."

Trevor had spent many years exploring this Mystic Desert, and he disagreed with the local Paiute. If skin walkers indeed existed, and if they indeed frequented the clay flats, it is not because death ruled. It was because there was a *power* there, one much stronger than the power that danced within the average Earth-walking body.

It is death that rules in a rain forest, Trevor thought. *But, it is life that rules in a desert.* He knew that very few people would likely agree with him. Then again, they hadn't spent years thinking about it, and living it.

So here Trevor was, trying to understand the great spiritual and religious mystics of the world, by coming to and *becoming the desert.* Just like in his dream. *To find out what the clay teaches, where it comes from and where it goes.*

And while after sleeping out here for three months, Trevor still didn't agree with the native, he *did* understand that there *was* an energy source here, and it was *very* difficult to live right in it. It was exhausting, and not due to the heat. It seemed like the ground itself was sucking the life force from him. He often woke much more tired than when he went to sleep.

He imagined the desert speaking to him in a deep whisper:

"I am, the desert, I am, and I power all of life. There would be no dreams born without me. I am the waves of the ocean, the flats of the wastelands. I am the very distance between the stars, the fire within volcanoes. I birth the dust that the stars are made out of and I dance between the electrons that hold your body together. If you want to see a glimpse of God, you must first see through me."

Trevor shivered. No, even the coyotes usually avoided this place.

It was starting to heat up, so Trevor headed back to the tent, unzipped it.

"Hey Lisa, wake up!"

"What time is it?" Lisa groggily asked.

"I don't know, somewhere around 7:30 maybe."

"It's already hot in here," she complained.

"I know, that's why I was surprised you were still asleep. Come on, let's get up, and drive out to Shoshone for some coffee, ice tea, and breakfast."

"With what money?" she asked.

"We still have a few bucks left," he replied.

"That sounds good."

--- --- ---

-

Lisa was a Mainiac, and so the desert was new to her. She was used to the blueberry covered hills, the rainy days, the green country sides, and the beautiful Maine coastal tides which brought an endless supply of delicious lobster.

She had thought she had fallen in love, and to one of those tall, dark and handsome men that just seemed to promise her the world with his dashing smile. He promised the world, yes, but what did he give her?

He gave her Las Vegas, black eyes, swollen lips, and a God-awful heroin addiction. In fact, she met Trevor having just sailed and crashed through a wall, at the hands of her fiancé. Trevor, by coincidence, just happened to be visiting someone in the next apartment.

Lisa was very tiny growing up; her growth, in fact was stunted, and she turned out quite short; everyone always used to call her Happy Feet when she was little. Well, she took advantage of her auspicious meeting with Trevor to move her little happy feet out of there. She didn't know how she had gotten so lost to begin with.

The biggest problem was the drugs. She considered going down to the methadone clinic. Having told Trevor, he thought he had a better solution. Trevor seemed to be just like a miraculous big brother who had just appeared out of nowhere into her life.

"It's going to be a rough week or so, but if you're willing to quit, I believe that I can help your body with the physical craving."

"How are you going to do that?" she asked.

He said, "One of the biggest problems with heroin, is that once you manage to break the dependency, every time your body goes through any change, the heroin that is stored in your body is released; just enough to make you feel like you absolutely have to use. This can go on for years, even if you manage to somehow resist the craving."

"But, I've been studying a substance for quite a few years that helps the body naturally detoxify itself. Although I can't prove it, I believe that it can, and will, actually pull out and neutralize the heroin stored in your body. If you can tough out that first 72 hours, I think you can kick it."

Lisa knew one thing: She wanted to be free. Free from *him*, the pain, the drugs, and the entire lifestyle. She was willing to do *anything*. Since she no longer had a place to stay, she decided that she could probably crash on a friend's couch, and just grin and bear the withdrawals.

"Is that what you do for a living? Are you an herbalist or something?"

Trevor laughed. "No, no... Right now, I'm currently helping to write and edit a pilot's flight manual for a small passenger airplane."

"Wow," she said, "That sounds very interesting. Are you a pilot, too?"

"No, I'm not a pilot! And actually, I think it is the most boring thing I've ever done; it's driving me crazy!" he laughed.

Later, Trevor brought her a few gallons of this milky grey-green water. It had a mildly pleasant taste, but was a bit chalky.

She didn't remember much of the next week; most of the time she was just curled up in a little ball, in the fetal position. It was terrible. The only thing she did was drink green clay water, as much as her body could handle, when it could handle anything. Day after day: Clay water. Sometimes she would throw it up. Then, she would just wait for her stomach to settle down a bit, and then she'd just drink some more. No food at all, just three (or was it five?) days of drinking clay water.

Then, her body stopped seizing up. Her stomach settled. Her mind cleared. Her strength returned.

She never craved, nor used, heroin again for the rest of her life.

Lisa ended up at a woman's homeless shelter. She didn't mind that much, because she was free from the hellish life she had been drowning in not one month previously.

That's why, when Trevor asked her if she wanted to take off and spend some time in the mystic desert, studying it, clay, and meditating, she didn't even hesitate. She was already a clay disciple.

Trevor told her, "My life as it is now is absolutely not working. Work is driving me crazy and I just feel like I'm surrounded by an impenetrable wall. I want to take off to the desert, and spend some time drinking in the silence, meditating and simply *being*."

She laughed and left and never looked back at her old life.

Later, she would consider this strange desert the place of her rebirth.

They were done with breakfast and ready to hit the road by 10:00 am. Trevor glanced at the fuel gauge in his truck. Under ½ tank. Not good, but not bad to the point to warrant desperation.

Just as long as the truck didn't run out of gas out on the road, everything would work out. This time of year, nobody was out here. If a car passed at all, as often as not, it wouldn't stop. *This* stretch of road was extremely dangerous; dangerous, that is, according to Tim (or Timmy as his *much* younger girlfriend would call him), the "Silver Streak" California Highway Patrolman.

The road itself leads between Death Valley Junction and Baker (better known to us as hell). Whether trying to blast through the Nevada border from California, or vice versa, the road was a criminal's one shot at freedom. If a fugitive could beat the highway patrol to the Pahrump turnoff, freedom was all but guaranteed. It was a dice roll as to whether the CHP in Inyo County was down near Independence or Death Valley National Park, or patrolling near Shoshone to Baker. With nothing to lose, people are often known ready to roll those dice without a second thought.

Trevor didn't see it though. The danger, that is. Someone running would be moving very fast through the desert, with law enforcement not that far off. Still, it did become evident that people who frequented the highway believed it, and they really wouldn't stop for anything.

"Thinking about the gas situation?" Lisa guessed.

Trevor shrugged. "There's not much point in worrying about it, right?"

"What shall be, shall be. What is, is. What is not, cannot..." she said.

Trevor set his eyes back onto the road. Up ahead he saw a strange sight. There was actually a man walking down the side of the highway, with his thumb sticking up. Trevor had never seen anything like it. Not this time of year. He wore black cowboy boots with metal tips, blue jeans, a black button-down shirt (long sleeved) and a black cowboy hat. He had a sack swung over one shoulder, and a guitar case swung over the other shoulder. It looked like he was slowly *limping* forward; or even dragging a leg a bit behind him as he walked.

Lisa said, "Oh my God, would you look at *that*," she pointed as if Trevor might miss the sight.

Trevor drove slowly, imagining that it was a sawed off shotgun in the case, rather than a guitar.

"Trevor you *have* to stop and pick him up," Lisa said.

"Pick him up. *Right*. And then do exactly *what* with him? Take him home with us to our nice house on the beach?"

Lisa was silent, thinking.

The stranger had stopped, set his guitar case on the gravel, and was slowly waving his thumb back and forth. Trevor passed him by, driving about half the speed limit.

He drove a few more miles down the road, then pulled over.

"What the hell is that guy doing walking out here?" Trevor knew that he could last about four hours in the raging heat hiking through the terrain. But that was Trevor, and he had a few tricks the stranger wouldn't be aware of. And Trevor was also clearly at least twenty years younger than the stranger.

"It's insane. The man is on a suicide run," Trevor finished.

"Trev, we can't just leave him there."

"I know, Lisa, I know."

Trevor turned around, and went back to where the man was standing. He rolled down his window.

"Hi there, where are you headed?"

The stranger pointed down the road. "That way," he said. "Down to Baker. Then, up over to Los Angeles."

Trevor had to smile at his sense of direction, and the thick accent. The cowboy, however, looked like he was ready to collapse. It didn't look like he would last out in the heat. He took a step toward the truck, and winced. He was clearly favoring one leg.

"What's wrong with your leg?" Trevor asked, imagining that the stranger had maybe gotten shot during a shoot out with God knew who.

"I'm diabetic," he offered. "The foot's got an infection. The doc told me to get to some antibiotics when I got the chance, but even then he reckoned I was gonna eventually lose the foot."

"That don't bother me none, not as long as I can get to Los Angeles to visit my daughter. I ain't never got the chance to meet her yet. And that's the only thing that counts, least in my book."

In his hand, he held out a picture of the cutest 12 or 13 year old, and offered to me as if it were a carte blanche transportation pass of some sort.

Just then, my perception of him softened, melted a bit.

"Listen, you look dehydrated and exhausted. Let's go back to Shoshone for a bit, get something ice-cold to drink, and get out of the heat." Trevor said.

The stranger nodded, and lifted himself into the back of Trevor's truck.

They went down to the Red Buggy Café, which was completely empty. Robin looked up as all three entered the café.

"Hey there, you two, you've been my only customers today, and I see this time you guys brought back a stranger. I saw you meander by earlier. I was wondering how far you were going to get."

"I don't think he was going to get too far, Robin. Can we all get some cold water, please?" Trevor asked.

"Iced tea?" she asked.

All three wanted ice tea, and all three took a moment and introduced themselves to each other.

"Charles, can you tell me a bit about that foot?"

"Well, it's been this way for four or five months. It just keeps getting worse, bit by bit. There's a hole the size of a quarter on the bottom of my foot, and it goes right up to the bone. Sometimes, the prison doc cleaned it out, scraped it clean before putting some antibiotic ointment on it."

"Has the infection penetrated the bone yet?" asked Trevor.

"No, I don't think so," replied Charles.

"Charles, look. I have a really bad feeling about you and that foot. Even though you're at most two days outside of Los Angeles, by the way you were looking on the side of the road back there, I don't think you're going to make it."

"Well, there ain't no doctors up here, right? And I ain't got no money to pay one with, anyway." Charles said in a matter of fact tone.

"No. You should either go down to Pahrump, or you could consider letting us try something with your foot. We have access to a therapeutic clay that I believe will help you immensely; and it would only take us about six hours to know for sure." Trevor said.

"You should see what this stuff is capable of doing." Lisa chimed in.

"What's that, some kind of Indian stuff?" asked Charles.

"Yes, I guess you could say it is," replied Trevor.

"Well, from what I done heard, Pah-rump don't sound like no place I want to visit any time soon."

And so it was settled.

Trevor and Lisa arranged (with Robin's help) for Charles to stay out of the heat for the afternoon. They were to return later, as they had to prepare the bentonite clay for use.

--- --- ---

-

The sun was beginning to set upon the hot calm of the desert. Trevor, Lisa, and Charles sat out by Trevor's tent.

Charles removed his boots, and revealed his foot.

"Those socks have to be thrown out," Trevor said. "I have an extra pair you can have."

Gangrene was setting in, and the foot stank. The toes still had circulation though, and there was no dead, black tissue to be seen. The area around the tunneling infection was bright red and inflamed. Trevor was worried that it was close to being septic, but they didn't have a thermometer to track Charles' body temperature.

Lisa brought out a sizeable glass container filled with hydrated clay, and some clean white rags.

"Don't you need to clean it before you put your stuff on it?" Charles asked.

"Well, in an ideal world you'd have an MD debride the wound before applying healing clay. As it stands, the clay will actually do that job extraordinarily well, and without all the pain and tissue damage associated with debridement."

"Well, I hope you two aren't some crazy Charles Manson followers. He was supposed to hide out here in these parts at one time, right? Still some of them boys got to be out here, wanderin' around," Charles said, joking.

Trevor laughed. "You got us nailed. We brought you out here to feed our pet Coyotes, and to pawn off that guitar of yours."

"Alright," said Trevor. "This is going to feel cold and uncomfortable."

He took some clay gel and carefully placed in inside the hole in Charles' foot. Some people would pack it in there, but Trevor knew it was better to ever so gently press it in, without actually compressing the clay. Then, he took another sizeable glob of clay, and covered the entire bottom of the foot with clay packed about ½" thick. For good measure, Trevor placed clay on top of the foot, directly over where the tunneling infection was.

Then, Lisa wrapped the foot in clean cloth. She used two ace bandages to secure the dressing to the foot, so that the ace bandages weren't pressing on the clay over the infected area. She tied off both ace bandages.

"Well, I'll be. That wasn't bad at all. Nothing like when the doc cleans that sucker out."

Trevor kept an eye on the dressing to be certain that the wound wasn't draining out. The clay could stay on as long as the wound wasn't draining too much; if it were, then a new clay poultice would need to be used.

Minutes passed. A half-hour. An hour. An hour and a half.

"By God I just noticed somethin'," said Charles.

"What's that," asked Lisa.

"The pain. It's gone. There ain't no more pain at all. It don't feel too heated, it's not achin'. Nothin'. Even a bit warm and soothed."

Trevor removed the dressing and carefully examined the clay. The clay was filled with pussy, gooey, even bloody muck.

Lisa had gotten a bucket of fresh hot spring water directly from the spring source. She carefully cleaned the wound, and the bottom of the foot.

Trevor looked at the foot. The wound itself was completely clean. It looked absolutely perfect. Even better, Trevor noted, was the bottom of the foot. The whole sole of the foot was snow white. *An endothermic reaction around the wound site*, thought Trevor. *They clay is successfully correcting a deficiency.* He nodded, satisfied.

"I'm not a doctor, Charles, but I think the infection will be complete gone within 72 hours, if it is not already. We need to pack the clay again for a few more hours, and then do one more treatment for the night."

They repacked the foot, and everyone visibly relaxed.

"So Charles, if you don't mind my asking, what were you in for?"

Charles looked down, and sighed.

"You know, I've had a long time to think about the perfect song to express what I done."

No Shade Between Heaven and Hell

"Rather than say it, if you two don't mind, I want to grab my guitar. Like I said I ain't got no money, but I figure we could all use a good song right 'bout now."

So, he skillfully began strumming, and then singing:

"It was Della and the dealer and a dog named Jake,
And a cat named Kalamazoo,
Left the city in a pick-up truck.
Gonna make some dreams come true.
Yeah, they rolled out west where the wild sun sets,
And the coyote bays at the moon.
Della and the dealer and a dog named Jake,
And a cat named Kalamazoo.

If that cat could talk, what tales he'd tell,
About Della and the Dealer and the dog as well.
But the cat was cool,
And he never said a mumblin' word.

Down Tucson way there's a small cafe,
Where they play a little cowboy tune.
And the guitar picker was a friend of mine,
By the name of Randy Boone.

Yeah, Randy played her a sweet love song,
And Della got a fire in her eye.
The Dealer had a knife and the dog had a gun,
And the cat had a shot of rye.

If that cat could talk, what tales he'd tell,
About Della and the Dealer and the dog as well.
But the cat was cool,
And he never said a mumblin' word.

Yeah, the Dealer was a killer; he was evil and mean,
And he was jealous of the fire in her eyes.
He snorted his coke through a century note,
And he swore that Boone would die.

And the stage was set when the lights went out,
There was death in Tucson town.
Two shadows ran for the bar back door,
But one stayed on the ground.

If that cat could talk, what tales he'd tell,
About Della and the Dealer and the dog as well.
But the cat was cool,

And he never said a mumblin' word.

If that cat could talk, what tales he'd tell,
About Della and the Dealer and the dog as well.
But the cat was cool,
And he never said a mumblin' word.

Two shadows ran from the bar that night,
And a dog and a cat ran too.
And the tires got hot on the pickup truck,
As down the road they flew.

It was Della and her lover and a dog named Jake,
And a cat named Kalamazoo.
Left Tucson in a pickup truck.
Gonna make some dreams come true.

Yeah, yeah, yeah.

If that cat could talk, what tales he'd tell,
About Della and the Dealer and the dog as well.
But the cat was cool,
And he never said a mumblin' word."

Charles did a Brilliant job with the song; *better than even Hoyt Axton*, thought Trevor.

"Now, I ain't gonna tell whether I was the cat or the dog or the lover; you gots to figure that out for yourselves."

Lisa was mesmerized as the song sank in. "Well, Charles. In court, what was your defense?"

"Me? I didn't have no defense. Sometimes, bad things happen, and just the fact that you don't stop 'em, don't say a word, just walk away... Sometimes, that makes you just as much to blame as any man who pulled the trigger..."

"Charles, you are fantastic with that guitar. Did you spend your time playing your music and writing songs?"

Charles paused, and looked Trevor straight in the eyes. "Not one chord, not one chorus, not one lyric."

And that was the last thing Charles said that night.

Trevor said, "Charles, tomorrow after breakfast, Lisa and I will drive you down toward Baker, and drop you off as far as we can; some place where there is shade, where you can wait for a lift."

Hmph, thought Charles. That clerk back in Independence said there weren't no shade out there 'tall.

--- --- ---

-

Morning came and went. Trevor and Lisa sat in the cab of the truck, while Charles sat in the back.

Trevor studied the gas gauge as if staring at it would magically keep it from going down.

Lisa said, "We are going to have to get gas, you know."

Trevor said, "I know, I know. But I promised that man I'd drop him off near a shaded area, and I do mean to keep my word."

Mile after mile passed. Not one scrap of shade. They passed Dumont Dunes. Nearly an hour had rolled by.

"I can't believe there wasn't one shaded area on that whole stretch of road. Unbelievable! We just drove all the way to hell," he said, as they drove into Baker.

For Trevor and Lisa, Baker was hell. It was the last place anyone would want to be. Baker was someplace that you stopped at if you had to, but there was something completely *wrong* about it. Trevor sensed it.

But as they pulled into a gas station, they glanced back and saw Charles' face light up at the sight of the dozens of semi-trailers cruising down the nearby highway.

No doubt to Charles, this was heaven. If not heaven, then perhaps it was the gateway to heaven. No, to Charles, where he came from was likely hell; sitting back there on that road, near *our* heaven.

He handed Charles their last container of clay, and some pure raw clay. "Keep packing it, Charles, if you can. It will heal. If you can, add a little bit of this raw clay to your water; a little bit each day, and drink it."

Charles said, "I can walk on it perfectly and it don't hurt none. I don't rightly know what I can do to repay you for your kindness."

Lisa smiled to him and said, "Just go see your daughter, Charles. Make her smile. That will be plenty of thanks."

And with that, Charles put his hat on, and started walking *that way*.

"Who would have ever thought?" said Trevor.

"Thought what?" asked Lisa.

"Who would have ever thought that there was no shade between heaven and hell."

"You know Lisa, it just now really dawned on me. All this journeying I've been doing… We've been doing. I finally get it. The only thing I can do for my fellow brothers and sisters on this planet? It's to help them get to where they most need to go. It is that simple. No more. No less. So very simple."

Everything changed in that moment for Trevor.

Perhaps, Trevor thought that is what the desert was doing for me all along… Helping me get to where I most needed to go.

And it was then that Trevor knew it would soon be time to move on.

"Trev, you know we are going to have to put our very last dime into the gas tank just to get back home."

Trevor smiled. "Yes, I realize that. And you know what Lisa. It's ok. It's all going to be ok."

The Singing Chef and the Sorrowed Finger

Tom loved three things most of all in life. His only regret was that he couldn't do all three at once.

First, Tom loved to eat. Italian Food. Mexican Food. Thai Food. Chinese Food. Actually, Tom couldn't really think of any type of food he didn't like.

Next, and luckily, Tom loved to cook. To him, cooking was an art form that took equal parts of creativity and science to do properly. Therefore, Tom considered himself both an artist and an artisan; if not a culinary genius, then at least a culinary master. Again, luckily, he lived in a city that loved good food: Las Vegas, Nevada.

And finally, Tom loved to sing. He wasn't good enough to land a Vegas show or anything, but he *was* good enough to get a second call back from American Idol. He actually thought he had one tiny bit of a chance. He had a big voice. Unfortunately, he had an equally large body frame. *Still*, he had told himself, *look at Meatloaf*. His brief singing career, however, ended quite abruptly with a scowl from Simon Cowell.

Fortunately, cooking and singing went along fine with each other. In fact, Uncle Tom, as his associates nicknamed him, always told his regular customers that it was the music that made the food taste as good as it did.

"Just a roast beef sandwich today, Mick? What, A Billy Joel New Yorker, or maybe a Bob Dylan & Willie Nelson Heartland today?" Tom asked one of his regulars.

"I'm not in any New York state of mine today, Uncle Tom. You pick."

"Sure thing, Mick," Tom replied.

"Still can't see why you left the strip; I have no clue what you're doing cooking down here." Mick asked.

"Because, Mick, this place is no place. I'm tired. Tired of the rat chasing the cheese, and tired of the cats chasing the rats. I just want to do my thing."

The truth was that Tom felt like he was getting old and tired. More tired each day. The energy just seemed to drain from his body, and he was having trouble catching his breath all the time.

Yes, Tom loved to eat.

And that's why, not so luckily, he collapsed shortly thereafter.

Tom had heart attack after heart attack. Twice, three times, four. Terrible months followed terrible months. Tom was on the heart transplant list, but it took him nearly three years to get a new heart.

After the successful heart transplant, he also developed Type II Diabetes.

Tom took his wake up call (or wake up calls) in perfect stride, though. He changed his diet and developed a sort of hybrid cooking style, blending the more healthy cooking habits of the raw organic food followers, with some macrobiotic ideas, and borrowing from the latest super food studies.

"My new job," Tom would say, "Is to make rabbit food taste good and then make the rabbit itself healthy enough to eat!"

Still, he had a very rough case of diabetes, and he still couldn't manage to completely control his appetite. He felt a lot healthier, but he was still heavy. The drugs that he had to take on a daily basis also took their toll.

So, the next thing that got Tom into trouble wasn't his eating, it was his singing. He couldn't sing that much in the years before the heart transplant, but now that he had his lungs back, the lyrics that played inside his mind for so long would simply pour forth.

He was in the kitchen, slicing up some cucumbers. Billy Joel was keeping him company:

> "Anthony works in the grocery store
> Savin' his pennies for someday
> Mama Leone left a note on the door,
> She said,
> "Sonny, move out to the country.""

Tom closed his eyes, and took a giant breath.

> "Well, Workin' too hard can give you
> A heart attackackackackackack..."

Abruptly, Tom stopped dead in his tracks. His face turned white. Just a second before, he felt the sharp blade of the knife slice into his left index finger. He replayed the moment in his mind, and didn't know how he'd managed to stop the knife from slicing straight through.

He didn't think he had sliced it straight through. He was afraid to look to down. So, he closed his eyes, took a deep breath, calmed himself, and *then* glanced down.

The Singing Chef and the Sorrowed Finger

Blood was pouring out everywhere. *Lunch is ruined*, Tom thought to himself. He could move the finger fine, and the bone wasn't broken; it was a flesh wound straight to the bone, but just that. He shook his head and grinned at his clumsiness. He must have done the same thing a hundred times.

Tom finally started to feel the finger throb and ache. He grabbed a small towel and wrapped the finger.

> " You oughta know by now
> And if he can't drive
> With a broken back
> At least he can polish the fenders..."

He sang while cleaning off the work table, soaking up all of the blood. Finished, he closed down the little café, and drove to the hospital.

The doctor tortured the finger for a good ten minutes. "We have be certain the wound is clean," he told Tom as he sowed the finger up.

Then, the doctor put an ointment on it. "That will prevent an infection," he said.

The doctor dressed the wound, and then wrote him a script for some antibiotics. "And that's just in case. With the anti-rejection drugs you have to take because of your heart transplant, your immune system isn't working up to par. Not to mention the diabetes."

And with that, Tom went home.

Later that night, the finger started to hurt. Bad. Then worse. And worse.

By the next morning, Tom was back at the hospital.

The doctor shook his head. "Yep. It's infected."

Tom again went through the agonizing procedure of getting the wound cleaned, closed and dressed.

The doctor was confident: "She looks good now!"

But nearly two months had now passed, and she wasn't looking good. She was feeling even worse. The doctor had done a good job at aggressively keep the finger in the best shape possible, but they were getting nowhere with the treatment. Tom could barely handle the pain. He couldn't sleep, he couldn't enjoy anything, and he couldn't use his left hand at all.

"Well Tom," the doctor finally told him. "There *is* nothing else we can do, except take the finger off. That might be the only option, considering your condition and all. We've done a good job caring for the finger, but it just won't heal and keeps getting re-infected."

Tom, again sitting at home doing nothing but moping around, was considering it. It's only one finger, he thought to himself. But then, what happens if the wound at the finger stub won't heal? What then? And what do I do when I get an infection in the toe? The other hand? Will I be like those other diabetics, having pieces chopped off of me until, eventually, there's nothing left to chop off?

The next morning, the phone rang. An old friend called to check up on him. He told his friend about his wounded finger, and mentioned he was considering having it amputated.

"Oh God, don't do that!" his friend said. "Look, I know this guy that will give you some of this strange stuff to put on it. I kid you not, you'll be extremely glad you contacted him."

Tom didn't see what he had to lose. His friend arranged for Tom to drive over and pick up some of this "stuff" from a gentleman named Brett.

Upon arriving at Brett's home, Brett greeted him with a smile, and a sealed glass jar filled with some green stuff.

"Here you go," Brett said, handing him the jar. It was heavy, and the stuff inside had a strange bounce to it.

"What do I with this stuff?" asked Tom.

"It's very simple and easy Tom," Brett said. "You remove the dressing from your finger, and gently clean off whatever is on the wound site. Then, you take this clay gel, and you pack your entire finger with it, ¾ to 1 inch thick, all the way around the finger, and covering the entire finger. Then, you wrap it up just like it is now. You can secure the dressing with tape, or by simply wrapping it and tying it off at the base of the finger."

"Hmmm," said Tom. "It sounds simple enough. Don't you want to take a look at the finger?"

"Not today," said Brett. "I hear that the doctor is considering taking the finger off. I bet you've been in a lot of pain. Keep doing this, repacking it every two to four hours, or whenever you can. Put a fresh clay pack on before bed. Change it out in the morning. If it still hurts in 48 hours, *then* I will want to see the finger. But I bet the pain will be gone. If the pain *is* gone, then keep doing the clay pack for a total of five to seven days. If there is no pain, give yourself that amount of time *before* going back to see the doc. You don't want him to needlessly take the finger off, so give it a chance to show some excellent signs of recovery."

"What is this stuff, by the way? You called it clay? Like, the clay you make pottery with? Cement clay?" asked Tom.

Brett laughed, "Well, kinda yes and no. It's actually edible clay; it is a green calcium bentonite healing clay with a long history of successful use. This is specially formulated with an oligodynamic silver hydrosol (a special silver water) and a special natural water."

"Silver like the jewelry metal?" Tom asked, puzzled.

"Yes... and no. The silver is much purer, and in a different state. The water contains micro-fine silver particles in colloidal suspension, as well as isolated and negatively charged silver ions. The clay will work to pull the infection, the silver will work to quickly kill it, and then both will work to stimulate wound healing and speed healthy tissue growth."

Tom said. "Hmmm... That seems all very strange to me."

If Tom's friend wasn't so damn reliable, Tom probably would have driven away with a "thanks" and deposited the jar of clay in the garbage.

"I'll give it a try!" Tom said. "What do I owe you for this?" he asked. The alt med and herbal people were sometimes a hundred times worse than the doctors. Only, at least he had insurance to help pay the doctors.

"You don't owe me a dime, Tom. Don't worry about it, just heal the finger." Brett said.

Tom did what Brett had advised him to do. At first, it was a bit confusing to work with the clay gel. But, it became surprisingly easy after the first treatment. The clay gel was wet, but it held together easily. It was also very malleable; easy to mould to and apply.

By the second day, Tom was astounded. The pain that had robbed him of his life for the past months was gone. The mobility of his finger was even returning. The swelling was down. Tom was overjoyed, and felt that he had a strange new lease on life. *Maybe the diagnosis of diabetic wasn't a slow death sentence after all, maybe there are things I can do*, Tom thought.

Then, Tom got mad. He headed toward the door, then caught himself, and sighed. He had promised Brett that he would wait a week before going back to see the doctor.

For a week, Tom's blood boiled.

The week was up, and Tom stormed in to see the doctor. The doctor didn't seem to notice Tom's body language at all.

The doctor unwrapped the dressing on the finger. "Hmm... Lookie here. How about that? It looks like we finally got things under control. That is just great. Can you move it? Good... Good. Does it hurt?" he asked.

Tom said, "No. It doesn't hurt. It's healing up just fine."

Then he screamed at the doctor: "YOU WANTED TO CHOP MY FINGER OFF YOU USELESS BASTARD. I HAD THIS GUY GIVE ME THIS SILVER CLAY. IT HEALED THE PAIN IN TWO DAYS. I PAID YOU THREE HUNDRED DOLLARS ON TOP OF INSURANCE MONEY TO TORTURE MY ASS. HE GAVE ME THE STUFF FOR FREE. WHAT KIND OF RACKET ARE YOU RUNNING HERE?"

Tom was loud. The doctor looked scared. A nurse came in alarmed.

But as quickly as he heated up, he had cooled down.

"God that felt good!" Tom said.

The doctor, now paying *very* careful attention to Tom's body language asked, "What did you do to the finger?"

"This researcher gave me a green clay gel made with silver water to put on my finger. I did. It worked. I brought some in; do you want to see it?"

"No... No, that's all right. Silver, eh? Well, here then."

The doctor picked up his pad, and wrote out a prescription, and handed it to Tom.

"Everything looks perfect. Get that filled at the pharmacy, follow the instructions, and see me again in three weeks to be certain it's healing up correctly."

And with that, the doctor put away his pen, and walked out the door.

Tom looked at the script. It said, "Silver Sulfadiazine."

Tom left hospital, but he chose never to see that doctor again.

He called Brett to give him the good news about his finger.

"...and then the stupid doctor gave me this cream. I use it, but it doesn't take away the aching, or seem to do much."

Brett laughed. "Silvadine, eh? What an idiot. Now, Silvadine is a great product, but not for your kind of wound. So he didn't even want to look at the hydrated clay you brought in?" Brett paused, shaking his head.

"Typical," Brett said. "I've seen it over and over again."

"But who I really feel sorry for, though, is that doctor's *next* unresponsive patient. The patient who is going to lose the toe or the finger to the infection. That is the real tragedy."

The Tribe of the Sacred Clays

Grandfather looked over the great Los Angeles City from the vantage point provided by the North Hollywood Hills. The city was still. Not one vehicle moved along the roadways below. Not one light shone from street or shop. The international airport's usual roar was silent. *One could almost hear the crashing of the surf, the swaying of the ocean*, Grandfather thought.

He liked to imagine that the city was actually dead. For not so long ago, all of the cities had nearly been destroyed; all of mankind had nearly been wiped clean off of the face of the earth. *No, the city is not dead today*, he thought, *it is simply resting-- waiting*.

As the sun finished its retreat over the ocean horizon, Grandfather started to notice small fires, newly lit, dotting the landscape below. They looked like tiny flickers produced by miniature lighters from his vantage point. *Others are gathering, just like we are*, he thought.

Starting today, all over the world, in every city across every nation, the power was turned off. Every ship sailing every sea was silenced; every airplane's engine powered down; every orbiting satellite quieted; every possible source of man-made technology was stilled.

The only exceptions were emergency services, such as hospitals, which remained powered; but even they had to have the outside of the building completely covered, so that no artificial light shone out; shielded so that no EMF frequencies penetrated the lead cocoons encasing the hospitals. The numerous nuclear power plants also needed to remain online even though they would not be producing any usable power.

Designing the shielding for the world's nuclear powered technologies had nearly bankrupted the nations of the Earth. However, since the very survival of Earth depended upon absolute compliance, the resources were found.

Lastly, the world's defense computer systems remained on alert, all equipment in shielded bunkers. Satellites quietly listened both to the quiet song of the Earth below and to the (hopefully) empty silences between the planets of the solar system.

Ironically, thought Grandfather, *the war against terror which the west had fought for so long was ended in less than 90 days*. Twelve years of failure, and then, *just like that*, it was over. Tens of thousands of people had to be killed; in a few cases, it almost took genocides.

The Tribe of the Sacred Clays

There was no more room for any isms or ianities, not for the first five days of each month, six months out of the year. If an individual couldn't set aside his or her isms, gripes, and whatever other rights that may or may not have been previously bestowed upon them by God or Country, then the individual was killed immediately, and without a trial.

No, nobody had any rights or privileges during these days. During these days, everyone was a member of the New Tribe.

Today, and for the next five days, he was Grandfather. For the remainder of the month, however, he was Lee Marcus Jones, a now retired computer sciences engineer who specialized in room temperature superconductivity computer technologies. He was also President and Chief Global Advisor for the United Governments' Council of Xenoglobal Foreign Affairs.

He was six feet two inches tall, and still had an incredibly wide shoulder frame, with chiseled arms, deeply wrinkled skin and high cheekbones. His eyes were vibrant blue, and shone with a fierce intelligence. Every last hair on Lee's body was snow white; his deeply wrinkled face appeared as if wisdom itself was carved in the wrinkles. He was eighty-three years old. His voice carried both authority and age quite well. He had seen more happen in his lifetime than anyone should be allowed to see; that is, see and remain sane. Lee was tired, but he had to remain strong tonight for the telling of the stories.

As the late afternoon became evening, Grandfather's campfire began drowning out all other light sources. The bonfire had become huge, and there were a good thirty or thirty-five people chatting quietly nearby. The young and the older were here, present for the telling of the stories.

He lifted up a jar made of a glass silicone polymer (he liked to call the substance Silly Glass, but only in his mind – who ever heard of glass that you could throw off a ten-story building, and have it bounce down the street unharmed?). The jar was covered in a special thick paper which actually neutralized light and any form of radiation, electromagnetic or otherwise.

He turned it a bit in the air, and let the firelight dance off of the jar. He opened it, placed his left hand in the jar, and took out two fingers full of hydrated clay. He smeared clay down one side of his cheek. Then the other. Then, across the forehead. Then, down his chin. The clay appeared as if pale white on his skin; he looked eerily ancient and authoritative in the dancing firelight and rising moonlight.

He spoke, and as he did so, people quieted.

"The stories told are our heritage and our inheritance. They contain the promise of that which we truly are, the hope of what we shall become, and the sadness of our short-comings. And we cannot forget our own betrayals, even as we embrace our own triumphs. My story starts with the very earth itself; the very ground walked upon."

Grandfather paused, looking again at the jar.

"Selectively transducing, self-organizing, scalar-field projecting, hydrated, colloidal, charged nanocrystals. Scientists call it a monatomic element collector; a selective ion pump, and many other things. But it is, in truth, the very essence of all life on Earth; the fire of the universe. It is plant food. It is birthed by the ocean, and birthed from the Earth's very core. Scientists now *know* that this sacred earth was at the very least responsible for the formation of the first semi-permeable cell walls; the same cell walls that made complex life possible. The same clay that for reasons that still baffle the brightest minds on Earth, seems to hunger to support higher and higher forms of organized life.

"My ancestors," continued Grandfather, "Called it Ee-Wah-Kee, which means the earth that heals."

Grandfather closed the jar and handed it to the closest person sitting around the fire. He stopped talking, and listened to the gentle breeze blowing softly.

It was too easy for Grandfather to get lost in his own thoughts these days. *I'm getting so old,* he reminded himself. He continued to let his thoughts wander as the jar of clay passed from person to person, where each person took their two left fingers and removed clay from the jar.

Glancing at the individuals around the fire, Grandfather noticed that a seven-year-old child had a watch—a Mickey Mouse watch – strapped to her wrist. He walked over to her and–gently but sternly—removed the watch from her wrist, and tossed it into the fire.

The adults nearby did not say a word. The child put her right hand over her newly O-shaped mouth. Grandfather returned to his thoughts.

All around the world (it *seemed like just yesterday, but in truth it has been nearly three years*) the indigenous "first people" of every continent had been given what is now called Equal Rulership Rights and Privileges, based upon the system of government in place in each nation on Earth. In the United States, for example, there were now two Presidents sharing power, and for every settled-American Congressman, there was a Native Congressman, indigenous to the state of representation, or at least representative of the native tribes in that region.

The Australian Aborigines eventually fit into the parliamentary system quite well. Mexico had serious integration problems, mostly due to the original corruption of the Mexico system of government. Ultimately Mexico came through it all quite well.

Many other countries were not so lucky. This new global law caused the total collapse of more than one government. But again, since the survival of humanity depended upon it, change rushed forward; the selfish fell, fell hard, and fell fast. The United Governments of the World (the UGW, which replaced the obsolete, defunct, and corrupt United Nations) would quickly step in with overpowering force and restore order. Local governments *needed* to be comprised of local people; autonomy had to be maintained. Furthermore, the local leadership *was required* to be educated in order to effectively run a government that would have to work in unison with all nations on Earth.

This new world required true statesmen. It was as if, overnight, there was no more room for politicians in politics. Grandfather chuckled to himself. *Perhaps that was what was meant by the Old Testament phrase 'the meek shall inherit the Earth'*, he thought.

In those early days, sweeping changes, like raging wildfires, rushed across the human landscapes, wave after wave. And everything that humanity needed to accomplish – and accomplish *now*—caused panics that ebbed and flowed like flooding waters crashing against levies. The biggest problem was that the changes required were so *expensive*.

Humanity had the resources and manpower, but nobody had the money; with each day of new expenditures, inflation raged. There wasn't enough money to do what needed to be done.

The UGW had approached Lee with the dilemma, and it was clear the greatest minds of the time had no clear answer as to what to do.

"The answer is obvious," Lee stated in a matter-of-fact tone. "If there is not enough money to accomplish what needs to be done, then... Simply abolish money completely. Problem solved."

And so the UGW did just that. In its place, a temporary system was set up that was the exact opposite of money. You didn't pay to get things. When you got things, the people you got them from received payment in the form of points.

Points were created by demand and supply for goods, services and ideas; there was no limited amount of points issued to begin with, they were simply created out of thin air as needed at the point of need, and tracked by one of the enormous global super computers that had become almost commonplace.

A team of highly qualified theoretical economists watched the economic trends in real time, and reported all trends to the UGW on a weekly basis; unbeneficial trends considered actionable by a country's government were dealt with, and with no red tape at all.

Points had no established material value, but powerful voices on the new pan-global political (and military) scene argued that one day, once the Effort (as the whole human transformation program was called) had been completed, there would be a vast payback, with interest. And because everyone *was too scared not to believe it because the alternative was certain death*, everyone treated points as more valuable than the old money everyone had been born using.

Under pressure from the old way of doing things, the UWG approached Lee with a problem. "What about the corporations?"

The corporate entity instantly became the poorest thing on the planet.

Lee patiently explained. "Corporations have nothing to give; since they have nothing to give, they should have no actual tangible value. Since they have become materially valueless, everyone can finally see the only true value of a corporate entity: Structure.

"So, henceforth, let the people structure businesses as needed, but without the burden of corporate asset possession. It will take time, but future generations will see that the idea of ownership is simply a useful illusion. Let the use prevail and let the illusion fail. The future we are building is one of abundance, not lack. Let the people working for the corporations earn the points based on their contribution to the Effort."

Thus rich fat cats became poor cats. Small farmers became very comfortable; workers became middle class. Technologists became upper middle class, and creative geniuses of all types reached a kind of demigod status as heroes for a new tomorrow.

Multitudinous problems constantly presented themselves.

For example, the poor class was eliminated by Government Mandate. It became illegal to be poor.

The Tribe of the Sacred Clays

That wasn't working out very well, so the UWG sought out Lee once more. "Jailing the worlds poor can hardly be considered humane. We are failing to bring all of the people of the world out of poverty."

Lee nodded to them. "Again, the answer is quite simple. Now that you have made it illegal to be poor, you simply need to make it illegal for *people to allow* people to be poor. Let all of the people accept the burden of the Effort."

Since the rich and the comfortable would be jailed if the poor remained poor, the rich became very creative in dealing with poverty. Necessity is the mother of invention. It soon became clear to everyone that the best solution to the problem was the oldest one: Neighbors helping neighbors.

For humanity could not afford to be poor, not and survive. People had to be well fed, well cared for, and well connected—both to themselves and with each other. There were to be no excuses.

So that is when Lee wiped out the fractional banking reserve system, and flushed it down the toilet of history. Not even the bankers looked back.

The UGW again ran into a dilemma. Again, Lee was called in to consult.

"People are still fighting over the rights of ideas. We have technologies that need to be developed, owned by companies that cannot afford to develop them, trying to negotiate with the economists about how much points an owned idea might be worth."

Lee chuckled, thinking to himself: Ownership, ownership, ownership. What was the old saying, possession is 9/10 of the law?

"The answer is self-evident. Declare all patents null and void, and limit copyright capabilities," Lee directed.

A new system of authorship and inventorship was enacted in place of the old laws. This system rewarded new ideas immediately, and made them available to any entity that decided to develop the idea or invention. When questioned about the need to protect massive investments, Lee was called in again.

"If Business A were to spend two years developing a technology, and Businesses B, C, and D were going to do the same, and none had a clear advantage, what would the only intelligent solution for all four companies to do?"

One of the UGW representatives quickly nodded. "Of course, the only solution would be for all four companies to partnership."

"And what if one had a clear developmental advantage due to production capability, or distribution?" Lee asked.

"Cooperative mergers and trades based on capabilities, of course."

From that point on, during the Humanity Restoration Period, what one man created belonged to all of mankind.

Grandfather returned to the present time, and stoked the fire. He took a deep breath, and realized that only a few moments had passed since he had stopped speaking.

He resumed his monologue:

"But the saddest thing was that our great people, who had once been masters of clay use, lost the art completely when the British and European settlers came and took over the land. It was they who rediscovered the use of clay here in North America, and it was their children's children's grandchildren who ended up teaching us about clay therapy."

"But even then, as the 20th Century progressed, new medicines and powerful life killers were born from science. Alternatives to traditional medicines (soon called modern medicine) replaced nearly all natural medicines. People largely forgot about the living clays. It seemed like the whole of natural medicine would leave mankind with a soft whimper."

Grandfather paused, as the last person sitting around the giant bonfire finished with his jar of clay. He knelt down and took the clay from what looked to be a 14-year-old boy, who was busy licking his fingers.

Grandfather's voice began to show a slight edge of irritation. "It didn't matter that clay, when applied and left on during the night, would somehow kill the virus which caused warts," Grandfather's voice raised, even as he raised one arm up.

His voice grew louder. "It didn't matter that there was no medicine that could heal a sunburn as fast and thoroughly as hydrated clay, preventing tissue damage and reducing the chance of acquiring skin cancer later... It didn't matter that clay could do these things *and* that no modern medicine could.

"It didn't matter that, when good healing clay was used on wounds, the wounds never became infected. It didn't matter that swelling was rapidly reduced and that pain, pain which even the strongest pain killers wouldn't numb, would always rapidly vanish, as if were just washed away!" Grandfather's hands swept across his chest.

Grandfather's voice reached a feverish, intense pitch. "It didn't matter that sometimes life-threatening cancers would vanish under the influence of clay. It didn't matter than our earth-that-heals could quickly cure poisoning; either by food or insect bite; even such toxic, damaging bites as were caused by the brown recluse. No. Mother Earth's medicines were not *convenient* enough. Mother Earth Herself could not be patented, and thus, selling earth was not *profitable*, and giving earth away (as if someone could own it) was considered *not wise*." Grandfather took a breath and looked around.

Grandfather now whispered, but to those listening, it was like he was screaming: "It... didn't... matter."

He paused for a good two minutes; nobody broke the silence. He took a deep breath, and then loudly sighed.

"But then something happened," he stated. "Something terrible."

Lee held the attention of every eye around the campfire. He met each set of eyes with the fury of his own; his azure eyes shone like blue fire opals in the firelight.

"Something terrible yes. But not something unexpected. Our ancestors knew that the following events would occur; that modern civilization would cause a great imbalance in the forces of nature... That mankind would not heed the ancestors' warnings, and that things would get worse. Even our ancient Mayan brothers foretold the future by ending their calendar. "Something terrible, yes. Mankind began poisoning the Earth, and in turn, poisoning the self. Doctors tried treating the poisoned condition with more poisons, which, in turn, ended up dumped into the waters of the world where we all drank them. Mankind poisoned the skies, and tried to save the skies by dumping more poisons into the clouds, where we all breathed them. Mankind had robbed the very nutrients from the lands, and thus began starving the animals of the world, and thus themselves. The doctors tried to cure the malnourishment with more chemicals. Obesity became a true abomination, a sign of the sick nourishment of mind, heart, and body. Mankind poisoned the Ether with electric noises of all sorts, and the doctors tried to cure all of the ensuing insanities with drugs that caused even more insanity." Grandfather spit into the fire in marked disgust.

"As the Twentieth Century ended, more and more people suffered; suffered long, slow deaths in some cases, quick and shocking deaths in other cases. Cancers, arthritic conditions, auto-immune disorders, neurological conditions... Weak bone disorders, personality disorders... As time marched on, the problems became worse. The medicines of modern man started breeding angry and lethal diseases which started to march against humanity, slowly and painfully deadly. Mankind was powerless, *powerless* to slow their marching hunger to consume the slime spreading across the Earth known as mankind.

"Painfully slowly people began to realize that technology, and the civilizations driving technologies forward, that ran contrary to the laws of nature, already contained the seed of that civilization's destruction.

"People, one by one, started to rediscover the truth; the same truth of the Ancestors.

"As people learned, they started going back to natural ways, yes, but only because they were the only things that actually *worked*!

"People started their own gardens, and started using small amounts of clay to re-naturalize manufactured soils. People gave clays to their pets, and put it in their feed and drinking water. When that worked so well, small organic farmers started to give clay to their livestock."

"The medical world was very ineffective at dealing with the metal toxicity and chemical toxicity that was the underlying cause (or at the very least, the single co-factor) for most of modern man's chronic illnesses; in fact, doctors were mostly in denial, hypnotized by insurance companies, drug companies and the regulatory bodies ruled by the special interest groups.

"Bodies poisoned with heavy metals and chemicals began to recover. Sometimes quickly and dramatically and other times painfully slowly, countless people began to reawaken to nature, began to heal and to breath. People returned to the Earth, bathing in it, playing in it, drinking it. And these people rediscovered a calm serenity long denied to them.

"Diabetics were miraculously able to fend off the infections storming their hands and feet; through internal use, their metabolic function improved and the metabolism became far easier to effectively regulate. They grew healthier, happier, and felt empowered by the very earth itself.

"Super bacterial infections fell to the power of good healing clay as well; MRSA, pseudomonas, and even flesh eating bacterial infections.

"Clay use, topically, via baths, compresses, poultices, and as an internal supplement, seemed to improve nearly any condition it was used for. Tens of thousands of people began to re-discover how to *integrate* clay into their regular health regimes.

"Even those poisoned with radiation responded well to clay use; people suffering from acute toxicity at the site of chemical spills responded well to clay use; clay helped people reverse chronic degenerative conditions, such as osteoporosis.

"Some of best, state of the art plastic surgeons even learned how to speed tissue healing and reduce scarring by the use of clay-filled complex colloids.

"Illites, calcium montmorillonites, sodium bentonites… Sacred clays were slowly unearthed and found their way into the natural health movement. The successful use of clays continued to *lead* people back to a way of life that was more harmonious with life and nature. It was as if clay itself possessed a guiding, intelligent force; one that people began listening to."

It seemed like Grandfather could go on forever talking about healing clay. But a small voice, issued from the far side of the fire, interrupted him:

"Grandfather, but then something happened next, tell us what happened next, Grandfather!" there was excitement and awe in her voice, and it was clear from looking at the group that it was time to move forward.

Yes, something did happen, and that something has kept mankind in an uproar ever since. In fact, it amazed Lee that for all but five days a month, six months out of the year, humanity was a sea of chaos, but then, for these five days… Everything was at peace; everyone fell into a quiet, awe-filled serenity.

"Yes, tell us Grandfather, what happened on that night then, after all of this!" chimed in another youthful voice.

Grandfather paused for a good minute with his eyes closed. He took a breath.

"Yes, yes. It turns out, that the movement back to a harmony with the natural world was far too little, far too late; although nobody knew it at the time.

"It was near the middle of December, 2017. It was a cold evening. I was preparing to speak at a very large trade show exhibition currently being held just outside Delores, Colorado. Delores was the location of an experimental, newly developed space elevator that was to begin construction later that year. The foundation, and the two stories beneath the earth required to maintain and run the massive elevator had already been completed. I created the computer system which regulated the tension beams according to wind shear and other environmental factors.

"Just then, and without any warning, the sky turned bright white, then became filled with flashes of blue. The major TV networks, previously bored stiff with hours of jargon filled lectures, were stunned back to life. Cameras swept in all directions as everyone tried to source the nature of the disturbance.

"Then, the sky was still once more. But, sitting as quiet as could be in front of us all, was a strange rounded triangular vehicle, hovering just above the ground. It was as if it just appeared in a flash of light.

Grandfather paused, and looked at the faces of the young ones in the crowd. Their eyes were open in absolute terror. *Good*, thought Grandfather. For the children here would have to grow up and complete the great work that the elder generation had started. *It was good that they felt both fear and awe.* Grandfather knew that the children were listening to the story of the past, while at the same time shivering at the thought of what would happen on the sixth and seventh days of this month.

He continued. "A ramp that seemed like it was made from light appeared from the strange vehicle. Seven individuals appeared at the top, and began walking down the ramp, slowly, gazing at the few hundred people hushed before them. Cameras rolled. Commentators with microphones whispered intently.

"I was startled. The figures which approached me directly looked familiar. They wore full headdresses, and their faces were painted with wild berry war paint. The figure in front was obviously a chief, and he carried a spear with a glistening point. A simple loincloth adorned his torso, and nothing covered his feet. He was as tall as I.

"He walked directly up to me; my microphone was still live, and it was the only thing between him and me. He ignored the entire crowed, and spoke, gazing into my eyes.

""I am Chief Ranahazum, of the Anasazi, returned home after a long journey far away. We have come home to the place of the Ancestors, to the world of our birth, which was, and ever remains, ours." The chief had paused for effect, but then continued, "As a first people tasked as friends of the Ancients, we have been returned by the Star Brothers. We have been returned to pass judgment upon you. We are here to be your judges and your executioners. We are seven horsemen, and as we look upon the wasteland of our homeland, we see only: Legion."

Grandfather paused from the story now, as was tradition. There was no need to recount the thousands of crimes against humanity and against nature that the Anasazi read off, one by one. This story was not about the failure of mankind; everyone could read about that in the New Histories. This story was about the hope of humanity. The chance for a new beginning: The struggle for both survival and for redemption.

The small crowd which gathered around the fire didn't think Grandfather's voice could get louder or more powerful, but it did as he began to chant:

> "Neither stars nor stripes
> Nor religion's old gods
> Nor the science of the odds
> Will disturb the calm on these five days–
> Not the hammer or the sickle
> Not one electronic trickle
> Not a rock or a hard place
> Nor excuse or abuse
> Will disturb our painful stay
>
> We cannot halt our new ways;
> When the star brothers come
> With the barrel of a gun
> For the star dust pure
> On the sixth and seventh days
> From the tribe of the sacred clays
> When the angels from the skies
> Look down upon us with no eyes
> It's the tribe of the sacred clays
> That will save our human race."

--- --- ---

-

Grandfather paused, again becoming lost in his own thoughts.

Thus humanity's first contact with intelligent life from another star system was, in fact, the completion of the Ancient Anasazi Trail, the return of the lost tribe of the ancient ones.

While the returned natives gave their opening speech, dozens of starships fell into orbit. Everyone had been too stunned to panic. The Anasazi outlined every last flaw of humanity's civilization over the last four centuries, and then, he had asked Lee (and the rest of the world via the live global telecast), if humanity had any defense.

In shock, Lee remembered saying something absolutely stupid: "We had thought you disappeared in the great Black Rock Desert."

The Chief hmph'd, and said, arms folded, "We did. And that is exactly where we returned; only, it seems that nobody got the message we had left; nobody was there to greet us. And so we came here, to the space elevator, where we knew there would be a big party."

It was that moment that Lee knew that the people of this world had a chance; he sensed it. He sensed he had a friend in the Chief, not an enemy.

Lee had looked directly into the amused face of the Anasazi chief: "There is no defense against the forces of nature and evolution," Lee spoke very carefully. "Our own very nature redirects us to discover the earth, the universe, life itself, in each and every breath we take; for we too are nature. That this sacredness might be lost to the children, does not mean that the sacredness is, in fact, actually lost."

Then, Lee had issued his own challenge. "Our defense, then, can lie only in the value of what we *have* created, who we are *in process* of becoming, and *what*, finally we have actually *overcome*, in order to arrive in this exact time space."

The Chief did not give in so easily, however. "The dictates of *nature* and *evolution*? And what of the dictates of Great Spirit, so easily and conveniently ignored, and the dictates of the rains and sunlight, which speak but plainly to the ear ready for listening. My people were always able to listen, despite the dictates of so called progress and evolution." He paused.

"And yet, it is true, there are many seasons, each having a place. Therefore, I hereby charge you and the nations of the world to demonstrate the value; the value of the discovered earth, the civilizations, the philosophies, the religions, art forms, sciences or whatever else may possibly pass as *value*.

"And because we share a common past, we will assist you in trying to discover this value you speak of. However, I warn you: Judgment has but already been passed, as the Star Brothers have visited this world often enough to see its decay, and the time has come when you grow strong enough to threaten more than this small world."

Grandfather snapped back to present time, and then realized that he must have just spoken the story of First Contact aloud.

He spoke, this time with full intent. "All of the feeble attempts of the peoples of the world to show off humanity's accomplishments were met with either disinterest or complete disdain. A week passed, then two, and finally the visitors orbiting Earth grew weary, and made a decision.

"In one heartbeat, a scorching fire exploded across an entire content, and billions died within seconds. In fact, all organic material had been incinerated. Dry ash was all that remained."

Grandfather paused, watching the small group of people. He saw painful memories in the eyes of the older people, fear and wonder in the eyes of the younger generations.

He whispered. "All seemed to have been lost. Humanity had no recourse, and while many screamed in anger, or in fear, or hate, nobody important cared to listen."

He spoke up once more. "Then, the Cleansing of the Earth's Surface, as the Anasazi called it, suddenly halted. I was called before the Seven Horseman (as the media quickly adapted to calling the representatives of the Anasazi).

"The Anasazi had brought a map, and were pointing at an area near Russia. After a few puzzled moments, I recognized it. "That is Chernobyl" I said, voice trembling. I thought this was to be the final, ultimate embarrassment before the final wrath of the Star Travelers was unleashed upon the world. "It is the site of a nuclear reactor meltdown of devastating proportions," I continued.

"The Chief stated, "Yes, we can see that. But why is not as hot as it should be? We cannot exactly tell what has happened to this area. There's something strange there. We're sending drones down to investigate."

Grandfather paused a moment, breathing.

"That is when it dawned on me that thousands upon thousands of tons of smectite clay, most likely bentonite, were dumped upon the hot nuclear reactor, shortly after the nuclear meltdown. The clay adsorbed much of the radiation, and helped to seal the reactor beneath the earth.

"Within several hours, the Anasazi had samples of the clay, and were studying it intently. "This substance has become something the universe has never seen before!" he noted with a touch of awe in his voice. "The scientists describe the clay as being in a state of quantum decoherence. Wave form after collapsing wave form slapping the unstable isotopes make it nearly impossible to even study the substance. A new science has already been created just to study the effects."

"Within a week twelve or thirteen quarries containing unique clays were discovered, and samples obtained for study. Several days passed, when I received a Sat phone call from a very hushed Chief Ranahazum. 'The council is very interested in all of these clays. They have seen nothing like them before, anywhere,' the Chief stated. I replied, 'But how is that possible? This galaxy must be filled with clay; even just this solar system must contain an over-abundance of clay.' The Chief nodded, and responded, 'Yes, but the clays cataloged to date share only the properties of average, un-noteworthy crystals. They are not alive, not like the clays found here. There is even debate that the clays contain a super-evolved consciousness, one that is of course very foreign to our standard non-mineral, organic-based idea of intelligence. They are stating that it will take thousands of years of study to even develop the necessary technology to study the multi, inter-dimensional properties of the clays.'"

Lee took a deep breath, and concluded his story for the night.

"And that is how healing clays saved the human race, and how the Tribe of the Sacred Clays was born."

--- --- ---

-

Lee sat down as the group began chattering amongst themselves. His thoughts quickly moved forward, however, caught in the telling of his own story. The group was satisfied with the brief account, but Lee was still caught up in the drama.

He had been stunned to silence by the Chief's insistence in the clays' unique qualities. But the Chief continued, still in a hushed voice, too quickly: "Lee, but you must act quickly now. Favor has been granted to the clays of this world, but not to its inhabitants."

The visitors, Lee realized, still planned on wiping out the human race, and claiming it as their own prized possession. Lee, as the sole appointed spokesperson for the world (at the insistence of the Anasazi), had ready access to the world's current leaders. They quickly developed and quietly executed a plan to spread the world's nuclear arsenal amidst the valuable clay deposits.

Once this was accomplished, Lee contacted the Chief, and demanded that all starships leave, except for the Anasazi vessel, and maintain a distance outside of the moon's orbit. The Star Travelers quickly realized that the humans would destroy the clay deposits.

Lee and his Anasazi ally were instrumental in negotiating and signing a peace treaty that included a limited trade agreement. The arrangement included the trade of non-interstellar technologies to humankind, which would, Lee thought, be instrumental in being able to lift humanity out of its dark ages.

However, the peace treaty also included demands that the human race restore and care for the planet and all of its inhabitants, including themselves. The agreement also prevented any space travel beyond the moon's orbit. It gave humanity a fleeting chance to raise itself up to the standards of the star-traveling civilizations; a temporary reprieve from certain death.

Furthermore, the Chief explained that the clays were so sensitive to electromagnetic energy, the Star Visitors demanded that they be mined and stored completely pure, without contamination, electromagnetic or otherwise. Any resonance fields created on the surface of the Earth, the human scientists quickly learned, were carried rapidly world-wide, embedded in the Schuman resonance fields of the Earth's electromagnetic field, carried through the air, by the sea, and even bounced back off of the stratosphere and ozone layer.

The seven day cycle was thus created, where man would mine and store clay for five days. On the sixth and seventh day, the giant transport vehicles would land; we would load the clay without direct contact with anyone, and then the transports would depart.

Humanity, it would seem, was finally going to have to learn how to be quiet.

Year after year Lee watched them come and go; had many secret meetings with the Anasazi, who always seemed to have an answer to the latest catastrophes threatening mankind's future. Each time the visitors arrived, Lee and his Anasazi friend wondered if they were here, finally, to wipe the Earth's surface clean once and for all.

Each year, they came and went, and upon leaving, Chief Ranahazum would say: "Perhaps, then, the healing clays have a greater plan for us, still!"

Then, he too would disappear into the distant stars.

Author's Note

I wanted to include a science fiction story in this small collection, but I didn't know exactly how I wanted to do it.

The initial story idea for *this* story was completely comprised around the idea of a Native American telling stories to a captive audience around a camp fire. I needed a story that I could insert a bunch of tiny clay experiences into, whenever I wanted to. This would give me the ability to throw in tidbits of healing clay uses that didn't warrant a full story.

I felt I could accomplish this in a manner that was creative and entertaining, and without simply having a list about what clay has healed or could heal.

Then something very irritating happened. While researching material for Book II, I began reading "More Precious than Gold", by Ray Pendergraft. The book starts out positing this question: "What would you do if you found yourself in possession of one of the most precious substances ever known to mankind?"

At the same time, I had been dealing with a big perception problem when it comes to clay therapy. It was as if all of the written material described clay use as being important if you were far away from help, or otherwise had no access to modern medicine.

It was like the attitude toward clay therapy was: "Yep, if I was up in the mountains and hurt myself, far away from the comforts of a hospital, that's when I'd want to be sure to have clay handy."

A big part of book III is an attempt to modernize clay therapy. There are dozens of situations where people really need to change the thinking. The thinking should be, "Let me use this clay first, and then if I have continue to have a problem, then I'll go to the hospital."

I truly believe that many lives would be saved if healing clay therapy were to be restored to its rightful place in human health care.

So, a story involving the distant past, the turbulent present, and a strange future started to emerge in my mind.

In fact, the story took over my mind, and started telling itself. I literally lost control of it, and haven't really regained control of it yet.

Central to the idea of this story is an old story once told to me about an Aboriginal Australian. A younger aboriginal man found himself far away from home, with a very cold night approaching. The young man had plenty of food and water, but didn't know if he could survive the cold.

While walking, he stumbled upon a briefcase. He opened it, and became excited and overjoyed! His prayers had been answered!

In the suitcase was a million dollars. The aborigine man quickly set about using the paper to make a warm fire, and slept the night through, grateful for his good fortune.

Our perceptions color both our actions and our perception of those actions. I have always seen a parallel to the story of discovering that briefcase full of money and the undiscovered potential of healing clays.

Sometimes, we know not what it is that we possess.

<u>Never Look Back</u>

Rick could see each breath he exhaled as steam, but he couldn't hear his breathing. The rumbling sound all around him drowned out everything else. He felt the heat pouring out from the engine near his leather-padded legs. He felt the crunch of crackling dirt as he adjusted his feet beneath him.

He tightened his grip on the handle bars, tested his hand brakes, and then relaxed his fingers. Adrenaline began pumping as Rick began to anticipate the "GO!" signal. He hit the throttle with his right hand, just to confirm that the fuel and air mixture was just right and to hear the thunder of raw horsepower. His KTM 500 roared beneath him, and lurched ever so slightly.

The beast is hungry! Rick thought with a grin.

Rick was a competitor. He loved the feel of adrenaline which raced through his blood during a competition. He loved the heightened sense of awareness he would experience. He loved that, during the rush of a race, every second was like a fire in his heart; nothing existed outside of the moment.

Win or lose, his body saw each and every motion as a life and death struggle for survival. Rick's fifteen-year-old ego hungered for the attention of being the winner, but losing was its own prize. Losing a race just provided more fuel for the next competition.

He glanced out into the crowd, and saw his mother. Rick wished his father could see the race, but he was away on business. He would tell Rick, "How else are we going to pay for all of those repairs when you tear that beast apart on the raceway, eh?" His father always attended the races when he could. His father was his biggest fan.

Rick imagined his father telling him, like he usually would right before a race began: "Now, son, once you hit that throttle, don't ever look back. Not once. You just fix your eye on the road ahead, and the prize!"

Rick almost missed the start signal. In a second he engaged the clutch and pumped back on the throttle. He felt the g-forces trying to yank him off the bike backwards as he shot forward, dirt and gravel spitting out from underneath his rear tire. He leaned forward and down, lifting off of his seat a good inch.

He heard someone scream in the audience: "Let's go let's go let's go yah go!" in rapid fire.

Four other bikers had beaten him to the punch, pulling out a few yards ahead of him. Rick grimaced, as he knew they would have their choice of approach angles on the second turn of the track, which had a nasty set of moguls before a steep jump.

He took the first turn of the track, hugging it close, taking the inside turn with inches to spare before gunning his engine and catapulting himself to the outside of the track. That move gave him third place, although he was nearly rear-to front-tire with the third place contender.

In fact, he was just a little bit nervous at how close they were to each other, so he drifted out just a touch to give them both a bit more room. By doing so, he misjudged the set of small moguls in front of him and he hit them just a bit off, causing his bike to torque just a bit. He was off angle as he approached the second turn, but if Rick wanted to gain on the current leader, he was going to have to gun it, and try to adjust his position on the approach.

He knew his mistake just before it happened, but he was powerless to change course. His rear tire lost traction and he fishtailed ever so slightly. When he hit the jump, he hit it at an angle. The bike started to twirl in the air, off to the side and back, carrying Rick along with it. Rick soon found himself in the position of the bike being on top, and him facing the ground.

In the calm, surreal moment, Rick launched himself off the bike by pushing against the handlebars. He didn't feel hitting the ground, but rather, he heard the screeching of his helmet being scratched by the gravel and dirt as he crashed to the ground. In another second, he saw the bike come slamming down; he saw it bite into his right leg, crushing and twisting and mangling it.

He didn't feel a thing. Then, another moment passed, and he blacked out.

He awoke to his mother screaming into a telephone. Or was she screaming at the man in the white coat? He couldn't be sure.

He then realized that he had been coming in and out of consciousness for the last few hours. He was in the hospital. The man in the white coat was a doctor.

"But the doctor says his head is ok. Right, Dr. Schmidt? Only a mild concussion," his mother said. Rick realized that she was probably talking to his father. "No, damned it, Sean. His leg must have picked up every infection in the hospital. He's running a temperature of 105 degrees. They've got him on every antibiotic in the book. Christ, he's only fifteen years old, Sean!"

His father talked for awhile. Rick didn't like the sound of any of it. He tried to rise up, but he was so dizzy and weak that he just collapsed back down without making much progress.

"Goddamn it Sean, how the hell do I know? They say if they don't take the leg off, he's going to die! It's gangrene," she paused, listening. "Tomorrow morning, they have already scheduled an OR room. If he hasn't improved, I told them to go ahead and take the leg," she paused, again listening.

"Well, Jesus, Sean, you're NOT here, what do you want me to do?" she screamed at the phone, closed the flip lid, and threw it at the ground.

Everything faded out, and Rick lost consciousness.

--- --- ---

-

Rick woke up again. The room was nearly dark. He saw someone in the room. It was his father.

"Dad..." Rick said, weakly.

"Don't you worry kiddo, I'm going to get you out of here. Everything is going to be just fine."

"What are you doing, Dad? Is my leg better? I feel hot.... Errr, cold..."

"Everything is going to be fine, your leg is going to be perfectly fine, don't worry... I'm not going to let them chop it off," his father said.

"Where's Mom?" asked Rick.

"Shhhh... She's asleep, she had a very rough few days. Let her rest."

Rick unhooked the IV drip from the central line in Rick's arm. He then removed the central line, and used a bandage to protect the puncture.

"Dad, what are you doing?" Rick asked.

"Shhhhh... Don't worry kiddo, we'll have you as good as new in no time."

And with that, Sean lifted Rick out of the bed, and took off down the hall. He passed a nurse who exclaimed, "Excuse me, sir..." as they passed, but Sean ignored her.

Don't look back, Sean thought. Not even once, keep your eyes on the road ahead.

He didn't want to wait for the elevator, so he took the stairs down.

His car was parked at the emergency room entrance, still running.

He opened the back door, and laid his son down on the seat. He got in the driver seat, and they took off.

He drove all of the rest of that night, and well into the next day, only stopping for gas and coffee.

Sometime during the morning hours he told Rick, "Don't worry son, I'm taking you to someplace special. I have a few friends ready and waiting. It wouldn't make any sense to you if I tried to explain, so just hang in there, son."

Rick didn't have a choice. The pain in his leg was mind-numbing. He felt as if he were on fire and freezing at the same time. The drive out into the middle of the desert was the longest ride of his life. He was sure he spent most of it softly whimpering and moaning.

--- --- ---

-

Mouri and Art saw the old sedan pull up. They were waiting out on Mouri's patio, sipping some coffee. Sean got out of the car, and grabbed Rick, carrying him inside Mouri's home. He laid him down on the floor, and Mouri and Art began removing the dressings from the leg, rinsing it and gently peeling off the gauze.

"Gangrene alright," Mouri said.

"Ain't that so," Art agreed, shaking his head. "I ain't never seen a leg chopped up like that before. And no broken bones, that's something."

Sean jumped in, "What do you think? I didn't know what else to do, where else to go. They were going to take my boy's leg off. Is it too late? Can we do anything at all?"

Mouri was quite calm, and not stressed in the least. "Son, can you wiggle your toes?" he asked.

Rick, panic rising at hearing his father talk that way, did so. "Yes, I can."

"Well then, I don't see any problem at all," Mouri said with a very calming smile.

Rick's panic turned into confusion. "What are you going to do?"

Mouri brought over a big plastic bin; a garbage bin. He let Rick look inside. The inside of the bin was filled with what looked like a grey-greenish mud. He was puzzled for a moment, and then it dawned on him. "You're planning on putting my leg in that dirty MUD?"

"Oh no. Oh no you are NOT! NO way!" Rick shouted.

"Now, don't worry Rick…" his father said. "This is going to feel fantastic."

"No. Not dirt! Not a chance. Not ever am I going to put my leg in that!"

Just then Art, Mouri and his father lifted him up. He started squirming and yelling. It took all three of them to get that Rick's leg into the clay, and then to hold Rick still.

Rick stopped fighting as he tried to understand what he was feeling. The clay was extremely cooling… Or was it warming? In a few short moments, the pain Rick was filling just sort of melted away.

"The pain is gone!" yelled Rick.

Sean and his friends helped position Rick more comfortably. Seeing his son smile, the stress melted away from Sean. He sighed.

An hour and a half later, Rick's temperature was back to normal.

Mouri checked twice. "Yep. Just like we thought! We'll do this clay here for three days, soak it in the mineral springs, and then we'll send you back home with enough clay to finish the treatment. I'll bet you that leg is as good as new in three weeks time, Rick!"

Rick's father sighed. "Well, I suppose I should phone your mother, kiddo. I don't think she's going to be too happy with me at the moment."

Art shook his head and whistled. "What are you going to tell the little lady?" he asked.

"I'm going to lie through me teeth!" Sean joked. "Maybe tell her that Rick was kidnapped… hmmm… abducted by aliens, that's it!" he joked.

Rick's mother was furious. Rick could hear her screaming through the phone. "…called the police…didn't know where the hell…"

Rick's father: "Well, honey, you wouldn't have let me…" more screaming. "Now, I know you have every reason to be upset, it's ok." More yelling. "No, he's fine, he's just fine!" pause. "No, no, honey, there's no need for you to call a lawyer, please calm down just a bit!"

The conversation seemed to go on for ages, and Rick grimaced through the whole thing. After the phone line was dead, Sean looked exhausted and defeated.

But, in the end, his mother forgave them both, and was right there, as usual, at the racetrack exactly three weeks later as Rick snapped his helmet on, and sat down on his newly refurbished KTM 500.

Yep. The Beast is hungry, Rick thought, as he pulled down on the throttled and shot forward, swearing he was never, ever going to look back.

<u>Sally's Shattered Brow</u>

Paul and Jonathan, sitting on the front patio, watched as an old station wagon pulled up in the driveway. Jonathan had called Paul earlier, asking him if he would be willing to take a look at an injury sustained by a girl during a baseball game.

"Well, Jonathan, have her parents already taken her to see a doctor?" Paul had asked.

"Yes," replied Jonathan. "That's the first thing they did. The doctor consulted with a specialist surgeon, and both agreed that the best action would be no action. They just want to wait and see how she fares on her own."

"Well, then, great. Have them cover over," Paul had replied.

"Great, will do. I'll come over to your place, and have them meet us there."

Now that they were here, Paul's curiosity was peaking. Most parents wouldn't even consider questioning the advice of a doctor, let alone consider using what must seem like a radically strange and completely unorthodox holistic treatment.

Sally hopped out of the car first, and came over to where Jonathan was sitting. She gave him a big hug. Jonathan was an art teacher, and she had been one of his students since she was nine years old.

"How are you feeling, Sally?" asked Jonathan.

"I'm okay," Sally replied. "My eye hurts, but not as bad as it did yesterday."

She turned around toward her approaching parents, and for the first time Paul got a chance to see her injured eye. That she had a black eye was an understatement. The eyelid itself could barely open due to the swelling of the eyebrow. The area beneath the eye was a dark black and blue. It looked as if someone had taken a baseball bat to her eye.

Her parents greeted Jonathan, and after introductions, Sally's father explained exactly what had happened.

"Sally was at bat the day before yesterday. The pitcher threw a fast inside slider that didn't break in like it should have. The ball hit Sally square in the eye. The baseball completely shattered the brow bone above the eye, but didn't break the bone below. The doctors told us she was lucky not to have been blinded."

"It's amazing that the skin wasn't broken at all," Paul noted, carefully examining the eye.

"Exactly," replied her father. "The doctor said that surgery would be too risky to the eye itself, and the bone was so severely shattered, that the surgeon wasn't sure what he could do anyway. They suggested we just wait, and hope that the area starts to heal without infection."

"Jonathan speaks very highly about your research work, and thought that maybe there was something we could do to help her injury to heal correctly," he finished.

Paul nodded. "I'm just amazed that you are willing to consider anything outside of the box; especially *before* serious complications have occurred. Usually, people don't start exploring other options until the doctors lose control of a situation, and desperation sets in," Paul commented.

"Well, we believe in approaching things with both common sense and intuition," he explained.

"That's excellent," Paul replied.

He turned to Sally. "You know what, Sally? I got hit right here in the forehead with a baseball when I was about your age. Only, I was the pitcher, and the batter hit my fastball... a line drive right square in the forehead. I was knocked out before I even hit the ground."

"Ouch!" Sally grimaced.

"Yeah. I had a huge knot on my forehead for a few weeks. Sadly, I didn't have this therapeutic clay to use, like I do now."

"Clay? What will it do?" Sally asked.

"If past experience is any indication, the first thing it will do is remove the pain. Then, in a short time, say by tomorrow, the swelling will go down, and you'll be able to open your eye all of the way. The clay applications will speed up the healing process, and will likely prevent any infection from occurring."

"It will stop the pain?" she asked incredulously. Paul knew that she had probably hoped that the doctors would help get rid of the pain. She was probably quite disappointed at the effect of the over-the-counter anti-inflammatory drugs that the doctor recommended she use.

"Yes. You won't even need the ibuprofen," Paul replied.

"Wow!" she said.

Sally's mother chimed in. "Paul, have you ever used therapeutic clay on anything like this brow before?"

"No, I haven't," Paul replied. "I've never seen anything like this at all before. It looks to me like the area is currently free from infection, which is excellent. Since there is absolutely no risk in doing so, I really see little to lose and quite a lot to gain by attempting clay therapy," he said.

"Let me tell you one quick story," Paul continued. "I met this gentleman out in the desert that had the cleanest bullet wound scars you've ever seen. He told me that he had had the unfortunate experience of getting shot in the shoulder. Luckily, the bullet had gone straight through the shoulder."

"Wow," Sally interjected. "Why did he get shot?"

"Well, Sally, I don't know. By the looks of him, I decided I didn't want to ask him, and he never volunteered that information to me. He did tell me that he couldn't go to the hospital. So what he did, is he took this clay, and he packed the entire wound from front to back. He kept packing the clay into the bullet wound hole until clay started coming out of the wound in his back, where the bullet exited. He then just kept doing clay packs on the outside of his shoulder, front and back, for three weeks or so," Paul said.

"What makes this story interesting and maybe relevant to your situation, Sally, is that the bullet must have severed a tendon, because his whole arm was limp. He had feeling in the entire arm, but he couldn't move it. And yet, one day, a few weeks into the treatment, his arm just started working again," Paul finished the story, shaking his head.

Sally's one unhurt eye was big as she pictured this mean looking stranger with a gunshot wound getting healed up so perfectly well.

"Personally, I didn't want to believe it. I carefully looked at the scars. I concluded that this gentleman wasn't the kind of person that felt a need to lie about anything. This isn't the only report that I've come across where healing grade clay appears to exhibit extraordinary regenerative properties," Paul said.

"And, if you and your parents are willing, Sally, you may help prove that exact point."

It was clear to Paul that Sally's parents were ready to try the natural approach. Their body language seemed calm and sure, settled and determined.

Sally's father asked, "Well, what do you think, Sally? Do you think you want to try this clay?"

Sally said, "Yes, absolutely!"

Paul explained to Sally and her parents that the clay should be gently applied about ¾ to one inch thick. Since the area was so fragile, Paul suggested that they just apply the clay directly, and not worry about using a dressing to cover it.

"Just keep applying the clay for at least an hour at a time. When the clay is finished, you'll see that it looks like it is ready to fall off. Just remove the clay that comes off, and re-apply fresh clay. Keep that up, as often as possible, until you go back into the doctor for your follow up x-rays. If the pain doesn't go away or if it gets worse, or if the swelling doesn't start to go down, please let me know immediately."

Paul didn't hear anything from the family for over a month and a half. Then one day, Jonathan and the small family came over.

Sally's eye looked completely healed.

Paul's father said, "The doctors said they'd never seen anything like it. The bones knitted perfectly, and the brow began healing a lot faster than they expected. We didn't tell them about using clay. But it worked exactly as you thought it would. Since the application of clay took away the pain so quickly, we didn't have any problem getting Sally to wear the clay over the three-day weekend. By Monday, since she had school, we only did treatments after school, at night, and once in the morning," he finished.

Sally spoke up. "The feeling was amazing! I loved putting the clay on, because as long as I kept it on, the pain went away!"

And that is how Sally became one of the youngest clay disciples Paul knew.

Book 1 Part B: Correspondences

Introduction

This section is comprised of e-mails, letters, and other correspondences that the author feels would be valuable to those interested in researching natural medicine, alternatives to contemporary medicine, healing clays, and related topics. After all, I've always felt that clay therapy begins with a technical user's manual, but it ends wherever the individual journey itself does. I cannot know where you are coming from or going, but I plan to design this whole work to help you get there.

There is much critical information to be presented that simply doesn't belong in a clay user's guide or the scientific, technical section, but that may be invaluable research information.

Some documents have been included simply because I felt that people might find it enjoyable and interesting to follow the correspondence.

This entire book, from the author's perspective, is about *opening doors*, not closing them. I do not wish the reader to read the user's manual as if were a law book or scientific textbook. Rather, I'd like the reader to use the clay user's guide as a starting point, very much like I, so many years ago, used Raymond Dextreit's work as launching pad which began my explorations. *It is creativity which opens the most interesting doors.*

I've left room open for letters, although I have no plans, as of yet, to include any in the section. I'm hoping that in the future, individuals will submit their own material, in the form of testimonials, or even tutorials. As they say, build it, and people will come!

Some items I have included because I felt the items may be of some minor historic value to some future researcher.

The names of the individuals involved in the correspondences have been changed, unless otherwise specified by the individual. The author has taken the liberty to edit the material as needed to provide the most useful, concise and accurate accounting of the material itself.

Finally, I'd like for the reader to keep in mind that the material in this section is dated, and therefore the research should not be considered definitive; rather an exploratory beginning to topics of interest.

Date:........ 7/2008
Format:... Email
To:...........Jason@Eytonsearth.org
Topics:..... Dietary philosophy, Digestive Health and pH

Hi Jason,

1)   If the stomach can properly digest food then the body will normally be in the alkaline side of the pH scale, and able to withstand some normal acid foods/drinks without problem (so long as the acid stuff isn't consumed in huge amounts, daily)

2)   You had a digestion problem but cured it. How?

3)   As I've never had digestion problems, and don't even know what heartburn feels like, I'm assuming that when you say take 3 HCL Betaine tablets, eat food and if there is no discomfort then there is a digestion problem? Which means, if there is discomfort then that means everything is working fine and I've just added too much acid to the normal amount of stomach acid?

4)   Is there a way to cure the digestion problem without resorting to having to take HCL tablets the rest of your life? It would be better to do what is necessary to change the body and then keep it that way, rather than continually just "helping" the digestion process.

Response from *Jason@eytonsearth.org*:

1)   In most cases, yes. When the digestive system is functioning correctly, the body can tolerate and eliminate acidic waste. However, one must also consider that mental and emotional stress can contribute to acid-forming states in the body, as well as physical trauma. Preservatives and chemicals likely also contribute to a chronic state of acidosis. So, when I say acidic foods are ok, I don't mean processed, over-cooked, pesticide and hormone filled foods. That said, when one does manage to restore health to the digestive system and restore proper function to the body's metabolism, tolerance to such foods can return. However, it should be noted that the soft tissues should

be very close to neutral, neither overly alkaline nor overly acidic.

2) I combined quite a few dietary philosophies. I still have to make dietary adjustments on a regular basis. I studied the raw, paleolithic diet for quite some time, and ended up adopting some of the ideas presented, but I was far more impressed with the less radical thinking presented in *"Restoring your Digestive Health"*, by Jordan S. Rubin and Dr. Joseph Brasco, M.D. I certainly would never recommend eating raw meat without ozonation just prior to consumption... We might have been able to do this safely prior to the industrial revolution, but risks associated with eating raw meat are growing by the year. There are many raw meat eaters who simply accept the increase in parasites in their body as "natural", but I'm far too sanitized to appreciate this viewpoint except on an intellectual level, and I do not agree that there are no potential health consequences. Furthermore, raw meat and raw foods can, under the wrong circumstances, cause catastrophic illness in the body. There is no such risk with programs such as the "Gust and Glory Program" and similar programs that attempt to address digestive crisis that may exist in the stomach, small intestines and large intestines. The Weston Price-Pottenger Nutritional Foundation also presents some excellent research and information on how to develop truly healthy eating habits.

3) When you take any HCL supplement, no discomfort means that a deficiency exists. If you are taking, as an example, 1500 milligrams of HCL, and you DO experience discomfort, you have too much acid in the stomach. During the next protein filled meal, you take 1000 mg. Then 500 mg... If at 500 mg (or whatever 1 capsule/tablet provides), you still experience a heartburn-like sensation, then you don't need any HCL or acidic supplementation (although there is always some benefit to taking digestive enzymes if needed, and if one has remaining food intolerances). This is simple and accurate science. It takes the guesswork out of this particular issue. And obviously, if the stomach is not producing enough acidic for digestion, it won't matter what dietary system an individual might use; it will fail. Supplementation is self-

correcting. If one is taking 3 tablets/capsules WITH a meal, and the individual experiences no discomfort, the day will come when this changes, and one feels the heart burn. One then drops down to two tablets... Then down to one... And finally, the digestive aid is no longer needed. Henceforth, if the diet is correct, ideally one would never need the HCL supplement again. However, rarely is a person's diet correct these days! Every once in awhile, it is a good idea to take one with a meal, and see if there is discomfort. OR, once the initial deficiency has been corrected, THEN one might consider simply integrating natural foods with each meal to address potential problems (such as ACV, Pineapple, and other natural digestive aids rich with living enzymes).

4) Without a diet rich in raw foods, I don't believe that good digestive health is possible without supplementation. Some people, traditionally (such as Gandhi did) "cheat" by including a lot of raw fruit in the diet to compensate for a weak digestive system.
When the stomach is capable of breaking down food properly, and when the small intestine is capable of adsorbing nutrients, then good healing clay used internally should be able to provide complete relief from any remaining digestive problem, if the pH balance of body's soft tissues are correct and the individual is not living on junk food. It just may take some time.

To summarize, many supplements that would normally be effective won't work if the biological terrain of the body, and the metabolism which drives it, are not functioning due to pH issues in the body, or due to digestive failure, or due to hydration issues.

The same can be said for any formal dietary philosophy. For example, if an individual does not have the digestive enzymes and/or HCL to digestive a given plant food, then such a food which may normally be healthful can actually become toxic.

Therefore, individuals who are suffering from chronic illness may actually be suffering for malnutrition. The digestive system must be repaired prior to experiencing any healing.

Determining whether one's digestive system is functioning well is very simple. For every major meal an individual eats in one day, the individual should experience one well formed bowel movement the next day. The bowel movement should also be effortless. If this is not the case, then there is at least some dysfunction occurring in the digestive system.

With all of the dietary fads out there, an individual truly needs to research all of the philosophies, but only adapt what actually works for the individual. When good dietary changes are made, results are very quickly demonstrated via an overall improvement in well being.

I strongly recommend that individuals ignore actual nutritional ideologies, and operate from observable nutritional realities.

Far Infrared TDP Mineral Lamps, Qi Gong, and Clay

Date:........ 4/27/09
Format:.... Email
To:...........Jason@Eytonsearth.org
Topics:...... Qi Gong, Gou Gong TDP Mineral Lamps, Far Infrared and Healing Clay

Hi Jason,
We have been having a really difficult time trying to establish just which company and which TDP lamp is the genuine "Gou Gong" as mentioned on your website:
http://www.eytonsearth.org/tdp-mineral-lamp-clay.php
We have had one here for nearly a month and I must pay for it or return it if it is not the real thing.

I followed the links on your website to find suppliers and the company that manufactures them and I found, first, the company that makes the one I have here, made by the Chongquing Xinfeng Medical Instrument company. They call this lamp a Heating Lamp in the user's manual.

The link below seems to be to a company listed as THE ORIGINAL inventors of the Gou Gong Lamp.

http://china-tdp.en.alibaba.com/aboutus.html

Are you able to identify by these names whether they are the real deal? If not do you have a contact who could advise me.

Is it mainly the warming aspect of the lamp that is effective? As I guess it doesn't give off the true "far infra red "spectrum; or does it?

Response from *Jason@eytonsearth.org*:

Please keep in mind that all of the products marketed as Gou Gong TDP Mineral Lamps seem to be effective as far as what they are designed to do; and all of the mineral plates appear to be fine. The only difference I have been able to identify is in the components used for the heat generating circuitry. The cheap units work fine, but the heating circuitry burns out in about a year due to lower quality components.

I am not certain who the actual originator of the Gou Gong Lamps is.

There is a book called *"Pain Free with Far Infrared Mineral Therapy"* by Kara Lee Schoonover. If you can get a copy it may greatly help with your understanding on how and why the mineral lamps work, and it also gives a great overview of what, traditionally, the lamps have been used to treat.

Also, as your customers become fascinated with the ideas central to Qi Gong, you may wish to suggest they read a landmark work called *"The Healing Art of Qi Gong"*, by Grandmaster Hong Liu. This is probably the most significant work published in English about truly authentic, traditional Qi Gong. It is extremely rare to read such a work written in English; and since the Chinese Government had at one time banned any and all Qi Gong books in China, it is probably even rare in China!

It is also a must read for those involved in cancer cure and prevention research, as a professional or lay person. Most of my own advanced studies and thoughts regarding healing clays are in the exact context of Qi Gong... translated as "Working the Energy". Hong Li was an actual medical doctor in China; when he moved to the United States, he did not pursue an actual medical degree, so he cannot use the medical title here.

The TDP lamp is unique in that it produces a far infrared electromagnetic emission. So, yes, it emits energy in the far infrared spectrum, but also much more. It contains the electromagnetic "signature" or frequency of the clay minerals in the plate itself. While many uneducated (yet highly degreed, published, etc.) authorities claim that such ideas would be fringe or even junk science, this is demonstrably not the case.

In the forward to the interesting book entitled: *"Biological, Chemical, and Nuclear Warfare... Protecting Yourself and Your Loved Ones: The Power of Digital Medicine"*, written by renowned ex-Soviet scientist Savely Yurkovsky, MD, a profound scientific experience was mentioned by the scientist who conducted it, Professor William A. Tiller of Standford University.

Bear with me for a moment, and let me quote Professor Tiller:

> "It is well known that placing colloidal particles of silver into a beaker of water that contains bacteria will kill the bacteria. What is not so well known is that placing these colloidal silver particles in a nearby gas discharge tube, and focusing the electromagnetic emissions from such an operating tube onto the beaker, will also kill the bacteria. Thus, physical contact between the bacteria and the silver is not a necessary condition for killing the bacteria. Further, if one looks at the optical spectrum of silver and then combines the magnitudes of the optical output for several light sources of different frequencies so as to closely simulate the silver spectrum, such a beam of electromagnetic radiation will also kill these bacteria. Via this simple example we see that it is the specific information pattern inherent in the silver atom and not the physical contact that is killing the bacteria..."

This is similar to how the TDP lamp works... The energy source that carries the "information" is a far infrared emission.

This is also how I believe the clay works in situations where, frankly, nobody can find an actual method of action. The clay is a transducer more complex than anyone but a very few complex laboratories can even record, let alone understand from an intellectual or scientific viewpoint.

All of this is often lost to those who practice clay therapy, but in my opinion, it should be at the forefront of thinking. For, even when clay is effective, there is an idea that there is a causative factor underlying the condition that ought to be addressed; and, in a situation where clay is not effective where we believe it should be, then we need to have the clues to lead us to understand what is missing. If we consider clay therapy in energetic terms, I have found that the answers we seek present readily!

Even if we consider the possibility that the minutest clay particles can somehow enter through the skin and reach a problem site in the body, in some cases I am intimately familiar with, it would not have been possible. For example, in one case, there was no drainage in the lymphs of a leg and circulation was nearly non-existent. Pitting edema was prevalent. Even so, the clay was effectively topically used to successfully address an actual bone condition.

As my understanding of clay progresses, I always revisit key experiences that have long defied reasonable and rational explanation.

For example, in a possible bone marrow cancer case, in order for the body to heal, three miraculous things had to happen:

1. The lymphatic system needed to be unclogged and stimulated, and

2. The cause of the cancer, likely cell starvation (poor biological terrain) or cell toxicity had to be reversed, and

3. The cancer cells needed to be replaced with healthy cells (the cancer cells had to die, and be replaced by healthy cells).

I hope you do have the opportunity to read about Master Hong Liu's work with cancer, as I believe that his theories, coupled with the ideas presented by Professor Tillman, go along way to explaining how... not one, but all three... of these events occurred, and occurred within a 72-hour period (in my watch case example).

This is also why I always find myself saying: "Use the best water you can find..." to hydrate clay with! So that one can be reasonably certain that the clay itself has all of the necessary "building blocks" to work with. It's also why I spend so much time studying the waters of the world.

So, to try to bring this all back on track...

Many years ago, a dear friend of mine, who had placed himself in remission from Hodgkin's disease... relapsed almost instantly and catastrophically. As usual, the clay had more lessons to teach us. This particular experience really got me to strongly focus on "subtle energy" research to begin with.

My friend's leg had completely failed him. I was living at the time at some hot springs, helping to manage a resort and doing some research... Not only could he not return home from the visit, but he could not walk at all.

I would make fresh clay hydrated with the hot springs water, and wrap the entire leg with clay about ¾" inch thick, and I would leave that on for three or four hours a time. When I removed the clay, each time, the whole leg was ghost white. I had never seen anything like it (perhaps I had never paid careful enough attention to notice such an event). I thought privately to myself, my God, the clay is not enough; my friend is not going to recover.

I realized in an instant that clay had two diametrically opposite potential reactions with the body, endothermic or exothermic. When needed, it either drained the heat or other energy from the body, or attempted to provide energy (perhaps in some cases, both) to the body.

In my friend's case, I became worried that the body needed more energy than the clay had to give. In his case, thankfully, the clay eventually was able to supply enough healing energy to the body... It was three or five (alas I cannot remember) days later when I finally removed the clay and the leg itself was back to normal skin color (more or less). I instantly knew that the clay therapy had worked. My friend was able to walk to that day, and return home the next. He has never experienced another relapse.

Of course, the relapse was never confirmed to be actual Hodgkin's Disease; but my friend insisted it was so.

Since that time, I had been on the lookout for effective, scientifically substantiated, conjunctant treatments to use with the clay, specifically to help address problems of deficiencies within the body (energy deficiencies). The Qi Gong (or Gou Gong) far infrared mineral lamp was an exact answer to this "prayer" of mine. I theorize that the lamp imparts an abundance of very information-specific energy to the clay, and the clay processes this information and transduces it, as needed, to the human body.

I have not proven this theory in practice, as I have not had the opportunity. But I really wanted to try to give you some background information, so that, as the opportunities present themselves, you would have some knowledge to work with!

Please let me know if you'd like me to expound further upon anything.

So, to close, an individual can use a far infrared sauna for general health and detox, but use the Mineral Lamp for pinpoint treatments.

PS: The lamp I purchased was one that burned out after one year. My only complaint about it was that it burned out after one year of use.

Not all Water is Created Equal

Date:......... 06/12/08
Format:... Yahoo Group + Email
To:............Jason@Eytonsearth.org
Topics:...... Ionized Water, natural waters, home-made alkaline water, purified water, alkalizing, dietary philosophies

I am recently re-enjoying a Bikram yoga practice that I used to experience about 10 years ago & almost forgot how fun it was!

It is done in a heated room from 100 F to, at times, 112 F with humidifiers cranked throughout room. Doors are opened at times depending upon teacher and ability level of class.

Yes, you do sweat your buns off and my towel at times is easily as wet as when removing from the washing machine and it feels GREAT! The heat does help me with getting deeper into postures and forces me to be aware of my conscious rhythmic breathing through nose and remain calm under the extremes. At times you do get dizzy and enjoy a great light show and if too intense I will listen to body and surrender to savasana or child's pose to slow down the heart rate then continue.

Currently I am drinking fresh coconut water from the shell (several a day), Emergen-C, Goji berries in water with fresh lemon. I eat Sushi also several times a week.

Also, often afterwards, while in shower I grab a couple of handfuls of dry bentonite and scrub the body down vigorously and leave it on briefly. I haven't started ingesting clay yet as I don't know where to begin but am interested and feel within there is something "special" about it.

Any other suggestions, brands of products that would assist mind/body and where to purchase them would be much appreciated!

Also, do you suggest a water alkaline machine and if so what brand?

As always, kind thanks for sharing your wisdom...

Response from *Jason@eytonsearth.org*:

It's great to hear from you, and your heat Yoga practice sounds fantastic.

"...fresh coconut water from the shell (several a day), Emergen-C, Goji berries in water with fresh lemon." It's hard to beat that combination, Don.

Water is a giant topic. I've been studying it for years. What can I recommend to everyone but to: Pay very careful attention to the water!

I don't often like to "over-comment" on the issue, because my views evolve as I gain more experience and knowledge. However, this once I'd like to indulge, just a bit!

Unless you are an individual who greatly values convenience, I wouldn't buy a standard water ionizer, such as a Jupiter, etc.

Why? Because if you are going to go to that much trouble for your drinking water, you might as well do it right, and without having to spend a thousand dollars.

None of the water ionizers I've seen come with sufficient filtration technology, and in truth (especially in places like Las Vegas), high quality Reverse Osmosis or steam distillation, combined with water ozonation, is truly required to sufficiently protect one's health.

At one time, I thought we might be able to take a few shortcuts, but my recent research indicates that there are contaminants in our drinking water supply (even after "filtration") that are harmful to humans in the *parts per billion* range, such as xenoestrogens from plastics.

Therefore, it is imperative that you start off with a high quality water source. There are of course, some high quality deep well sources for water (not around here though), and some high altitude locations that have minimal contamination (there is no surface fresh water left on the planet that is not at least in part contaminated).

If you are stuck in the city, this means you have to fully filter the water, or steam distill it, and then ozonate it.

Even if you buy steam distilled water in the store, or high quality bottled water, you really still should ozonate it yourself, because there is no way to determine if the plastic has leached out or out gassed into the water (in parts per billion), especially in a place like Las Vegas, where the water may have been stored or shipped in a non-climate control environment (heat is seldom good for plastic). Ten minutes of ozonation with even the simplest water ozonator prior to use guarantees your safety.

Otherwise, you can find a water store that does at least seven stage reverse osmosis water filtration plus ozonation; this gives you control over the proper transportation and storage of the water.

Now you are left with clean, but a very unnatural, denatured water. There are troves of companies just waiting to sell you outrageously priced additives to your water, with various claims that are mostly misleading (I'm being kind here). They talk about alkalizing; they talk about structure; they talk about minerals; but most don't know what they are talking about, as would be evident if you tried to ask them some questions.

Even if you manage to structure or alkalize the water with commercial additives, there is no guarantee that the structure will be beneficial to your life, and there is no way to guarantee that the "alkalization" will not simply be eliminated before being adsorbed into the body (unless *you know* exactly what the additives are). Furthermore, some products use chemicals that are not the best for alkalization, due to the potential of delivering bone/and/or metabolizing changing substances (such as unnaturally derived *calcium*) into the body.

So, what I currently do is I first start by *slightly* remineralizing the water, then I alkalize the water, and without making soap. One product that I use to do so is Concentrace (trace minerals from Utah). I do not, however, use as much as they recommend. I am not an advocate of drinking "mineral water" just because it has an abundance of minerals. I prefer very clean water; and the water one drinks should definitely *taste* clean. I'll use between 3-15 drops of Concentrace per five gallons of water.

To alkalize the water, I personally use Potassium Hydroxide (USP Grade, 50% in liquid). This is a controversial method, and it scares some people who are not very familiar with chemistry, but it is the only method that I've found that actually safely titrates throughout the body. Potassium hydroxide is only K(OH)-. The only thing that makes it dangerous is misuse; in its concentrated from, it is *extremely* alkaline. I use between 10 and 25 drops per 5 gallons of water, depending upon how alkaline I want the water.

My normal target pH using this method is between 9.5 and 10.5 on the pH scale. However, if I am not consuming acidic drinks (such as coffee), then my target pH is usually between 8.0 – 8.5.

When you are doing these kinds of modifications, you truly need equipment to be certain you haven't accidentally "messed up". A good purchase is a Hanna PWT ORP combo meter.

Ok, what we have at this stage is a "wetter" alkaline water with trace minerals, that tastes exceptionally clean at a pH of 9.0. Since all of the minerals added are in ionic form at this stage, we have an active and chaotic water (that some so called experts wrongly call "structured"). There is still nothing to hold the structure of the water, and it is still has, relatively speaking, a low energy level. The water might even appear to be beautiful if photographed (such as demonstrated by Dr. Emoto's work).

Actually, to try and be more scientifically accurate, we now DO have "structured" water, but the structure fails in milliseconds, only to reform into another structure. There is no stabilization.

Why? Because you absolutely cannot hold structure in H_2O without the presence of some form of nanocrystals or perpetually collapsing wave forms.

Penta water is the only water that been scientifically proven (at least to my satisfaction, via the research done by scientists in Russia) to hold a structure through the bottling and storage stages, that has a measurable difference in human health, based on the structure of the water.

Although the researchers at Penta would not speak to me to either confirm or to deny my hypothesis (I suspect they didn't know one way or the other), I believe that the high pressurization in their process caused the formation of extremely minute calcium crystals in the water. It is these calcium crystals (the water measures *less* than 0.4 uS on any good PWT meter) that I believe hold the structure of the water. And it is the extreme pressure that provides the energy source for both the structure and the oligodynamic activity of Penta water.

People have mentioned that sunlight is a good way to "power" water; I disagree, at least in part. Any energy imparted from sunlight into water would only last for a very short period of time.

I prefer to power my water with oxygen.

Let me rephrase: Silver activated oxygen. I take roughly one tablespoonful of ~10PPM colloidal silver and add it to the five gallons of water. I then add between two and fifteen drops of 35% hydrogen peroxide (USP grade) to the water. But one should note that more is NOT better. Again, 35% hydrogen peroxide can be even more dangerous to handle than the potassium hydroxide.

As some of you may be aware, you can power a race car with pure silver and high concentration hydrogen peroxide.

Again, up to the point that you add the silver, you are only dealing with an ionic solution. This means, that if you take your water into a pitch-dark room, and shine a laser light through it, you will not see a "beam" (or what is called a tyndall effect). You have dissolved mineral solids in a dihydrogen dioxide solution.

Once you add the silver, it's likely that you won't be able to see a tyndall effect, because of the small amount of silver used. But once you add the H_2O_2, and wait for an hour or so, you'll get a beautiful, bright tyndall effect, if it's been done correctly; and that tyndall effect is caused by the explosive reaction between the silver and the H_2O_2; it will easily last as long as the water does (considering that ideally one is actually using the water). A similar, albeit smaller reaction happens as water cascades over rocks in a briskly flowing river.

Now, again, there is not enough silver in the water to exceed EPA drinking water guidelines (or have a therapeutic effect in and of itself), and there is not enough H_2O_2 in the water to be considered "H2O2 therapy" (or cause the infamous upset stomach). We're not trying to make a medicine here, just fantastic drinking water with oligodynamic properties; More is not better!

Now we have an energetically charged solution, with some colloid characteristics, as we are making some interesting and exotic silver and oxygen crystals in the water, as well as an abundance of activated oxygen (O -).

This is the point that I find is the best point to ozonate the water. Ozonating five gallons of water for about 15 minutes, as a matter of convenience, is fine.

Then, there is one last stage:

Add five to ten *grains* of your favorite healing clay. Grains! Not even enough to taste, or even enough to turn the water cloudy. Just enough to turn the whole thing into a highly powered transducing colloid.

Last, process the whole thing with your favorite sonic holoforms. Whether that is classical music, prayer, Qi Gong, Tai Chi, Sunlight, or light patterns.

You now have a very, very advanced and healthy, pathogen free, xenoestrogen free, oxygenated, highly and perpetually organized and reorganizing, hydrating solution, that is being organized by one the most natural water structuring substances on the earth: Healing Clay.

It will cost you far less than buying any gimmick (I've tested most of them).

But, don't stop there. Once you have an understanding of everything you've just accomplished, you might decide you need a bit more X or a bit more Y... or that you'd like to add *minute* amounts of other substances (i.e. maybe you've determined you need a bit more magnesium, so you might add ½ drop (or a flake) of magnesium chloride to 5 gallons)... Use the water taste test to gauge your success, as we are all individuals with different needs.

Now, there are times where you might want to change it up a bit, so let's talk about water ionization.

Water ionization machines are very simple. You have two metal electrodes (a minimum of titanium, not silver, copper, steel, or anything that reacts with electrolysis when low direct current is used). You have a two-chamber container, with a semi-permeable membrane between the two chambers. One electrode goes on one side, the other on the other side. You pass a current through the two electrodes.

The acidic substances all are drawn to one side, while the alkaline are drawn to the other.

But remember: Any garbage that is in the water, stays in the water.

Therefore, when I make ionized water, I still start with ultra-purified water, and do everything up to adding the H2O2. Instead, I'll ozonate the water and then use sea salt for my alkaline minerals, and I use... MSM for my acidic minerals.

If you don't have enough acidic *or* alkaline minerals, the water will *not* ionize correctly. But why settle for junk as your acidic substances, when natural, healthy sulphur (MSM) will work just fine?

I usually ionize water overnight, and I measure both the pHs of the acidic and alkaline water, *plus* the ORP (Oxygen *reduction* Potential). The ORP will fall off quickly in the alkaline water, and even faster when exposed to light, so the water must be stored in complete darkness, and consumed with a day or so. The acidic water makes a great cleanser. And since you now *know* that the acid is only sulphurous, you know that it will be great for your skin, for your hair, even to clean your kitchen floor with.

A basic ionization kit can be found for about $150.00.

Remember *not* to add any oxygen to the process after ozonation, because ionized water has an *oxygen reduction* potential. Consider this water to be exactly *opposite* of the water created previously (oxygen-rich).

Apparently, there is something about properly ionized water than some people really need. If you are one of those individuals, you will be able to feel it when you start drinking ionized water.

But don't let your imagination stop here, this is only the beginning.

Oh, and since you are doing all of that "sweat" exercise, consider also enriching your diet with some Vitamin E and Selenium, as well as adding healthy doses of Cilantro in-diet, as exercise, sweat, and the right substances in-body definitely help to reduce heavy metals.

Enjoy!

--- --- ---

-

I have another water question for you. Someone on a list mentioned a web site, which I forgot to save, but it talked about a product they made that basically mimicked acid water from an ionizing water machine. They went on to talk about the various ph numbers of the organs and how the stomach is acid, and the reason most people start having digestion problems when they get older is because their stomach stops producing enough acid to digest food.

All well and good, and true. But their idea was that by drinking a glass of their water (product mixed in water to make the water more acidic) on an empty stomach, first thing in the morning, and then not eating anything for a half hour, would re-acidify the stomach.

Then they went on to say how eating certain foods would help to alkalize the body, which you would want to do. Only the first part of their article made it sound like drinking alkaline water and eating alkalizing foods was a bad idea, unless the stomach had the right amount of acid.

This makes sense. But considering that most people are too acid to begin with–which allows disease to develop–then drinking acidic water would be a bad idea. Unless it actually would do the body/stomach good to drink one glass of acid water first thing in the morning to help the stomach re-acidify, and then drinking alkaline water the rest of the day to help the body out of the acid state and into an alkaline state.

I guess what I'm asking is: What do you think of this process? I know that many people swear by the alkaline water, that it gets rid of being too acidic in the urine, and helping to get rid of disease. So normally they say to ONLY drink alkaline water.

But the stomach does have to be acidic. Hence many people take ACV with their meals, or those hydrochloric acid tablets, to help with digestion. So, would drinking one glass of acidic water first thing, on an empty stomach, and not taking in anything else for a half hour actually rebalance the stomach to what it should be–which in turn would make digestion and USE of nutrients from foods better, and to drink alkaline water the rest of the day?

It would almost seem that one would cancel out the other. But on the other hand–it does make a sort of sense. I'm wondering what you or anyone else thinks of this.

--- --- ---

-

Response from *Jason@eytonsearth.org*:

That's a great 'topic'.

I can't comment on drinking the "acid water", because I don't know exactly what the acid in the water is.

When I use an ionizer to make acid water, I use pure water and add MSM for the acid. In such a case, the resulting low pH is made exclusively from sulphur, so I don't have to worry about what is in the water to make it acidic. Natural sulphur is not a toxic, metabolic waste product.

It's far easier to use a HCL/Betaine supplement to provide acid support in the stomach and to stimulate the production of HCL in the stomach, because one can rapidly determine if one actually has a problem with the HCL production in the stomach. The healing process itself takes the guess work out of the treatment.

For example, if you take three HCL tablets, and experience no "heartburn-like" symptoms after the meal, then you know that you have a problem, and that it would be wise to continue. There is no guesswork. In such a situation, you can bet that the entire digestive system is compromised, specifically due to the fact that ingested proteins are not being properly broken down.

When such a condition exists, and it is corrected through supplementation (even with the acid water if that actually does work), one will be able to record a fast correction in the acid/basic balance of the biological terrain/soft tissues. In other words, *just by making certain that the digestion system is working properly is actually an alkalizing practice.*

As I personally corrected this issue in myself, I was able to easily eat 3 times as much acidic food and still maintain a proper pH level in the biological terrain (the soft tissues of the body, not blood or organ levels). Most high fat high protein food sources are acidic.

Of interest, Alpha Omega labs used to sell an interesting acid water that I enjoyed using. I believe that it was made via water ionization.

The product manufacturers claim that the water is actually hydronium, H_3O. If so, then the idea itself is correct: Simply use the hydrogen atom itself to adjust the acid levels, for again, hydrogen would not be treated as a metabolic waste in the body.

Such a product may be used orally, but in *very* small amounts. Anyone who enjoys playing with exotic waters/solutions would probably enjoy experimenting with H_3O.

As far as how much alkaline food and water a person needs? There is no one size fits all formula. It all has to be based on the individual's state of health, metabolism, etc. Using pH strips to test the body throughout the day (saliva and/or urine), and recording the effects of different dietary changes/therapies, is the only sure method.

As long as the stomach is producing sufficient HCL, it won't really matter how much alkaline water or food you eat. It won't compromise food digestion. The alkalizing group of minerals/elements is simply absorbed through the stomach walls. In other words, the cause for the lack of production of HCL in the stomach is usually over-consumption of acidic food (especially colas and acid drinks, and likely processed foods full of nitrates used as preservatives), but certainly *never* from alkalizing.

To directly answer your question, I would prefer the HCL tablet method over the once daily acid drink, but only because I can then tell within an hour if I actually needed the supplementation.

---   ---   ---

-

I can attest to the truth of this statement from my own experience. For years, while I was very sick with CFS, I could not move off the high acid report of my morning pH strip–which would be actually stripped of its yellow to look white.

Having found various ways to promote good digestion, I now consume about a pound of meat/fish every day, and lots of saturated fat, and testing invariably gives me a very high alkaline report – not just green but sometimes the dark blue that healthy children test with (and I'll be 70 in Oct.!).

---   ---   ---

-

Response from *Jason@eytonsearth.org*:

(Previous correspondence not included due to space constraints, only the edited response follows)

In many cases, yes, when proper digestion is restored, then the body can tolerate a moderate amount acidic food without any difficulty at all. However, one must also consider that mental and emotional stress can contribute to acid-forming states in the body, as well as physical trauma.

Preservatives and chemicals likely also contribute to acidosis. So, when I say acidic foods are definitely ok, I don't mean processed, over-cooked, pesticide and hormone filled foods. However, when one does manage to restore health to the digestive system, and restore proper function to the body's metabolism, *tolerance* to such foods can return, and *health* can be derived from acidic foods properly prepared, such as meats, acidic fruits, etc.

Yes, I cured (or at least have greatly improved) my digestive problems by combining quite a few dietary philosophies; I still have to make adjustments on a regular basis. I studied raw, Paleo diets for quite some time, and I learned a lot about nutrition; I ended up adopting some of the ideas, but I was far more impressed with the less radical thinking in *"Restoring your Digestive Health"* by Jordan S. Rubin and Dr. Joseph Brasco, M.D.

I certainly would never recommend eating raw meat without ozonation just prior to consumption... We might have been able to do this safely prior to the industrial revolution, but risks associated with eating raw meat are growing by the year. I know a lot of raw meat eaters who just accept the increase in parasites in their body as "natural", but I'm far too sanitized to appreciate this viewpoint except at an intellectual level, and I do not agree that there are no potential health consequences. Furthermore, raw meat and raw foods can, under the wrong circumstances, cause catastrophic illness in the body. There is no such risk with programs such as the "Guts and Glory Program" and similar programs that attempt to address digestive crisis that may exist in the stomach, small intestines and large intestines.

Next, that is correct. When you take any HCL supplement, no discomfort means that a deficiency exists. If you are taking, as an example, 1500 milligrams of HCL, and you DO experience discomfort, you now have too much acid in the stomach. During the next protein-filled meal, you take 1000 mg. Then 500 mg... If at 500 mg (or whatever 1 capsule/tablet provides), you still experience a heartburn-like sensation, then you don't need any HCL or acidic supplementation (although there is always some benefit to taking digestive enzymes if needed, if one has remaining food intolerances).

Without near-raw food, I don't believe that digestive health without supplementation is possible. It's all about enzymes at this point, and over-processed and over-cooked food simply doesn't have them.

Some people (such as Gandhi) found a way "cheat" by including an abundance of raw fruit in the diet. This can, evidently, help compensate for digestive problems, but now we're delivering a lot of sugar carbs into the body.

When the stomach is capable of breaking down food properly, and when the small intestine is capable of adsorbing nutrients, then a good healing clay used internally should be able to provide complete relief from any remaining digestive problem, if the pH balance of body is correct and the individual is not living on junk food. It just may take some time.

Yes, many supplements really won't work if the biological terrain and metabolism are not functioning due to pH issues in the body. People, I suspect, flush thousands of dollars of unneeded supplements down the toilet due to their lack of knowledge concerning digestive and metabolic processes.

Your friend is not alone with severe reactions to dietary changes. Some people are so toxic, with compromised digestive systems, and organ problems (even organ failure), that all progress must be done slowly, carefully, and with a lot of trial and error. Fluids are always the most important considerations to start with in such situations.

--- --- ---

-

Wow, pretty detailed info on water et al and thank you for that. One of these days...

I recently read somewhere an opinion that alkalized water or substances to add for alkalinizing the body; like baking soda for example; may interfere with the necessary acid condition of the stomach needed for digestion.

This is a rough approximation of the concept, but it did strike a chord for me that an over simplified idea of changing acidosis by ingesting quickly highly alkaline substances may not be 'big picture' balanced.

There are a number of views on the measurement of pH as per Reams and the more advanced like the Biomedx.com people and their biological terrain 'flow systems' approach.

Perhaps it depends on the need and situation, as so much does, but might there be a long term impact from drinking a man made overly alkaline water?

--- --- ---

-

Response from *Jason@eytonsearth.org*:

I personally would not use baking soda, as it is *very* reactive in the stomach. Doing this would be one of those cases where a little bit of knowledge can be dangerous.

Yes, your point is well taken.

However, in my opinion the issue is critical enough that an individual would be wise to shift the pH of the soft tissues with any method possible, and then work on using whole foods to achieve the same thing. Many people with these severe digestive and metabolic problems are dealing with life and death situations, and, again in my opinion, and speaking from personal experience, one should correct severe electrolyte and pH balances in the body in any manner possible, and as quickly as feasible and safe.

Using diet alone to correct pH can be a very lengthy process, requiring a lot of core lifestyle changes. It has taken me personally 15 years to make these changes, and I'm not done yet. I don't think I personally would have lived long enough to make the changes, as I did have cancer when I first started addressing problems with digestion and the pH balance of the soft tissues (also sometimes called the biological terrain).

Many people cannot just simply do these changes overnight.

When manmade waters mimic high-grade natural waters (as closely as possible), then the concern is far less. As an example, one of the highest quality bottle drinking waters that I personally tested was Trinity (now out of business). The water had a natural pH level of about 9.6.

Furthermore, those who have chronic pH problems have such a toxic overload that water is a key ingredient to help the body detoxify. Fluids definitely help flush the system.

There are some people who are so sick, that their body cannot tolerate a change in diet, so water modifications may be the only first step possible.

It is a *very* individual choice. But I believe individuals really need to take the issue seriously, especially those people who have been eating processed foods for years on end which are loaded with acid forming chemical preservatives; those who have eaten over-cooked or otherwise destroyed foods; smokers; heavy drinkers and chronically over-stressed individuals.

Both issues should definitely be addressed. Many people have both problems: acidic biological terrain and a compromised digestive system.

I do not believe that drinking the more inert alkaline waters impacts the body's ability to produce HCL in the stomach. However, if this issue is a great concern, then one can use lemons as an alkalizing substance. Lemons are also used as a digestive aid. They hit the stomach as an acid and the acid is converted into a base before digestion is complete.

Finally, I do want to acknowledge that making water is definitely an alternative medicine, rather than a natural one. I just hope that by using a common sense approach, an individual might live long enough to enjoy a more natural approach.

As I have a long lasting love affair with the waters of the world, I am always open to learning new information, and hope to explore the issue further in the future.

As a final example, the ultimate step in water re-naturalization would be employing the use of flow forms, along the lines of the work done by Victor Schauberger, even Nikola Tesla.

Clay Baths Cause Severe Reaction

Date:......... 6/06/2008
Format:... Yahoo Group
To:............Jason@eytonsearth.org
Topics:...... Clay baths, heavy metal sensitivity, Melisa Test

Hi. I am a 43 year old male, and I am from Madrid, Spain. I would like your opinion on my experience with clay baths.

Three months ago I contacted an individual for assistance, as I am very ill, chronically, with a recent diagnosis of DYSAUTONOMIA which they say causes every possible symptom. I basically have always been diagnosed with anxiety/depression/insomnia disorder and later with C.Fatigue Syndrome, Fibromyalgia, etc, etc.

But last summer they did a Tilt Test on me and the severe reaction I showed was a disgnosis for this Dysautonomia thing for which there doesn't seem to be a cure and that is even questioned as an illness itself or part of the Chronic Fatigue Syndrome.

I had taken the Melisa Test 4 years ago saying I was very allergic to cadmium, molybdenum and mercury but never did much about it as there is no doctors or treatments backing it up. So, one day I was googling on Melisa Test and found a testimonial of an individual who said it saved his life along with the clay baths. I contacted him and he was very kind supporting and informing me about all of this.

He said that I might be suffering from those metals toxicity according to Melisa (not allergy but intoxication) and that I might try to remove it with clay as it had worked for him and many others.

He sent me some packs of the best clay, but while it arrived, I bought a cheap one here and took a couple of baths not noticing much.

But when his good clay arrived and I took a 20 minutes bath, I had a very severe reaction which was like an aggravation of my usual symptoms that I have experienced before, lasting for several days.

First of all, when I spoke with Dysautonomia experts in the U.S.A. they advised some things, one of them being never to dehydrate as the illness is potentially lethal. In this sense, it is also advised not to take hot baths, saunas, severe exercise, etc. But I just wanted to try since I am so hopeless.

So after the bath I felt good for a while as my chronic bronchitis, asthma and sinusitis felt better, but after 10 minutes I started to urinate non-stop for hours, felt extremely thirsty, very cold, weak, my head exploding, couldn't stand up very long, dizziness and loss of mental functioning as if I got blank.

Anyway, these symptoms are happening to me every day but with a much lesser strength. The bath only triggered a severe attack.

Speaking with the individual, he said he had never seen such a reaction and that people only benefits from the baths. He has suggested me to join here and ask in the forum if someone knows about this dehydration (or heart) (or electrolyte loss) problems when bathing in clay.

I will appreciate your comments if you know something. I found a wonderful hope but I could only take one bath and I am back to square one, meaning no hope.

Thank you in advance

--- --- ---

-

Response from *Jason@eytonsearth.org*:

First off, I don't know much about Dysautonomia. I do know that Familial Dysautonomia is a genetic disorder.

The testing methods I've viewed seem quite dubious, non-specific, and at best indicative of non-specific metabolic disorders. They apparently have several non-specific tests, that, when coupled together with the right symptoms, indicate "Dysautonomia".

As far as clay goes, let's apply a little bit of basic logic here.

You took clay baths with a standard clay, and experienced no ill effects. Therefore, we can rule out dehydration from baths, or "baths" in general as causing a worsening of your symptoms.

From this basic logic viewpoint, it is clear that the clay that was sent to you caused what is known as an exteriorization of the symptoms of your illness. Such things are usually expected in the field of Natural Medicine.

The fact that the clay bath at first resulted in your feeling better, and *then* caused an adverse reaction tells me that the clay is actually working... and yes, I've seen some pretty dramatic things happen with people and clay.

Your post-clay symptomology, in my opinion, mirrors what one would see with severe heavy metal poisoning.

I can neither advise you to continue with clay, nor advise against it... but I do have a few thoughts on the matter:

First, I recommend that you learn how to super hydrate your body, and also learn how to balance your own electrolytes. This is not a simple matter, but you need to pay close attention to the utilization of: Potassium, sodium, calcium and magnesium.

Drinking an alkaline water with the proper amount of alkaline minerals, made with fresh lemon water added, is a great way to begin.

Magnesium is usually the problem mineral for individuals. Magnesium supplements that are designed for internal are very problematic. I believe that using magnesium chloride (made from Nigari or other clean source) externally, either in bath or on the skin, is the best method to restore magnesium levels in the body.

Have you tried using the clay sent you internally?

Personally, I try to recommend that individuals start clay baths while also using a good internal clay, whenever possible, and for just this type of reason. You might consider starting off with a *very* small amount of clay added to a glass of water (1/4 tsp.) to start.

You can do some personal experiments... Try doing just a foot bath. Then, as all things go well, work up to doing a hip bath (If I remember correctly it was the famous naturopath Raymond Dextreit often recommended lukewarm hipbaths to help treat any cool, weakening conditions in the body).

You also really need to take a look at your diet, and see if there is anything in your diet that may be contributing to your condition.

Last, I refer to an abstract referenced by the Oxford Journals The abstract, entitled Dysautonomia, *A Heuristic Approach to a Revised Model for Etiology of Disease*, written by Derrick Lonsdale is refreshingly candid, and pinpoints another cause of this condition: An energy deficiency.

So, if we want to go in depth, what we are actually looking at is faulty neurotransmission. What can cause failed neurotransmission? Heavy metals in the nervous system can cause such neurological problems.

To quote the text:

> "Apart from genetically and epigenetically determined disease, evidence is presented that marginal high calorie malnutrition, particularly with reference to simple carbohydrates, is responsible for widespread dysautonomia..."

"...presented that loss of oxidative efficiency, particularly affecting the limbic brain and brainstem, is responsible for both the dysautonomia and possibly its associated organic disease. The underlying etiology can be genetic, epigenetic or due to imbalance between caloric and non-caloric nutrients as seen in beriberi, the prototype of functional dysautonomia..."

"...biochemical changes affect either the autonomic nervous system itself or its central control, leading to inefficient oxidative metabolism similar to the effects of hypoxia..."

If you do have Dysautonomia, and it is the genetic variety, then the only potential cure would be gene therapy; these controversial technologies are quite a ways off, and would likely involve using a genetically modified virus or nano-machine to correct the genetic coding at a cellular level. It's MOSTLY still the stuff of science fiction to date.

But one thing I do know is that when the medical model fails you, then you only have a few choices: Remain hopeless, or step outside of the model and explore.

Mysterious Splinters in Austin Texas

Date:…….. 8/30/2008
Format:… Email
To:………..Jason@eytonsearth.org
Topics:….. Mysterious Splinters Pulled Out by Clay

I have been regularly seeing dark splinters coming out of my body, mainly around my finger joints.

Recently, I was using some clay on a washrag which attracted larger splinters, tons of them, around my throat and chest. Giant ones came out of my breasts, sides, stomach, and butt.

Oh my God, they were HUGE !

½ inch. What is that stuff? Is that normal?

Signed,

Grossed out in Austin

--- --- ---

-

Response from *Jason@eytonsearth.og*:

Hi "Grossed Out":

Wow, that is strange! Repeated use of clay *can* cause objects which have been embedded in the skin to painlessly rise to the surface of the skin to be eliminated.

This used to happen on my hands for quite some time: Splinters, even a few small pieces of what I could only assume was glass.

What can I say but: It is likely far better that these foreign objects are being ejected from your body rather than staying within. Eventually, the body should get done eliminating them!

It is very hard to say what the origin could have been. Sometimes it's obvious, such as a case where one has been in an accident of some sort.

Please do let me know if you have any significant trouble with the experience.

Clay Facial Masque: Itching Skin

Date:........ 10/14/2008
Format:... Email
To:...........Jason@eytonsearth.org
Topics:......Clay facials, using essential oils, rosewood, triple facial

My two kids and I tried the clay on our faces. Is it normal for it to itch? I mean to the point that you just want to take it off because it itches so bad it almost hurts?

--- --- ---

-

Response from *Jason@eytonsearth.org*:

Remember, that although it may seem a bit counter-intuitive, the clay does not need to actually dry on the face in order to cleanse the skin. With some skin types, in fact, one would want to *avoid* letting the clay dry.
Here is a little secret that may help:
Go down to your local herbal store (or order online) and get some pure floral rose water (as opposed to essential oil). Place the rose water in a spritzer/spray bottle.
Now, once you start to feel the masque tightening a bit, spray a bit of rosewater on the face... Just enough to keep the clay hydrated. Do this for the entire 20/40-minute treatment.
Then, wash off the clay with a warm/hot wash cloth. Look carefully at the pores of the face, and you should see that they are still draining.
After *thoroughly* washing the clay off of the face with warm water, wash the face with very cool water to close the pores.
Then, gently towel-dry the face by patting it dry. Next, spray a very thin layer of rosewater onto the face.
If you want to experiment further with healthy face re-hydration methods, you can do things like adding a single drop of rosewood (as apposed to just rose) essential oil to the spritzer bottle.

Even if one dehydrates the skin, if the electrolyte balance of the body (the soft tissues) is normal, one's face will naturally re-hydrate within a few short hours. Providing a bit of insulation from the dry air and sun (by using just a touch of natural oils) is far better than the chemical insulation of modern skin creams.

Please let me know how that works out for you.

Now, some people really like to let the clay dry, and simply endure the "agony" of the itching.

However, if you apply the clay to the face thick (say ¼ inch thick), and you keep it hydrated so that it does not begin to shrink, and then if the skin *still* itches, it means that there are poisons/toxins or other contaminants in the skin that are being pulled to the surface and removed.

If you were to apply a thick clay poultice to a fresh spider bite, you'd actually be able to feel the clay pull the venom out within 15 minutes or so. It's a very "strange" pinching sensation.

For anyone who is pursuing the perfect facial, the following suggestion may be of interest:

First, take very, very small amounts of clay, and apply the clay to the face by massaging the clay deep into the skin. This should be an actual facial massage, hitting all of the acupressure points on the face and forehead, as well.

When this has been done, the clay should be dry, but there should be so little clay on the face that it would hardly been noticeable, visually.

Next, repeat the exact same thing.

After the second layer has been completed, the clay should be completely dry. One should feel a very slight pulling on the skin, but only mild.

Next, apply the third layer quickly and evenly on the face. The facial should be between 1/8 of an inch thick and ¼ inch thick under normal circumstances.

Finally, follow all of the above instructions to keep the clay completely hydrated for the duration of the treatment, and also for the clay removal.

Last, please remember that, especially for skin care, it is important to use a high quality water to hydrate the clay. A mineral-rich, natural water is best, and from a trusted source.

Aluminum Content in Clay

Date:........ 04/11/2006
Format:... Email
To:...........Yahoo Group
Topics:......Aluminum, detoxification from metals, mineral balancing, clay used internally

I have just started drinking water from clay soaked over night. I am a bit concerned that the second highest mineral is aluminum
Should I be concerned?

--- --- ---

-

Hi Group,

Dr. Lawrence Wilson, M.D. author of Nutritional Balancing and Hair Mineral Analysis suggests that bentonite clay will raise aluminum levels from his experimental analysis of hair and metabolic trends. I have been taking the clay in water since November. Prior to the consumption of the bentonite my aluminum levels had been very high, and on subsequent tests done every 3 months the aluminum levels had dropped. Just recently, I had a retest done after taking the bentonite and the levels of aluminum had climbed again, but the levels and ratios of other minerals had greatly improved, including calcium, magnesium, zinc, copper, sodium, and potassium. I finally started to eliminate toxic levels of copper as well. I will keep the group posted on my results I receive in May.

First glance leads me to believe that the fluctuation in the aluminum levels is just a compensatory way the body balances other minerals, and is not of much concern.

If anyone is looking for an inexpensive means of guidance, in relation to their individual nutrition programs, Hair analysis is the least invasive method I have found for the vast amount of information it provides, especially for correction of chronic problems rather than symptomatic relief. Please email me if you would like to see my results and discuss how this may help you.

Signed,

Dr. XXX

--- --- ---

-

Response from *Jason@eytonsearth.org*:

Almost all therapeutic clays are aluminum silicates. However, being afraid of the aluminum in clays does not support what we currently scientifically know about such clays, used internally and externally.

The aluminum silicate is a very stable crystal, and thus the aluminum is completely inert. When individuals have had lab testing done, the aluminum reading has always come back within normal levels.

Furthermore, most edible clays are completely inert in the body; the crystals pass through the digestive tract where they adsorb and absorb materials; where the clay acts as a catalyst, helping to regulate and normalize the digestive system (clay is a true homeostatic substance), as well as helping to regulate the body's metabolism. Then, the clay is eliminated in the feces.

Still, numerous prudent researchers and medical doctors have addressed the issue, such as Dr. Richard Anderson. Dr. Anderson consumed copious amounts of bentonite clay internally. Then, using hair analysis (which is not my favorite testing procedure) demonstrated that his body had lower than normal amounts of aluminum in his body.

Melisa testing has confirmed the same thing with clay use.

Even Dr. Grace Ziem (who used to do consulting work on occasion at John Hopkins Center for Environmental Medicine) used internal healing clays (bentonite) to help treat heavy metal toxicity.

To conclude, the aluminum scare, at least in regards to clean healing clays, is based on complete ignorance, and defies both the scientific analysis of the inert aluminum silicate crystal and the experience of those researchers who have tracked their aluminum levels prior to and after clay use. There may be clays that are higher in nascient aluminum, and may pose a risk. If so, however, they have not been among the clays studied, at least in North America, as edible therapeutic clays.

People Splashing Around in Clay Baths

Date:……. Various
Format:… Email, Yahoo Group
To:………..Jason@eytonsearth.org
Topics:…..Clay baths, mud baths, heavy metal toxicity, cleansing

From an individual who recovered from acute mercury toxicity:

I want to share with the group my experience using clay baths, and hope to hear from others.

I first must heartfully thank the parties that inspired the protocol that I followed: my mother, the inventor of the Melisa test, the people who have published the information on using clay for mercury detoxification and Google that allowed me to put the pieces together.

The infamous London Clinic sophisticated MRI having revealed that my brain was clear of any aneurysm (fantastic 3D images!!!); my mother is the first being (after been examined by countless eminent representatives of the medical establishment) that suspected my symptoms were a consequence of heavy metal poisoning. Google search on metal poisoning led me to the suggestion of taking clay baths, then another Google search on methods to detect metal poisoning in the human body led me to *www.melisa*.org which I immediately recognized as superior to other methods (hair analysis, blood/urine mass spectrometry, etc...). Melisa test results before taking a clay bath confirmed that the heavy metal was Thimerosal, a nasty mercury derivative commonly used in vaccines. Major symptoms disappeared immediately after my first clay bath, and 6 months later after I no longer suffered any symptoms, except occasional irritability, Melisa tests confirmed that Thimerosal was no longer detectable.

I must add that 6 months before I collapsed into coma due to mercury poisoning, a young energy healer in Nantes had warned me that I had an extensive "energy blockage" due to vaccination and that my health was in jeopardy. At that time, I simply confirmed that I did receive a series of vaccinations in the recent past, but because apart from tiredness I was feeling OK, I did not pay further attention. Soon after I was examined by the healer, he immigrated to Canada and unfortunately I could no longer consult him... He was absolutely right and I hope I will find where he lives now so I can pay him a visit one of these days to try understand what exactly he could sense.

I am now 53 and FULL OF LIFE. I shed 60 pounds (28 kg) and I am starting to train for the 2007 Las Vegas marathon. I did walk down to the Colorado River from the Grand Canyon South Rim last weekend (14 miles round trip + 1 mile elevation, in one day). I will do the North Rim descent to the river before the end of this month. Not bad for a dying man 4 years ago!!!!

Anyway, I have no hesitation to say that CLAY saved my life, or at least my HEALTH.

I am very pleased to see that autism is discussed on this group because since going through my resurrecting experience 4 years ago I am deeply convinced that clay baths may be of considerable help to these unfortunate victims of vaccines and other sources of poisoning... being industrial food, petrol/fuel burning residues, pesticides, household miraculous cleaning/shining sprays... mineral deficiency... and "natural energy" deficiency.

--- --- ---

-

Response from *Jason@eytonsearth.org*

From a chemically sensitive individual who enjoys therapeutic clay baths:

Although I've only been taking clay baths for a short time I feel they a highly effective means of detoxification. Along with the baths I also mix the clay in juice twice a day. I've noticed a definite increase in my energy level after just 3 weeks. When bathing there is noticeable pulling/pulsating sensation in my hands and at times other parts of my body. To me this signifies a pulling out of toxins.

After bathing I notice a huge difference in my breathing. My entire respiratory system feels very clear and clean. Almost as if extra oxygen were being pumped into me. I can breathe so much better, even though I wasn't at all aware of having a breathing problem.

Several times after bathing I've felt extremely dizzy and nauseous. But feel this is from the good work the clay bath is doing. When bathing I also do a clay mask for my face and the part of my neck that isn't under water. I'm thinking about doing my head as well but have hesitated because I'm not sure I want it in my hair.

People Splashing Around in Clay Baths

--- --- ---

-

From an individual with MCS:

I have MCS [Multiple Chemical Sensitivities] and to be honest, I never dreamed I'd be eating clay....but now feel like it's the very best thing I've ever done.

Showering after the bath makes cleanup a breeze.......just use your feet to guide the clay toward the drain. I'm too lazy to let it set only to remove later. No plumbing problems so far.

Give it a try...I think you'll enjoy it. My energy has increased by leaps and bounds. I can walk better and my hands aren't so stiff. I still have some reaction after the bath, but not as severe as the first few times.

--- --- ---

-

From a family experimenting with clay baths:

My wife and daughter did the clay bath. First they siphoned off the water and drank it. Well, my daughter didn't; she said it was putrid. Probably because I had put a cup of sea salt in it. My wife drank it and soon experienced strong bowel movements.

They soaked in the hot tub for awhile to open their pores, then they plastered the magma, which they described as a slime, all over their bodies. They then layed out in the sun for half an hour. Not wanting to have to clean out two tubs, they decided to hose each other off. After taking a shower, they felt very refreshed and energized and spent an hour cleaning the pool. I will try to find a good sodium bentonite clay and use the tub so I can see the toxins.

I took my clay bath today. First I soaked in the hot tub and brushed my skin to open the pores. Then I sunbathed for a few minutes. Then I plastered the magma on. I got it everywhere, including my eyes, hair and inside my mouth. I poured some of the magma in a Pyrex dish and soaked my feet in it. I stayed out in the sun for an hour, and then went inside after hosing off my hands and eyes.

I looked at myself in a full-length mirror and I looked like a primitive Cro-Magnon man. I drew a 4-inch deep hot bath and soaked for a few minutes, then rinsed off and took a shower. It took me half and hour to bail out the water till I got to the green and black sludge at the bottom.

I felt very energetic. I didn't have a problem with skin dryness even though I didn't use oil afterwards. My eyes are a little dry. I don't think I rinsed all the Bentonite out.

--- --- ---

-

From an individual new to clay baths:

I did a warm clay bath with nothing but white clay and water for around 25 minutes. After the bath, I let the clay settle to the bottom of the tub for an hour or so. When I started bailing out the top portion of the water in the tub and splashing it on the cement floor, I noticed a strong disagreeable smell as the water splashed around me. The smell definitely came from the water itself. Each splash of the water on the cement floor brought forth the bad odor. The smell reminded me of a mixture of rotten eggs and the smell of the skin on a hot sunny day. Something like that.

I went back to check the smell of a fresh batch of hydrated white clay to get its odor. The odor of the fresh bath smelled very clean, without any resemblance at all to the disagreeable odor.

When most of the water had been bailed out of the tub, leaving the clay residue, I could see the white clay not staying white but has a noticeable slightly brownish color. The original color of fresh hydrated white clay is really paper white.

Definitely my body was not that dirty or smelled bad before I took the clay bath.

--- --- ---

-

Response from *Jason@eytonsearth.org*:

To me, taking a clay bath is like immersing oneself in a sea of millions of the tiniest crystals imaginable. In my opinion, it should be more than just a therapeutic treatment, it should be a meditative, deeply enjoyable experience.

As such, this type of detoxification therapy may not be ideal for everyone; there are individuals who simply do not enjoy such things.

Also, it should be noted that it is a vastly different experience to place oneself in the earth, surrounded by tons of natural healing muds and clays, then taking a clay bath using a few cups or even pounds of clay. The natural experience is unmatched by anything we can create in our cities, but I continue to explore ways to create the most incredible clay bath experience possible.

People report very different experiences with clay baths. Some people notice absolutely nothing; others feel deeply refreshed, cleansed, and energized. Others report very severe exteriorizations which seem to indicate that the body is responding very well to the therapy.

As time progresses, we're learning.

As an example, an individual I've been consulting with has taken 45 clay baths using a standard technical grade sodium bentonite. Not leaving matters to chance, he's followed his progress with blood and hair analysis, and, while slowly gaining in better health, has charted continually decreasing amounts of mercury in his system.

When toxicity reaches the point that one is sensitive to electromagnetic fields, great lengths are often required to heal the body.

For the last two years, I've been slowly building a protocol to address extreme conditions. I'm hoping that one day, when the protocol is finished, there will be a method to the madness of recovering from extreme cases of chemical and heavy metal toxicity.

When advising people who are seriously building mud and clay facilities, I always STRONGLY encourage them to build them UNDER or INTO the Earth, rather than just above the Earth.

The difference, though subtle, I have found to be quite striking.

Dog Drinks Clay for Skin Cancer

Date:......... 11/03/2005
Format:.... Email
To:............The Eytons' Earth Forum
Topics:......Animals drinking clay, skin cancer, natural clay deposits

I feel it is my obligation to let the world know my experience with a red desert calcium bentonite clay. My 14 year old dog had a cancerous tumor the size of an egg. His lab work revealed that he may not make it through an operation to remove it.

My vet and I agreed to not remove it surgically. I started giving him clay and coral calcium. After a few weeks the tumor started to flatten out, but didn't change in volume. After 2 months the tumor was virtually gone... maybe the size of the tip of my pinky finger was left. Now, 4-5 months later I can't even find where the tumor was.

Before I started giving him the clay and calcium he couldn't hear practically at all...and now his hearing is better too. The cloudiness in his eyes has lessened also. Please remember he is a 14 year old dog...I can't tell anyone how much I believe in healing clay.

--- --- ---

-

Response from *Jason@eytonsearth.org*:

I've followed many such reports with a variety of healing clays.

Animals particularly enjoy ingesting clays. Most clay quarry owners I talk to can trace human use of the clay back to observations of animals frequenting the location to eat the clay, or indigenous native cultures (who probably first noticed animals ingesting the clay).

This report is unique in that the resulting improvement was through oral use only. Normally, one would use clay poultices along with internal clay supplementation.

Clay for Skin Use: Strange Reaction

Date:…….. 03/01/2005
Format:… Email
To:………..Yahoo Email List
Topics:…..Clay facials, herxheimer reaction, exteriorizations

My daughter and I recently experienced what we were told was a Herxheimer Reaction but I disagree. We used a Calcium Bentonite product as a clay mask. The reaction was a very small, two millimeters maybe, area on the corner of the mouth and the outside corner of one eye that became VERY sore to the touch, on the order of sensitivity of a herpetic lesion with no visible blister or swelling, but a very tiny amount of redness. The area on the corner of my mouth in a day or two developed a scab but I had not scratched it. It bleed a bit, scabbed over and seemed to heal then repeated. I used a Comfrey Calendula salve to heal both areas, Herbal Eds Salve to name the product.

My daughter experienced this twice, after healing the first time tried it again. Same experience only the second time she developed a very sore and large sty. When she applied a moisturizer made with this same product she got the same kind of lesion on her leg and her neck.

I am curious to know if anyone else has had this reaction. Could it be a mechanical irritation due to the mica or silica particles?

We both have used Ahava Mud Masks for years, some weeks she does them twice a day for five days in a row, with no untoward reactions other than a bit of dryness. But she was doing them for a bad outbreak of white heads and acne cysts.

The sellers of the product insist that it is a naturally pure product of Calcium Bentonite and that no one else has ever reported such an experience.

We do have sensitive skin but our use of Ahava and other facial soaps and lotions are without incident so we are not sensitive to everything under the sun as some people might be.

Thanks for any insights on this puzzling experience. Oh and she used both premixed and clay that I had rehydrated from dried.

--- --- ---

-

Response from *Jason@eytonsearth.org*

It is good to point out that there is a very big difference between a herx-like reaction and an exteriorization of an existing condition. A herx reaction is caused by die-off of pathogenic organisms, and the symptoms are the result of the subsequent toxic burden placed on the elimination system of the body.

An exteriorization is a latent condition, either currently "dormant" in the body, or isolated in the body and not currently displaying any symptoms, which, due to some action, either becomes active, or is "finally" being addressed by the immune system of the body.

Many people enjoy clay use without experiencing strange exteriorizations. However, I continue to see, year after year, the occasional baffling exteriorization. When they occur, I try to understand exactly what the clay is trying to "teach". I had a close friend that used to say, "Love brings everything unlike itself out into the light to be healed." One could, without excess exaggeration, state something similar about clay use!

It's good to note that "muds" and "clays" are two entirely different substances. Many therapeutic muds have a high percentage of "healing clay", but not all!

My experience is that clay will cause latent conditions in the dermal tissues to manifest when used on the skin. Some people will experience dry skin, which usually indicates the body is not properly hydrated. Some people will experience breakouts, which usually indicates that the there is an electrolyte imbalance, and/or a pH imbalance, caused by poor diet, toxicity, and related issues.

With these types of experiences, things become very tricky. One can pause the use of clay, and let the body go through its natural processes, and then resume; in many cases, clay use alone will work just fine at obtaining a good resolution to the exteriorization.

Or, one can dig in, and try to discover what the body needs, and support it, while either pausing or continuing with the clay use.

In this particular situation, the first thing that needs to be done is to restore the pH levels of the soft tissues. Liver congestion is the most leading cause of skin problems. Ph testing strips can be purchased quite affordably... For the soft tissues, one needs to test the saliva about an hour after eating/drinking. If the pH is below 6.5, then this must be corrected with an alkalizing program. Fresh lemon water is one of the best ways to start such a program.

It is amazing how many things *will* act as irritants to the skin when the body is not properly hydrated, or when the soft tissues are too acidic. This is because acids are being dumped out of the skin on a regular basis (rather than through the body's other elimination channels), which cause irritation and a biological terrain ripe for pathogenic organisms to proliferate.

"Solid" substances that have been embedded in the body's tissues, perhaps even from childhood, may also be pulled out of the skin with clay use.

Now, most skin moisturizers are not moisturizers. They are big problems waiting to happen. They "moisturize" *only* because they insulate the skin.

Healthy skin does not need moisturizing; when one is trying to restore healthy skin, it's first an "inside job". However, while an individual is... in process.. Pure Aloe Vera, with a touch of MSM and Chitosan, is one simple formula that can be used, usually even with for those with sensitive skin....perhaps with even a minute amount of Squalene added.

Others may find that olive oil, ozonated from between 10% and 50% creates a fine skin conditioner, with both the properties of olive oil, and the properties of the complex peroxides and activated oxygen.

To summarize, it is good to note that healing clays work best as a part of naturalized medicine, which seeks not to cover up problems, to suppress the body's natural responses, to drug it into a numbed complacency... but rather, to bring everything to the surface, heal it, and revitalize the body.

Jungle Rot, Clay Induced Illness & Experimentation

Date:........ 3/14/2003
Format:... Email
To:...........Yahoo Email Group
Topics:......Jungle rot fungal infection, experimenting with clay and other substances, and a caution about mixing clay with substances

We are very excited about the progress that we hope to achieve in the coming years in regards to understanding clay action.

One of my personal goals is to find a way to utilize clays combined with other substances to address rare fungal infections. Years ago, I ran across a few very severe cases of "Jungle Rot" that had completely resisted all known forms of treatment. Clays when used to treat various fungal infections externally, tend to be less effective than other types of infections, although treatment will always (from my experience) help inflammation of the non-infected tissue and speed healing.

Since that time I've been lucky to achieve a great deal of knowledge of a few other key substances which I hope will prove to be beneficial. However, caution needs to be used when combining clay with other substances; clay action can be so powerful that there may be unknown consequences when doing so.

One of the combinations I'd like to test in such situations is the DMSO/Silver/Clay combination. The problem here is that the DMSO reacts with the alumino-silicates that I've tested. DMSO will carry substances through the skin layers and into the body, and I'm concerned that the DMSO-clay reaction is actually "breaking" the aluminum silicate bond. Great caution must be used when mixing substances with DMSO.

If this is the case, then the DMSO may carry pure aluminum directly into the bloodstream or the lymphatic system, something which NEVER naturally happens, and something one should avoid. The consequences could be a breakdown of the immune system, localized to that area.

It is commonly believed that clay cannot act to carry substances into the body through the skin, but there is evidence (and striking evidence at that) that this is not always the case. I have not been able to find the research for quite some time, but there was a study done in

Africa by a talented scientist who was investigating an unusually high occurrence of a rare venereal disease among a native African tribe. He determined that it was natural clay that was indirectly responsible for this outbreak.

The people of the tribe would frequent an area rich in clays/volcanic ash (smectite / bentonite variety). Since these people did not wear any kind of shoes, their feet become covered with small amounts of clay. During their journeys, the feet would come in contact with various heavy metals from the ground. The clay sorbed (literally pulled) these heavy metals from the ground, into the clay, where they were then transported through the skin and into the body by the clay. Over time, this caused a complete failure of the lymphatic system in the legs, which resulted in a rare susceptibility to this disease.

The above story is one reason why I'm so adamant about "keeping clay pure".

However, there may be situations where experimentation may be the only thing left for an individual. The DMSO, clay and silver combination, where a very small amount of DMSO is mixed with clean clay hydrated with silver, might serve an individual well for short-term use in a dire situation.

Hydrating Clay with the Right Water

Date:......... 3/14/2003
Format:... Email
To:...........Yahoo Email Group
Topics:......Mixing clay with water, distilled water, natural waters, silver hydrosols and combining clay with other substances.

This is in response to something you said on another list. I'm assuming it is acceptable to quote your posts to the list here?

"The single problem is that for *skin* use (as apposed to poultice / clay pack use), distilled water is not the ideal water to hydrate clay with."

"My solution is to first hydrate the clay (about 50% of the total water by volume) with natural geothermal hot springs water and then add 50% colloidal silver. The difference in the end product is remarkable. Understanding that few have easy access to therapeutic quality hot springs, I'm working on safe ways to modify the water without sacrificing the effects of the clay and/or silver."

I have been using distilled water and/or CS to hydrate some "French Green Clay" from Now Foods (it is the only thing I could find locally) for internal use to treat a sick puppy who is experiencing explosive diarrhea.

We use distilled water for all our and their drinking water and of course for making CS. I had no idea that one should not use DW for hydrating healing clay. Is this true for internal use as well? What readily available alternative to "natural geothermally heated water" can I safely and efficaciously use for hydration" Also what is the problem with using the DW for hydration of the clay?

On your Eytons' Earth website you say not to use metal utensils in dealing with healing clays. Why is this? What damage will it do? I had always heard the same thing about putting CS into stainless steel containers, then just the other day, an individual pointed out that the "plating out" associated with SS containers had a very negligible effect on the actual silver content of the CS. From what he said it appears obvious that I didn't fully understand the issue of plate out as I had thought that it would continue at a rapid pace as long as the CS remained in the SS container.

Hydrating Clay with the Right Water

In the case of using stainless steel for mixing or holding healing clays I understand even less than I did about the plate out issue with CS. Should metal contact be avoid with both the dry and hydrated clay? For example, would it be acceptable to use SS measuring spoons/cups for measuring out the powder? In addition to the SS measuring vessels, I had been using a SS stirrer to mix the clay during hydration thinking it would be the least likely to interact with the clay. If not stainless steel then what would be the best material for measuring vessels and stirring devices?

--- --- ---

-

Response from *Jason@eytonsearth.org*:

The distilled water and clay is fine for internal use and even for clay poultices... What happens with the distilled water for general skin use, such as to treat acne or other surface skin conditions by simply applying some clay (such as one would use soap, or even a masque), is that the distilled water causes the skin to dry out rapidly; the distilled water is too corrosive.

The idea is to try to find beneficial ingredients to adjust the pH level of the "silver clay" and buffer it, so that the end result is vibrant skin; not dry skin. When one applies a clay poultice (clay applied ¼ inch to one inch thick or so), the clay maintains its own structure, doesn't dry as quickly, and doesn't interact with the skin in the same way. It's always better to use the highest quality water one can find, but distilled water works fine for internal use and for poultice use, especially if one does not have access to any high quality, natural water.

I've been testing (H_3O), acquired from Alpha Omega labs (I do not currently recommend mixing H_3O and clay), to bring down the pH level of the clay to between 4.5 and 5.5. This has been interesting, but the H_3O is reacting with the clay in the process, and this hasn't reduced the "harshness" of the distilled water.

The end idea would be to remineralize the water with natural substances that are compatible with clay use.

The clay reacts with stainless steel. If you take something that is stainless steel, and pack it in hydrated clay, you'll see the result of the reaction. I suspect that the only reported infection (neonatal tetanus) *caused* by clay use was due to improperly hydrated clay contaminated with stainless steel. I wouldn't worry so much about scooping the dry clay powder out with a stainless steel spoon, because the length of contact is quite short, and the dry clay is far less reactive. That said, however, why use metal when wood or plastic is readily available?

Natural ceramics, glass, and even plastic are OK to use, although I shy away from plastic, because the clay pulls all sorts of substances embedded in the plastic when stored for longer periods of time in a plastic container.

I did an experiment a long time ago, where I took a detergent plastic container, dumped some bleach in it for a few hours, dumped it out, and then cleaned that bucket until I swore it was completely clean. Then, I filled it will clay magma. It wasn't long before you could smell the bleach as the clay pulled it from the container walls; then, the smell was gone, but the bleach would burn the skin (not severely) if the clay were applied to the body. Clearly the clay pulled bleach from the plastic, and sorpted it into the clay.

As far as exposing clay to other substances, I often follow tradition very carefully, as there are *great* unknowns with clay. I personally take the information stated below very, very seriously.

To quote Dr. Randall N. Baer, who in turn is quoting the amazing Professor Cairns-Smith:

> "...Clays not only have the ability to grow and absorb other molecules, but they can then incorporate the information from those molecules and use it to alter and change themselves. Clays were also most certainly among the most abundant substances on the early Earth.... Cairns-Smith believes that it was clay itself that formed the first link between life and nonlife. In his book The Life Puzzle he sketches out a possible evolutionary description of three different species of clay..."

> "...Cairns-Smith believes that clays were the first "movers" on the face of the Earth. He also believes that clays and naturally occurring organic substances formed an early marriage and that it was as a result of this marriage that organic materials ultimately acquired the ability to reproduce and pass on inherited characteristics from their crystal forefathers.... Weiss has identified more than eight thousand different derivatives in which clays have acted as templates, causing chemicals like ammonium ions and alcohols to solidify into organic components. Cairns-Smith points out that such reactions could easily give rise to polymers with what can only be called genetically controlled configurations... Cairns-Smith believes that it was inevitable that the clay would ultimately

have assumed a secondary role, providing little more than a protective clamp, until at last, life broke free and started to form its own protective cell walls..."

I try not to delve too deeply into ideas such as morphogenic fields, crystalline matrix theories, and the like (at least not publicly), as such ideas are not readily accepted by the scientific community. Suffice it to say that clay can be demonstrated to do things where no one can find an exact method of action, i.e. that are impossible from a "chemical" standpoint.

Therefore, I believe it is wise to mix clay only with very pure substances which show no reaction when mixed with clay. Otherwise, one does not know exactly *what* one is creating.

For example, raw herbs react with clays, while the ultra-pure extracts (essential oils) do not seem to. Hydrogen peroxide ((H_2O_2) reacts violently with clay, while ozone (O_3) appears not to. When combining substances with clay, it is also necessary to point out the simple fact that one would want the clay action directed _toward the body_, and not the substance. Therefore, it is my long-standing opinion to hold with tradition, and to use substances that *do* react with clay, separately from the clay.

Book II Part A:
Clay Therapeutics

Introduction

The author has a very unique perspective on the world of clay therapy, in part because of the origin and the evolution of the Eytons' Earth ideology.

The Eytons' Earth website was the first internationally publicly available, free resource on the value of healing clays. It was created without any ulterior motives, and was to remain objective in the information it presented to the public.

My motive for putting together the Eytons' Earth website was not to promote a particular clay (or clay at all for that matter); it was not to teach people how to use clay or to suggest that people might want to use clay. The motive was very simple: Eytons' Earth was built so that I could learn about using clay from others, and having done so, make the knowledge freely available to others.

It was my hope that people would find Eytons' Earth, contact me, and explain to me how and why healing clays were effective. I hoped that someone would be able to tell me what, exactly, clay did, and exactly what healing clay was. In short, I was hoping that someone would be able to demystify clay, so that I could get on with my life.

Well, that didn't exactly happen. Day after day, month after month, I received email after email from people asking for help and support with clay use.

I helped everyone that I could, to the best of my ability. However, there was a huge logistics problem. The clay that I used was not yet readily available to others. Therefore, how could I know that the clay that someone else was using would work the same way that the one I was using did?

I could not know, of course.

I would also get the occasional email from small quarry owners or property owners who had discovered a clay deposit. Each one would swear that their clay was the best in the world, and so amazing that it was literally unbelievable. Each insisted that nothing could possibly come close to the effectiveness of *their* clay. The only problem was that they were describing experiences that I had been having for years with the clay that I had been studying.

After a dozen or so of these emails, I realized that there were many clay sources out there that had extraordinary healing potential. Furthermore, I realized that most everyone who had discovered their own prized clay became very single minded about it (even sometimes unreasonable). As information began to trickle through to the alternative and natural medicine community, a massive amount of confusion ensued.

I had felt that I could best serve the public interest by educating myself on the use of all clays. I also began to actively encourage clay enthusiasts to broaden their experience base, as well; I felt that an attitude of rigidity did not serve any higher interests.

At the same time, I had finally begun to meet others who were very advanced and/or experienced in the art of clay therapy. A great synergy was occurring, and I spent eight years studying everything I could learn from science and from other experienced clay enthusiasts; I am especially indebted to those individuals who were brave enough to test healing clay therapy on problems I had no previous experienced with.

Book Two is a statement of unity as much as it is anything. I wanted to bring together all of the key clay researchers of the world for the first time. I wanted to showcase those individuals who have contributed so much to the world of healing clays, and to make certain that the knowledge and experience they acquired would forever remain at the fingertips of those who needed the information most.

I also wanted to include as wide of a perspective as possible on the subject of healing with clays. I didn't want to get "locked in" to any single perspective or way of thinking. The best way to do that, I concluded, was to include this Book II. I wanted to present this as the second book, so that the reader would have a more comprehensive viewpoint to draw from when reading the third book.

This book shouldn't be considered a replacement for any work that the individuals themselves have done. However, it is my intent to be certain that all of the "key ingredients" from each clay researcher are presented here.

Now, then! Shall we move forward, and take a glimpse at Cano Graham's Crystal Cross Clay Healing Center?

Cano Graham, the Crystal Cross and the Clay Disciples

The Crystal Cross

**The Crystal Cross Therapeutic Clay Center as it is today
(now known as Poo-Ha-Bah)**

Cano Graham holds a very unique place in my heart. I didn't know it at the time, but his old stomping grounds (the desert just outside of Death Valley National Park) became my new stomping grounds shortly after he was forced to depart in the late 1980's.

I never knew what a friend I had in Cano Graham; not until meeting him years after I had first started studying therapeutic clays.

I had met some of the people in Cano Graham's book, *The Clay Disciples*, and I knew Cano by his small town reputation. In fact, it was Mouri, one of the people mentioned in Cano's book, who first pointed me in the right direction concerning my own research efforts. Mouri was one of the very "loveable old-timers" that Cano spoke so highly of during his stay in the desert. He was one of the most experienced clay users in the area at the time, and was never shy about sharing his knowledge.

Cano Graham purchased an old, rundown property once known as the "Ali Baba" hot springs resort. He had an idea to build a holistic healing center, but he didn't really have any clue as to what this center would look like, or what it eventually would offer. He spent some time visiting resorts all over California. He basically learned what he didn't want to build. He didn't want to build a fancy, high-priced spa that was designed to pamper people, he wanted to build something that would soothe the hearts, souls, and bodies of those who needed it most.

Cano rebuilt the resort, renovated it, and eventually renamed it *"The Crystal Cross Clay Therapeutic Center"*. It lived up to its name quite well. Many Las Vegas, Nevada locals remember the small center with a great degree of fondness. It was located off of the beaten path, in a very serene and unique patch of desert oasis. It existed without pretense. It was affordable. It was a friendly place; a giving, generous place. Later, I would learn to use many of those same words to describe Cano Graham.

That the vision of the Crystal Cross Therapeutic Clay Center was destined to fail was beside the point; it would leave its mark upon the world, and be a beacon of light for those able to see it. By the time I started studying the area, the Crystal Cross center was abandoned and eerily empty.

I spent many hours sitting on or around the natural stone sculptures that Cano had brought, through great effort, from Arizona. I would walk about the property, shaking my head as I glanced at the cracked and decaying old communal clay bath area. I sometimes felt that Cano's presence was here, as if waiting for something to happen next.

One of Dozens of Natural "Rock Sculptures" brought in by Cano from Arizona
Photo by Tony Aquilano (www.tonyphotoart.com)

    I would try to imagine what kind of a man Cano was, to have the insight to build such a facility. Very few people around the area saw what Cano saw; not then and not now. But it was obvious to me that Cano saw clearly, and that he saw what people truly needed as if it were self-evident.

    The clay bathing area (Cano called it a clay pit) was actually bowl shaped, and it was laid in concrete. Several tons of clay would be poured into the bowl, and then the natural hot springs water would be used to hydrate the clay. The design of the bowl allowed individuals to sit in hydrated clay magma up to the neck; it also allowed an individual to lay down in the clay, If they needed to, along the edges. A canopy made from old parachutes was used to partly block out the hot sun, while still allowing enough sunlight through to activate the clay.

Cano's Old Clay Pit as it Exists Today, Twenty Years Later
Photo by Tony Aquilano (*www.tonyphotoart.com*)

I would sit and imagine people soaking in clay for a while, and then rising out of the clay baths for twenty minutes of sunbathing. I would imagine seeing a grey colored person with dry clay cracking all over the body reaching for a hose to shower off the clay.

I would imagine them, dripping wet, heading off to the large, indoor covered pool. The flow of water in this pool was regulated in a manner that kept the pool at a very cool temperature. It might have been 110 degrees on a hot summer day; a cool mineral pool soak is just what everyone needed after sunbathing with clay.

Cano's Large Mineral Pool as it Exists Today
Photos by Tony Aquilano (www.tonyphotoart.com)

Cano's Hot Pool as it exists Today
Photo by Tony Aquilano
(www.tonyphotoart.com)

I imagined that after a ten-minute swim, cool and refreshed, people would emerge from the heavy, silky, mineral water and head over to the hot mineral baths.

The hot mineral bath room was small, as it should be, to act as a heat insulator for the winter months. The water poured into a single-person concrete tub; the size of the tub ensured that the energy (and heat) from the water was maintained with minimal water flow. It could also act as a contemporary style clay bath if desired. The little tub was designed to be extremely hot and to maintain as much of the therapeutic properties of the water as possible.

Then, the water would drain from the small tub into a larger tub. The larger tub was hot, but not so hot that a person couldn't spend twenty minutes or so soaking. There was plenty of room for three or four good friends in the larger tub.

The polished stone inlays in the concrete seats demonstrated just how much heart had gone into building the facility. That the entire vision was a labor of love was always quite clear to me.

Sandy Dann
Shoshone Tribe
Caretaker of the
Poo-Ha-Bah
Photo by Tony Aquilano
(www.tonyphotoart.com)

Having finished for the day, I would imagine a small group of people firing up the stone-built barbeque, and starting an evening camp fire, watching the sun set behind the mountains.

I was always quite a bit jealous that I could only sit and imagine what the place was like in its day. I spent quite some time trying to figure out why nobody since Cano's time could make anything work on the property. Eventually I was able to figure all of that out (but that is another story, for another book...).

Cano's old Crystal Cross Therapeutic Clay Healing Center was eventually purchased by the Newe Shoshone spiritual leader, Corbin Harney, who passed away in 2007. The property is still owned by the Shoshone, and is currently called the Poo-Ha-Bah (which translates as "Doctor Water") Native Healing Center.

It is the author's hope that one day, the original vision sourced by Cano Graham will be enacted; perhaps by the people who first settled the land.

Cano Graham, the Crystal Cross and the Clay Disciples

**The Therapeutic Healing Clay studied by Eytons' Earth,
Cano Graham, and the Clay Disciples
Courtesy of (*www.greenclays.com/*)**

**Cano's Cross (made from old mine beams), as it exists today,
overlooking the Grimshaw Natural Lake Preserve**

Cano Graham
5/10/1932 – 7/6/2009

Old U – We Wash Building, Tecopa Hot Springs, California
Photo & Creative Rendition by Tony Aquilano (*www.tonyphotoart.com*)

"I'm just gonna keep doin' what it is I do." Cano Graham would tell me.

A native of Shawnee, Oklahoma and a Texas transplant, Cano is a former actor, an author, and a public speaker. However, Cano became first and foremost a Clay Disciple.

It was as if Cano had allowed himself to be sculpted by clay; to be drawn along on an incredible journey that would eventually impact the lives of thousands of people worldwide. His book, first published in 2006, entitled "The Clay Disciples", is an excellent chronicle of his journey through life, as well as his transformation into a clay therapy researcher, practitioner and advocate.

Cano, like many of the modern day individuals who have discovered the healing power of clay, just happened across the subject, stumbling into it; he had no training in natural medicine. He also had no previous inclination to study balneology, balneotherapy or pelotherapy (healing with earths). However, when confronted with the idea of clay therapy, Cano rose to the challenge, continually struck with awe and humbled by this substance which was so simple to use and yet so complex to try to understand.

The first time I met Cano Graham, I soon discovered that Cano was generous to a fault, and often extremely intuitively insightful. We talked about clay therapy, the state of allopathic western medicine, and swapped stories for quite some time.

Cano's life philosophy was equally playful. He would talk about his life in a far more creative tone than most people. As an example, he would say things like, "Well, you see, here is how my career happened…" It was as if Cano found himself in a play, with the world happening around him, and he just jumped in at the places that were the most attractive to him at the moment.

Cano approached clay therapy in the wisest fashion: He allowed the clay to teach and guide him.

The section which follows is a simple chronicle of the discoveries that Cano Graham made, and how he used clay as a primary natural healing modality. Any reader interested in Cano's journey through life should consider acquiring a copy of his book, *"The Clay Disciples"*.

Small Hillside Deposit of Green Clay – Used by Tecopa Locals and Visitors

The Clay Disciple

Tecopa, California – Old Mining Railroad Town & Hot Springs Community
Photo by Tony Aquilano (www.tonyphotoart.com)

Although Cano Graham's mother had eaten clay when pregnant with Cano, it wasn't until Cano was nearly retired that he discovered clay. Cano's mother would eat black dirt and red clay gathered locally. She told Cano that she had learned about this common, global practice from a National Geographic's magazine.

After Cano had purchased the old Ali Baba Hot Springs Resort in Tecopa California, Mouri, a long-time local of the area, would visit Cano and talk about the curative powers of clay. Mouri was extremely well versed in using clay for health purposes.

Cano's first direct experience with the power of healing clay occurred after he had decided to allow a family to stay on his property for a week. The Hadley family had just lost nearly everything they had owned in a vehicle fire while moving. Claude Hadley had severely burned his forearm and hand. Sylvia, another Tecopa local, brought over some hydrated clay to treat the arm.

During this experience, Art, another local, had told Cano something that most of us who have spent years studying clay have all come to realize about healing clay: "...This has soaked up and stopped any infection we've ever seen. We don't know how, but it damn sure does it."

The clay completely eliminated the pain from the burn in a few short moments.

The same family experienced clay's powerful topical cleansing properties; they used the clay for facials and as a deep skin cleanser.

Cano also learned from the locals that clay could be successfully used to treat yeast infections.

It was clear that Cano's attention had been caught, and in a big way. To see someone in such immense pain, and then to watch that pain melt off the individual's face to be replaced with a calm serenity, is an amazingly rewarding experience.

However, it was Mouri that impressed a great need upon Cano to take the special healing clay seriously. Mouri explained to Cano that the local deposit of healing clay was effective for stomach conditions and dental problems, and also informed Cano that the local Shoshone natives had long used the clay for healing purposes.

Mouri, and many of the other old-timer's in Tecopa, sensed something great in Cano, and were literally electrified by the possibility that he would commit to doing something serious in area, which had become quite rundown since the mining business had faded away.

Cano was not yet committed to the idea of clay, though. He still had not grasped the significance of clay therapy, and he was probably still processing the experiences of the family he was hosting.

It was the same gentleman with the burnt arm that helped Cano build a cross made from old mining beams to replace a cross that had been vandalized by some kids. The cross, which sat up on one of hills overlooking Tecopa, originally served as a water marker. But for the local people, it seemed to hold a spiritual and religious significance.

It was that act of kindness that cemented Cano's place in the small community. Shortly thereafter, Cano was elected president of a local community organization, and henceforth dedicated himself to the practice of using therapeutic clay.

Cano's next documented experience with clay was with a gentleman who had feet problems; the gentleman, Mr. Al Simmons, had spent hundreds of dollars over a period of ten years to try to do what clay accomplished in very short order. The medical doctors he had visited suggested that an old injury (both feet damaged from wearing improperly sized boots) had turned into arthritis. Al Simmons was concerned that he eventually wouldn't be able to stand or walk. The clay started to remove the pain and heal the feet with a few short days of beginning use. Al used the clay by "slathering it on his feet", and also by doing hot foot soaks with clay water.

Cano was discovering what I had also been carefully exploring for years. When isolated injuries existed, even if a degenerative condition had henceforth developed, clay therapy often was dramatically effective, even if the initial injury was years, or even decades old.

Al Simmons' wife had a tooth abscess; Cano suggested she use clay for the abscess, but realized, upon Mr. Simmons' protests, that he didn't have enough information on what the clay actually was to suggest it be used in-body. Never-the-less, Al's wife independently elected to use clay.

She used it on the outside of the cheek, and described a strong pulling sensation, and believed that the clay was literally pulling the infection out. After a short hour and a half, the pain subsided.

Cano learned during a discussion with Mouri and some other locals, that clay could be used to eliminate migraines. A local resident regularly treated migraine headaches by using a clay compress on the forehead and covering her face; she often experienced relief in 30 minutes.

During the same afternoon, Cano learned that a Shoshone boy with a broken foot, Harold, used clay to heal the foot, which had been run over by a truck. A local miner packed the boy's foot in clay overnight, and in the morning, the pain was gone and the swelling was completely gone. The foot was fully functional after two weeks of regular clay therapy and mineral bath soaks.

Mouri had become Cano's teacher on the subject of clay. Mouri, being quite an intelligent person and with a great attention to detail, had devised a complete mythology on clay action, based on what little was known, scientifically about clay. While I strongly disagree with Mouri's conclusions about exactly how the clay was working, I do agree with Mouri's conclusions about the end result of clay use.

Mouri described clay particles as being so minute, that they entered into the body through the skin. Next, due to the surface charge of the clay particles, the clay would become attracted to, and travel to, the exact injury site (such as the end of a nerve). Then, the clay would provide whatever support was needed, including acting as a buffer against pain and infection; inducing a healing response; the reduction of blood flow constriction (increasing actual blood flow at the capillary level); direct to-cell nourishment; and reduction of the immune system response causing inflammation.

The clay, Mouri insisted, would travel through the bloodstream and act as a free radical scavenger, helping the body to eliminate toxic substances, acting as a traveling lymphatic system throughout the body while at the same time providing cell nourishment.

All of Mouri's conclusions were functionally correct, because his conclusions were based on years of watching clay in action. And yet, each conclusion about the method of action was absolutely wrong. The clay *did* accomplish everything that Mouri had stated that it did, but not by the method of actions that he imagined. I do not say this to belittle the work Mouri did; Mouri worked with the information at his disposal at the time, and I have immense respect for him as an individual.

Next, Mouri believed that healing clay was comprised of 100% trace minerals, and thus he implied a 100% cellular bioavailability. In fact, the clay crystals themselves are completely inert. There are trace minerals available in clay, in ionic form, but these exact minerals, in their exact form, are readily available in other supplement sources. However, using the minerals in other supplement sources does NOT result in the same great results as clay use. Therefore, the mineral content itself cannot explain any direct action.

The author will delve into these issues further in Book III.

After an afternoon lecture by Mouri about the healing properties of clay, Cano felt much more confident about using clay for healing. He began to feel like he understood clay. It was as if Cano's intellectual mind had something to grasp on to, and thus it began to settle down, allowing Cano to just go with the flow of events as they transpired.

Next, Cano met Curt Hibdon, who quickly became his close friend and trusted handyman. Curt broke his finger one day working on the property. He stopped working just long enough to pack the finger in clay, and then resumed work. The finger healed perfectly on its own.

Cano and his growing crew of disciples were never shy about trying clay on anything that would hold still for long enough. That included a mouse with a serious cut that was interfering with the mouse's ability to walk. The mouse improved within twenty-four hours.

The clay also healed a nasty gash caused by an iron frying pan to a local's head, caused by an angry wife. Cano used a popular treatment method of the time, which was to sprinkle dry powder on the deep laceration, and then cover the area with a clay pack. The individual would wait until the clay is naturally ready to fall off, and then repeat the process. In such a case, when the wound was treated shortly after it happened, the healing process would be extremely rapid; this case was no exception.

Next, Cano ran into a man named Al that claimed to have arthritis in one finger and in an elbow. After having clay on the finger for about thirty minutes, the pain was completely eliminated; the inflammation had disappeared. The elbow also responded well to the same treatment, that same day.

Al's "arthritis" was completely eliminated and never returned.

Cano mentions treating edema in the leg and foot of an individual successfully, but wasn't able to specify the cause, only that the individual continued treatments, every other day, to address the swelling.

When the time finally came for Cano to truly open up his healing center to the locals of Las Vegas, he did something truly amazing and unheard of. During a radio interview to promote his healing center, Cano offered an unconditional money back guarantee to everyone. This impressed a great many people, who would come to the center just to try to prove Cano wrong.

Cano's next experience with clay was with a scorpion sting. While the scorpions in the region weren't usually deadly, the stings were still far from pleasant. In this case, clay applied and left on overnight provided complete relief from swelling and discomfort by the next morning.

Cano came across a case of severe food poisoning when a couple pulled into his center one night, during a severe storm. The lady drank two cups of thick, hydrated clay water. A short time later, she was visibly relaxed but exhausted. She drank another cup of clay water that night, and was nearly completely recovered within two hours.

That same night, Cano helped her husband eliminate the stomach ulcers he had had for six years. The individual was instructed to drink a glass of thick clay water once first thing in the morning, the last thing before bed, and during the day when convenient.

Cano came across a man named Johnny Diamond who had previously had heart bypass surgery. The leg where the vein was harvested refused to heal. The leg was always at risk for a serious infection, and the medical doctors had scheduled a skin graft.

In short order, after applying clay, the leg felt like it was responding well; the swelling was reduced and the individual felt a very comforting soothing effect. In all likelihood, the clay would be the only treatment necessary to heal the leg.

Cano kept drawing a great deal of summer business to his therapeutic center, largely due to the clay pits that he built. This fact alone was very interesting. Usually, not a soul would brave the harsh desert climate during the summer months.

One of Cano's most unique discoveries during his exploration of clay therapy was its use for PMS. He advised women with menstruation problems to begin using the clay internally four or five days prior to their regular cycle. He advised them to continue to use the clay during the cycle as well. He recommended that individuals suffering from PMS to drink clay water on an empty stomach once in the morning and once prior to sleeping.

Individuals who experienced problems sleeping were encouraged to have a warm clay bath in the evening, as well. He encouraged women to use a clay compress on the face and the nape of the neck while in the clay bath. This usually felt very soothing and cooling in contrast to the warm clay bath.

A mouse wasn't the only animal that benefited from Cano's generosity. In one of his most amazing stories, he recounts an experience of treating a dog named Leroy using clay therapy. The dog was thirteen years old, and in enough pain that his owners were seriously considering putting him to sleep. The dog had an apparent severe case of arthritis in the back and in one leg.

Cano first mixed a small amount of clay in drinking water for his new companion. As is often the case with animals, the dog quickly lapped up the clay water. The next day, he gave the dog a clay water bath. After Leroy had recovered from the clay bath, Cano packed the dog's back and leg with clay. As the clay began to dry and tighten, Leroy became agitated, as Cano thought he would be as the clay dried and tightened. Cano rinsed the clay off.

The arthritic pain was quite obviously gone. Cano's book editor was so doubtful about the truth of the story, that Cano put a note in his book asking for similar stories to be documented with video from animal owners.

However, as one I will demonstrate in Book III, and even in one of the earlier stories in Book I, such things are a commonplace experience. And while, the method of action is still unclear, the actual effect in such a case is very easy to document.

Next, Cano met an old Shoshone native that lived out in Bishop, California, named Bob Daniels, who first experienced clay therapy in the 1960's or early 1970's. His father introduced him to clay therapy; it was likely that the Shoshone had long been using the clay in the area for healing purposes.

Cano's next encounter was very significant. He had the opportunity to see how quickly clay worked with a case of acute toxicity. Cano met Robert, who worked at a gas station. Robert was suffering from headaches. He also had open sores on his body that stung in the heat of the day.

Cano believed that the gas fumes from the old station were responsible for his toxic condition. He knew from a previous experience with a gentleman who worked in a chemical plant, that clay therapy would likely greatly assist Robert.

Cano had the early insight to realize that increasingly severe cases of Multiple Chemical Sensitivities would start to appear all over the industrialized world. He also had the insight to realize that clay therapy could offer one of the only treatments that could provide hope to its sufferers.

Eight days after spending one day at Cano's facility, Robert's headaches were gone and the sores had healed.

One of the most unique treatments that Cano describes in his book involves a serious case of Toxic Shock Syndrome. A lady named Cindy was in very bad shape, and had no easy way of reaching medical assistance that night. In the usual Cano-style, Cano shot from the hip; he had Cindy cover her body with clay gel. This seemed to help cool her down. He had her drink clay water which she managed to keep down. He had her do a number of clay poultices on the abdominal area. Finally, he filled a stocking with dry clay powder, and had the woman insert it vaginally.

By the next morning, the woman had fully recovered.

Cano's next story is actually quite sad. A lady showed up at his establishment with severe Multiple Chemical Sensitivity. Such individuals are triggered by nearly anything in the environment, including but certainly not limited to: Perfumes, sounds, electromagnetic energy, chemicals, and even certain foods. Cano mentions that detoxifying clay baths were working very well for her over the month that she stayed at his facility.

However, circumstances forced her to depart and she eventually committed suicide before she was able to return.

Next, Cano describes having the opportunity to treat an individual with an extreme steam burn which occurred via a truck radiator. Cano told the individual to keep applying the hydrated clay directly to the burn, then gently soak the effected areas with wet, warm towels, and reapply the clay.

He told the man to use a good Aloe Vera cream as a moisturizer once the effected areas were nearly healed. He instructed the individual to keep using the clay until new skin had grown back, and to drink clay water as well.

The burn healed quickly, and without any scarring.

In another highly dramatic situation, Cano was able to use clay after an automobile accident, before the arrival of EMTs. He used clay on lacerations to stop bleeding (one wound was gushing blood).

Next, Cano recounted the experience of Curt being burned by hot creosote while working on his property. Cano describes Kurt as having "cooking flesh". Curt was quickly told by the onlookers to strip down and jump into the clay pit nearby. Upon entering the clay pit, the searing pain was immediately soothed. Curt was just fine.

Cano ran into a lady (Laura) who had a severe fungal condition which had been present for eleven years. The fungus appeared as multi-colored blotches that covered her body, and appeared to be moving closer to her neck and face. Her husband (Carl) had a serious case of shingles on his right rib cage. Both used Cano's healing clay topically, and both fully recovered within thirty days.

Lou Caruso, a gentleman that Cano ran into one evening, knocked out a severe migraine headache in thirty minutes by sipping clay water and using a cold clay compress on the forehead and face.

Cano later ran into a very unusual and quite baffling situation. Pearl, an individual who showed up at The Crystal Cross, had a cancer operation six months previously. In the ensuing six months, she had put on thirty pounds, and her medical doctors told her that she was getting arthritis in every joint in her body.

Cano instructed Pearl to use the mineral baths, do some light exercise, and cover herself with clay on a daily basis. In fourteen days time, she was transformed and well on the way to what appeared to be a complete recovery. However, she was forced to leave shortly thereafter, and she was never heard from again.

The Dunsmuir chemical spill is probably the most interesting chapter of Cano's exploration of clay therapy. Cano believed that clay therapy was the perfect choice for herbicide and pesticide poisoning. However, he had no idea how effective it would be to treat severe and acute poisoning, until his experience with the sufferers in Dunsmuir.

A Southern Pacific Railroad tank car had jumped off track, and dove into the Sacramento River. The tank ruptured, and dumped toxic chemicals into the river. Cano spent part of a month assisting the locals with clay therapy.

Clay therapy worked to eliminate weeping sores, rashes, headaches, aching joints, and a host of other chemical toxicity symptoms. This was incredible, due to the fact that Cano arrived three months after the initial incident.

Cano would have any local brave enough to want to heal take hot clay baths, from between 45 minutes to an hour long, with one cupful of clay; he would have them drink clay water, and while in-bath, he would have them do cool clay compresses on the face and forehead and over the eyes.

After finishing a clay bath, Cano instructed those suffering with skin lesions and rashes to apply the clay gel wherever skin problems existed; he told them to just let the clay dry, and lie down on sheets.

Clay therapy was successful for those who utilized it, far beyond what anyone could have predicted.

To quote Cano:

> "The use of pesticides and herbicides, along with the byproducts of American Industry, sets the stage for a horrible payback for our progress and our avarice. Rachel Carson gave us fair warning in *The Silent Spring* fifty years ago. We Clay Disciples give you a promise: These are the old times. Learn how clay therapy can help you and your grandchildren's grandchildren survive. The Power created clay for the benefit of all living things."

From recovery from chemotherapy to curing pre-cancerous skin conditions, Cano Graham learned to live and breathe clay therapy. He is undoubtedly one the most dedicated, if not the single most dedicated, clay disciple to ever walk the planet.

Even when the government stepped in and seized Cano's prized oasis in the desert and incarcerated Cano, Cano managed to bring his clay therapy with him. The universe conspired with Cano, and he was able to sneak his healing clay into a federal prison, where he and a small band of Silent Disciples dedicated themselves to relieving pain and suffering.

**Harry Little (Cano) Graham, 2009
(Photo by Pam Belgarde)**

End Game

Cano and the Documentary Film Team
(Photo by Pam Belgarde)

When Cano was finally freed from incarceration, he quickly set about finishing and publishing his book, *The Clay Disciples*. He used this provocative autobiographical account as a launching pad to continue promoting his passion for clay therapy.

From 2006 to May 2009, Cano continued to educate people about the benefits of clay therapy. Specifically, Cano spent quite some time in Arizona working with the Pima Indians, and has focused on using clay therapy to address the many terrible problems associated with Type II Diabetes.

I met Cano in 2007, and he was nothing like what I'd imagined him to be. At least in Cano's case, I realized that I had to both ignore Cano's small town reputation while at the same time embracing it. That's Cano: Full of contradictions. He was a man who was born into a fabulous play, and simply decided to write his own part, one line at a time, and one day at a time. Cano always shot from the hip, but he wrote every single line of his life right from the heart, to the best of his very capable ability.

Cano mentions in his book that some people just don't like him, right off the bat. Well, that hasn't been my experience; everyone who met Cano, at least in my presence, simply loved him… right off the bat.

Cano was a great talker, and this was certainly a part of his considerable charm. But, in retrospect, I think his biggest attribute was the ability to look at people squarely, and to greet the actual being inside with his bright blue, kind eyes.

Cano continued his pursuits with utter abandon, right up until the very day he left this little globe of ours.

"I'm just gonna keep doin' what it is I do," he'd always enjoyed saying, followed by a "Go easy, friend."

And I think that that's really great advice, from a truly amazing individual.

After the publication of his book, having made a decision to focus on using clay to help treat diabetes and diabetes related health issues, he secured funding for a documentary film. The film was to feature the Pima Indians, healing clay and their diabetic health crisis caused by immense poverty. However, due to the economic downturn in 2008-2009, Cano lost his funding.

With funding for his film project done, he continued to attend speaking engagements and educate people on the uses of healing clay, right up until the day he was not physically capable of speaking.

On June 7th, 2009, Cano peacefully passed away after a long fight with advanced lung cancer.

Grimshaw Natural Lake Preserve, Mojave Desert, Tecopa, California
Photos by Tony Aquilano (*www.tonyphotoart.com*)

Ray Pendergraft, the Big Horn Mountains & Pascalite

Introduction

"High, high, up on Big Horn Mountain;
In ten sleeps more that's where I'll be;
Wounded Sioux must get to Big Horn Mountain,
To the Land of Ee-Wah-Kee.
Little Big Horn red with blood behind me;
Up ahead Red Man is free;
Make big medicine on Big Horn Mountain,
Make-well medicine of Ee-Wah-Kee"

- Lyrics to a song written by Ray

Ray Pendergraft (1905-1994), and all of those who have supported the Pascalite Odyssey since its discovery have contributed greatly to the knowledge of clay therapy in the United States. An amazing amount of exploratory work has been done with Pascalite.

Pascalite is a brand trade name given to the calcium bentonite discovered in the Big Horn Mountains of Wyoming. It was named after Emil Pascal who first attempted to mine and market the clay as a health-promoting substance. It is an off-white pale clay when dry, which hydrates into a grey-green clay when mixed with water. I classify Pascalite as a naturally occurring evolutionary calcium smectite with enough sodium to share many of the characteristics of sodium bentonite. It is very similar in appearance and function to the desert calcium bentonites mentioned in other parts of this book.

Historically, it is generally accepted that the animals that were indigenous to the Big Horn Mountains in Wyoming first discovered and used the calcium bentonite clay deposit for its amazing health benefits. Following the example of these often wiser-than-human animals, it is believed that the Native Americans, upon reaching the Big Horn Mountains, also used and traded the calcium bentonite with other tribes.

The Arapahos frequented the area, and likely frequented the clay deposit as well. There was also a strong Shoshone presence in the region. The Sioux were also very familiar with the territory. The Cheyenne were also reported to be in possession of medicinal clay that resembled the clay found in the Big Horn Mountains, and it was probably the same substance. The area had previously been Crow territory. The Blackfoot tribe had also been active in the area. All of these tribes were likely to have been the earliest human users of the calcium bentonite deposit.

A report from Army Major G.L. Scott's party, who traveled through the region by following the Sioux Trail, mentioned Pascalite as being "Indian Medicine". That was reportedly in 1868.

The first recorded use of the clay on a "white man", according to Ray , was with a writer named James Patten. Under the direction of Chief Washakie of the Shoshone, James was given some root herbs to chew and swallow. After consuming the herb, the native medicine man had James consume some very freshly mixed clay water. For his first meal, the now recovering man was given fresh chicken broth. That was in the summer of 1878.

Chief Washakie called Pascalite "Ee-Wah-Kee", which means the "Earth that Heals". He also called it White Powder Medicine.

However, it wasn't until Emil Pascal began to promote its use in the 1930's that the newly emerging civilization in the region began to take notice of the calcium bentonite clay. Pascal discovered its curative powers quite accidentally, after having battled with a steel chain-trapped coyote. Pascal, after winning his hand-to-paw battle with the coyote, had accidentally smeared the clay all over his painfully chapped and cracked hands. He left the clay on, and soon discovered its ability to soothe and heal.

Ironically, it was the American Great Depression that resulted in Ray 's involvement in Pascal's mine; Ray accepted a lonely job up in the Big Horn Mountains, mining Pascalite, after he lost his previous job due to the flailing economy.

One interesting bit of history is that Ray and his wife Peggie actually visited Cano Graham's Crystal Cross Therapeutic Clay Center (see Chapter 1). Ray and Cano got along very well, and spent quite some time exchanging information about their clays.

Ray had, of course, brought a sample of Pascalite for Cano to try. At the end of the s' stay, neither Ray nor Cano could really form an opinion on whose clay was better. They parted friends, and agreed that both of their prized clays were incredible.

Pascalite and Cano's desert green healing clay have very similar characteristics. Both are calcium bentonites/montmorillonites. Both share some of the properties of sodium bentonite. The clay described in Cano's book *"The Clay Disciples"* is a bit purer than Pascalite, as it was mined from a very pristine location where the clay had been protected by a Zeolite cap. Both have exhibited incredible curative powers.

There is a strong parallel between Cano's experience with the green desert clay and Ray's experience with Pascalite. Both discovered clay independent of any formal or informal education on natural or holistic medicine. Both embarked on an amazing journey of discovery. Neither Ray nor Cano had any early support for clay therapy; both had to learn about clay therapy by virtue of trial and error experience.

It took far longer for Pascalite to become a successful endeavor than it took Cano to establish a working healing center. However, it is only through Ray's immense decades-lasting struggle to get Pascalite recognized as a medicinal agent that we have a solid record of everything that has been accomplished with Pascalite. And this information and experience has proven to be invaluable.

In this chapter, I am not going to chronicle the entire Pascalite Journey. Those interested in the complete story should purchase the book "*More Precious than Gold*", by Ray. My goal is to highlight the important points, and provide the interested reader with both a concise reference to the important discoveries of Pascalite and to provide a broad summary of Ray's development of Pascalite, Inc.

Life Mud

"Three Scoops of Pascalite"
Hydrated Calcium Benonite Gel / Magma from Wyoming

When Ray first began using the calcium bentonite clay, nobody knew what it was. The name that they used was very uncreative and unseemly: "Life Mud".

Like most people who have discovered the value of healing clays, Ray learned to trust its healing power slowly, over time. While mining the Pascalite armed only with a shovel and a bag, Ray had plenty of little opportunities to experience the clay's remarkable healing power. After using it on various cuts, sprains, bites and burns, he started to truly appreciate its potential.

Ray documented what was likely the first U.S. case of an infected, gangrene leg turned septic, being cured by healing clay. The doctor in charge of the case felt that he would need to amputate the entire leg in order to save the life of the individual whose infected leg injury was poisoning his entire body. Clay poultices, and clay used internally, killed the infection and healed the leg in short order. This was probably the key medical case that kept Emile Pascal and the 's inspired enough to continue trying to promote Pascalite for so many years.

The first company formed, the "Pascal Products Company" failed. When the company failed, it couldn't afford to pay Ray's back wages, so Ray accepted payment in the form of clay products. Eventually, Ray bought one half interest in the mine from Emile Pascal. Still, neither Ray nor Pascal made any real headway in promoting their "Life Mud".

Ray's first minor success was from a Vanguard Press author Aaron Bacon. Ray had been writing and sending articles to prospective magazines for some time touting the benefits of the calcium bentonite. While Vanguard Press had gone out of business, Mr. Bacon was interested in studying the material. Clay samples were sent, and were studied by the Smithsonian Institute in Washington D.C. Mr. Bacon became interested in purchasing a share (half) in the mine. However, due to a mining claim dispute, nothing ever came from Mr. Bacon's interest.

About the same time, Ray started having problems with nasal staph infections, likely due to his involvement in his family's dry cleaning business. He eventually successfully treated the infection by using clay directly in the nostrils (never use clay powder directly in the nostrils). Ray would use a Q-tip covered with clay paste, and coat his nostrils with it. He also drank clay water several times a day. Ray reports that the infection was gone by the fourth day of treatment.

Ray eventually became Worland Wyoming's first Chief of Police. Shortly thereafter, Pascal sold his interest in the Pascalite mine to Carl Sneed, who worked as a policeman under Ray. Shortly thereafter, Ray and Carl finally changed the name of their product from Life Mud to Pascalite.

Pascalite

One day, a mining engineer by the name of Arthur Jones Sawyer approached Ray. He informed Ray that a group had been testing Pascalite at a health clinic in Thermopolis. Ray and Carl eventually gave him lease rights to the mine.

This was one critically important fact of the times, and it is one of the things that makes the Pascalite story very unique. During Ray's time, the FDA, the AMA, and the insurance companies didn't have nearly as much power as they do today.

Much of the extensive knowledge we have about Pascalite came from medical doctors who actually used the clay in their private practices. Doctors of that era felt much freer to practice medicine from both a scientific and common sense approach. If something was considered safe, and it was effective, a good doctor would not even hesitate to use it.

Sawyer's endeavor with Pascalite eventually failed, but it was clear that the "word" about Pascalite was finally spreading, and drawing an increasing amount of interest.

Ray eventually leased mining rights to another gentleman in Thermopile, Wyoming, Mr. Shakley. Mr. Shakley became a big advocate of Pascalite, and word of Pascalite spread all the way to the Eastern Seaboard through his efforts. However, very little substance materialized through his marketing efforts.

Shortly thereafter, Ray successfully published a cover-featured article about Pascalite in a publication called "Beyond Magazine". This became the first successful marketing effort that Ray had done. It was also the turning point in the Pascalite story, as word of mouth advertising would continue to grow their business from that point forward.

People began curing stomach ulcers, healing serious wounds, treating burns, solving mouth problems, and taking Pascalite daily as a mineral supplement.

In 1974, Ray had to go to court to defend his and his partners mining rights. The government was trying to claim that the calcium bentonite in the Big Horn Mountains had absolutely no value. After a lengthy trial, Carl, Ray, and the government reached an agreement outside of court, and they were allowed to continue their operations.

Most of us believe that Pascalite would have won in court, but it was clear that Ray and Carl didn't want to take any chances.

One of the most impressive testimonies was reported by a Dr. Sneed, MD. Dr. Sneed testified in a Wyoming State Court that Pascalite was the only known cure for a fiddle-back spider bite. At the time, there was only one other treatment, which was steroid injections (which were not very effective). The bite of the fiddle-back spider is necrotizing, and has been known to be fatal.

Through the efforts of Dr. Sneed, Pascalite also became known for its ability to rapidly and successfully treat brown recluse spider bites. He testified that Pascalite was the best possible treatment available for severe burns. He mentioned that silver might be superior, but he was not experienced with the use of silver. Ironically, nobody at that time realized that healing clay and silver could be combined together with very efficacious results.

Dr. James Summers, a veterinarian, also testified on behalf of Pascalite. Of interest, he actually made an injectable solution by mixing clay with distilled water, and then using the water after all solids had settled out. He also reported that he used Pascalite to heal wounds that were completely non-responsive to traditional wound care methods.

He reported that he actually injected clay-treated water in the bloodstream of a calf, and reports that the calf showed signs of improvement. He then injected the same solution intramuscularly. The calf was suffering from diphtheria. While the calf eventually died, the doctor reported that an autopsy revealed that there was no tissue reaction at the clay injection sites.

Another veterinarian testified as to Pascalite's successful ability to treat cellulites. The doctor used Pascalite poultices and IV antibiotics successfully on several occasions.

Ray recounted one individual's very interesting report that Pascalite used internally helped him successfully treat his alcoholism.

Finally, though, it was Walter Bennett, PhD., a California University graduate professor, that broke some truly amazing ground with a study he did on the properties of Pascalite.

Dr. Bennett first analyzed the clay chemically, and reported that the clay was a calcium bentonite containing silica, silicates, silicones; aluminum oxide; magnesium oxide; iron oxides; calcium oxides; complex sodium salts, titanium oxide, potassium salts, manganese oxide; barium oxide; zirconium silicates and zirconium carbonate;

strontium oxide and strontium celestite; cadmium oxide; copper oxides and copper sulfide; nickel oxide; gallium oxides and patronite; chromium oxide with iron, and boron borate and boron colemanite. He identified twenty elements, plus traces of sulfur, chlorides and hydrocarbons and 300 PPM of proteins.

He found that it was effective for topical application to skin disorders, including those associated with malaria, intertrigo, pruritus, fungus infections, sebaceous cysts, plantar heratosis and acne. He reported its effectiveness with bacterial infections, fungal infections and many forms of dermatitis.

He also reported Pascalite as being effective with burns, scrapes, minor wounds, bites, cold sores, corns, hemorrhoids and styes.

"…the almost miraculous recovery associated with the application of this natural material suggest a type of synergism which we do not completely understand." Dr. Bennett commented.

He further commented about the little known but extremely important role of metalloenzymes in the body, and made it clear that he suspected that the complex interdependencies of the *metal oxides* in the clay may, at least in part, explain clay's fantastic health benefits. He further iterated the importance of metal ions serving as key components of essential enzyme systems in living organisms.

He commented upon the presence of protein in the clay, and suggested that the presence of the protein indicated the presence of undisclosed amino acids. He felt that the presence of amino acids, even though present only in minute quantities, was extremely important.

He mentioned that Pascalite contained several types of fungi, but could only identify two: Penicillium and Actdinomyces.

Finally, Dr. Bennett concluded that Pascalite should be medically available to people with the following medical statements:

1. It is a valuable food supplement as a source of most essential minerals.
2. It is an effective topical treatment for dermatological disorders.
3. It is an essential component for cosmetics and beauty aids.
4. It is a safe, effective dressing for burns, abrasions, lacerations and punctures.
5. It is a safe, fast, and effective remedy for gastro-intestinal distress.
6. It has no contraindication to human health.

Pascalite was well on its way to becoming a well known aid to general health. It even started showing up in publications and independent studies.

Ray mentions a publication by Dr. Schmitt Jr. (DC) entitled "Compiled Notes on Clinical Nutritional Products". He recommended that individuals take Pascalite fifteen to thirty minutes before eating. He claimed that Pascalite would scrub and clean the small intestine, freeing it from mucous and debris that could impair the body's digestive function. He also claimed that by using the clay prior to eating, more surface area would be available in the small intestine for superior nutrient adsorption.

Ray received another very interesting report from Harvey C. Lisle, a chemical engineer specializing in biodynamics. He claimed that special "rock dusts", such as Pascalite, radiated energy 100 feet, and possessed the ability to negate noxious energies.

He recommended that Pascalite be placed above or below TV sets and microwaves, and reported that it cancelled out their noxious emissions. Furthermore, he stated that it neutralized the electrical field of a 12,000 volt transmission line that ran past his house.

He also reported that he considered clay as being enzymatic, possessing the power to change other substances chemically without changing the clay itself; and it thus acted as a catalyst. Finally, he reported that these special "live rock dusts" were being used to restore dead soils in Germany, Austria and Poland.

Finally, a Lakota Sioux Medicine Man placed everything in its most correct perspective when he told Ray: "There is some Pascalite in all of us."

More Precious than Gold contains many more wonderful stories about Pascalite. I've only included the significant ones in this chapter, to highlight the s' experience with healing clay and to include key research material about healing clay that isn't otherwise mentioned elsewhere.

> "The rock holds in its depth white clay which will come out milk-white from a cleft. Needlessly troubled people will not dare touch it, unaware that the foundation of the earth is clay."
> -- Quatrain 21, Nostradamus

Neal Bosshardt & Utah's Redmond Clay

The Redmond Clay Mineral Deposit

The Redmond clay deposit and the award winning Real Salt deposit are both located in Redmond Valley, Utah. This particular clay deposit is a mineral-rich mixture of sodium and calcium bentonite that had once been used by the local natives for the therapeutic and healing properties of the clay. The Fremont Indians of Southern Utah began using the clay deposit for health purposes after they observed herds of deer frequenting the deposit to eat the clay.

The Bosshardt family began experimenting with the clay in the 1960's. Their experimentation eventually evolved into a family business, and Redmond clay was born. Currently, Redmond clay is extremely popular in Utah. It also has growing reputation for its health benefits across the country. Neal Bosshardt, while not well known outside of Utah, is an extremely accomplished clay disciple.

Neal Bosshardt, founder of Redmond Clay and Noted Clay Disciple

Redmond Valley, Utah

Redmond clay has exhibited all of the properties commonly associated with therapeutic grade clays. It is clean enough to be safely used internally, and it works exceptionally well for external applications. The Bosshardt family has done an excellent job developing this mineral deposit, and they have collected a wide variety of fascinating clay disciple stories to tell.

This section of the book highlights a few of the more unique case histories shared by Neal Bosshardt. Neal wrote his own short clay usage guide, which can be obtained by contacting Redmond Clay directly (*www.redmondclay.com*). He also has an excellent short video of a lecture he gave.

External Use of Redmond Clay

Ankle Infection Healed

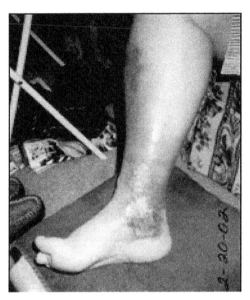

All therapeutic grade clays have an amazing ability to assist the body with healing trauma, no matter how severe or unresponsive the body may be to other traditional treatment methods.

The ankle in the image (left) had been infected for eight months. Note the redness traveling up the leg; the infection was at risk for sepsis. Often times, especially with individuals with diabetes, when an infection has raged for this long the eventual outcome is the loss of the foot, ankle, and even sometimes the whole leg.

Luckily, this individual discovered healing clay. The individual treated the leg by locally applying a clay poultice over the entire area affected. The entire leg was healed within two months.

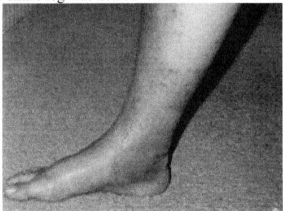

The Leg: Two Months Later

A Very Painful Torch Burn

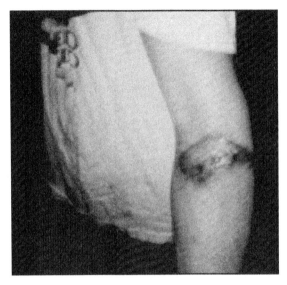

One of the most valuable uses for clay therapy is to help remove pain from trauma while at the same time eliminating any risk of infection. The image (left) depicts a serious acetylene torch burn. This wound should have hurt for days if not weeks. Luckily, the individual found some Redmond Clay. After ten minutes of clay application, the pain was completely eliminated. Within four days, the skin looked fantastic.

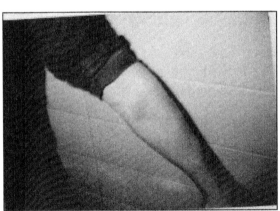

The Same Arm – Completely Healed

This is not an exceptional case with clay therapy, it is a common one. Results won't vary. The pain will be relieved and the injury healed, provided that the body has the needed nutrients and health to recover.

Road Rash from a Bike Crash

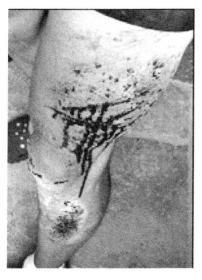

Clay has an amazing ability to cleanse sooth and protect abrasions. Wound debridement is seldom necessary with new wounds. This bike accident road rash (left) could have been a serious and ongoing nightmare. However, this luckily and wise individual simply applied some clay (bottom left) and rinsed it off two hours later. This individual's doctor told him that the wound needed to be professionally cleaned (a very torturous process) or he would have permanent tattooing due to the road debris embedded deep in his leg.

Two hours later, the leg looked terrific (bottom right). No debridement needed. Clay application was only done two more times, and the leg healed perfectly with no scarring.

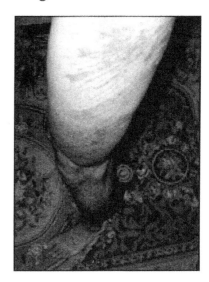

Internal Use of Redmond Clay

Although Redmond Clay works very well externally, Darryl Bosshardt, Neal's son, noted that at least 50% of Redmond Clay users use it as edible clay.

Digestive issues such as colitis have been reported to respond very well:

> "My colitis was so bad that I was experiencing constant, uncontrollable diarrhea. I didn't dare leave the house. I got a bottle of Redmond Clay and began taking it. After three days I couldn't believe that something so simple could help so much. My bowels are totally controlled now. Redmond Clay is a miracle and has given me my life back. Thank you." – DG

Another individual reported excellent, long term results using Redmond Clay to cure ulcerative colitis:

> "I am 45 years old and have suffered from ulcerative colitis for the past ten years. I am in a high stress profession and at times have been unable to work due to the debilitating symptoms of this terrible disease. Three years ago I went to see a colon specialist and contemplated having part of my colon removed.
>
> "I have been on every medication presently prescribed for this condition with little or no help in terms of relief or remission. Two years ago I was introduced to a product called Redmond Clay and from the testimonials, it appeared to have helped others who suffered from colitis. I began taking Redmond Clay in liquid form two years ago.
>
> "I stirred one tablespoonful of clay into a glass of water and then let the majority of the clay particles settle to the bottom and then drank the clear water. I did this religiously for three months. At the end of three months, I had no visible symptoms of the disease. Everything was normal and the blood and cramping subsided. I now take a few glassfuls a month but have not taken it on a regular basis like I did initially.
>
> "Last January I went in for my annual exam and was excited to hear the results. I was not surprised when my doctor told me there was no need to come back for three years due to the health of my colon. I have had no relapses in the last three years and I feel wonderful. I attribute my health to the Redmond Clay. I can't medically explain why, but I know it has helped me." – BR

Like any excellent healing-grade therapeutic clay, Redmond Clay doesn't just work to restore the normal function of the colon. It also works for stomach issues as well as helping to cleanse and heal the small intestine.

> "My son has suffered from reflux at a very early age. At 14 months he was taking adult doses of reflux medicine – Prevacid and Carafate. My friend gave me a bottle of Redmond Clay and told me of its healing properties. I was very uncomfortable with the possible effects of all the medicines on my son's liver so I decided to try the clay. I have been amazed and so pleased with the results. My son is doing great. He is no longer taking any of the medicines and shows no sign of any reflux complications. He sleeps better through the night, there are no more circles under his eyes, he is more active and he eats when he is hungry. Thank you very much for the quality of Redmond Clay. Now that my son is doing better, I feel like I have my life back. When he sleeps, I sleep". – KK

In fact, Brigham Young University did a study on Redmond Clay. Dr. Kim L. O'Neill and Joshua D. Stubblefield, working in the Microbiology department at BYU, studied Redmond Clay's effect on Aflatoxin B_1 and Cholera toxin. The report was completed on September 5th, 2000.

The microbiology team determined that the use of Redmond Clay would "…reverse the dehydration caused by secretory diarrhea by replenishing lost electrolytes and absorbing bacterial toxins; thereby promoting water reabsorption…" While acute diarrhea may kill over 5,000,000 people every year worldwide, it's not likely to do so for those who know about edible clay!

The microbiology team determined that the clay's most likely method of action was not due to any antibacterial properties, but rather, due to the clay's ability to quickly and safely adsorb and evacuate the toxins produced by the pathogenic bacteria. Further, based upon a chemical analysis of the clay, the scientists hypothesized that the clay could also be acting as an oral rehydration solution. Therefore, taking clay internally not only eliminated the danger presented by the pathogenic organisms, but also may help in providing desperately needed electrolytes to the body (in the small intestine).

The entire study has been republished in the references and studies section of this book.

Terramin: California Desert Earth Red Clay
Introduction

Fifty million years ago, as winter ebbed and the sun began to shine brightly upon the snow-capped Colorado Rocky Mountains, the snow began its seasonal melt. Beads of water joined to become trickles. Trickles of water became streams and those streams became rivers. River waters rushed down the mountains' canyons, carrying what would eventually become essential nutrient minerals. The mineral-rich waters eventually spilled into the mighty Colorado River.

As spring moved toward summer, the waters of the great Colorado River rose day by day. The river waters rushed toward and down into the Colorado River Basin, where the river began to slow its movement across the gentler, flatter landscape. Eventually, the river began to spill over, breaching the well-defined banks of the river. This "quiet water" overflow was gentle rather than raging. It would deposit only the lightest of minerals and the smallest particles along with the debris-free roily water onto the hot and dry regions of the lower delta.

This mineral-rich silt was composed of mixed silicate clays filled with alkaline, ionic minerals that eventually settled on the arid desert floor. The air was as pristine as the sun was cleansing. The wide landscape was open, hot and quiet. The mineral-laden water quickly dried atop the previous year's deposit, leaving yet another layer of mineralized clay. Simple and complex oxides formed as the blazing sun sucked nearly all of the moisture from the newly deposited earth.

Year after year, just like the daily tides of the Earth's great oceans, this cycle continued its ebb and flow, marking the passage of time not in days but in eons. For millions of years, the Colorado River dug deeply into the earth, forming great canyon waterways. The hydrolic forces of the water which layered the deeply red earth formed one of the most interesting and beneficial calcium bentonite clay deposits in North America.

The Terramin clay deposit was thus born.

Wild animals by instinct were the first to discover and utilize this rare deposit of nutritional healing clay. Eventually, indigenous people hundreds and maybe even thousands of years ago began to utilize the clay for its health-promoting properties. Today, California Earth Minerals, owned and operated by Ray Kong, sells this mineral supplement for human and animal use.

Hydrated Terramin Magma – A rich, smooth, creamy, chocolate colored gel

Neva Jensen, NASA and "The Source"

The Source

Modern intuitives, when presented with a healing grade clay deposit for the first time, often struggle for the words to describe what they perceive. Since these clay deposits are like nothing that they have ever encountered before, the adjectives they come up with are often along the lines of "The Source" and "Sacred Manna".

It is clear by examining his writings that even Nostradamus must have been exposed to healing clays. It is equally clear at how awed he must have been with the living power of clay when he wrote the following words:

> "The rock holds in its depth white clay which will come out milk-white from a cleft. Needlessly troubled people will not dare touch it, unaware that the foundation of the earth is clay."

This milk-white manna that he refers to has been written about for ages, but it actually has nothing to do with the color of the rock, but rather, what the rock contains, which has also long been referred to as the "Food of the Gods". In the "old world", most of the clay deposits containing this "sacred manna" where either white clay deposits (of the Middle East) or green clay deposits (of Europe).

If Nostradamus had more of an opportunity to travel in the "New World", he would have chosen his words more carefully. Unfortunately, since many intuitives actually see clay as glowing with rich, shimmering, white energy, the lack of clarity between the distinction of white powder, white energy, and white colored earth has caused much confusion. Rest assured that all known sacred therapeutic clays contain some form of this "manna".

To clarify and illustrate this point, consider the California Earth Mineral Deposit. Researchers have determined by comparative testing that while the entire clay deposit is quite vast, only a portion of this deposit has therapeutic properties. They discovered that the further away from the "center" of the source, the less effective the clay becomes as a health-promoting substance. While there is no proven scientific reason for this disparity, the difference could be linked to a more pronounced hydrothermal activity in the region of the "source" clay; it is directly above the San Andreas Fault.

Only "The Source" is marketed by California Earth Minerals Corporation in their line of clay products.

Neva Jensen: Hydro-thermally Produced Living Clay

Terramin – ION-MIN – California Earth Minerals

Neva Jensen, a very noteworthy clay researcher wrote a book entitled *"The Healing Power of Hydro-Thermally Produced Living Clay"*, copyright 1982. This book was written to document and explore the use of Terramin clay for health purposes.

This section has been written to briefly chronicle the knowledge and information contained in the book. Neva's book is still available from California Earth Minerals Corporation, and may be ordered through them or their distributors.

Neva Jensen was first introduced to the art of healing with clay by a Native American. She had long experienced serious health problems, and the Native American had her use clay taken with herbs to relieve pain and help the body function normally. Neva notes that the North American Natives used clay and herbs side by side, as an integral system of natural medicine.

Neva points out that native medicine men would give therapeutic clay as a gift, and that the location of the clay deposits were only known to those who gathered the clay. When Neva went on her own search for healing clays, she reported mixed results from the natural deposits she discovered. She also reported limited results with marine clays she experimented with.

In particular, Neva was searching for clay to help alleviate bone problems. Her bone problems, which had previously been rectified using clay, had recurred. She needed to find a clay source similar in therapeutic value to the clays that the natives had used and given her.

Eventually, she was introduced to Terramin, which founders Harry K. and Madeline K. Hebbard had been mining since 1946.

Terramin possessed the therapeutic properties she had long been seeking. The red montmorillonite smectite clay, hydrotheramally altered and aged by the arid California desert, began working exactly like the healing clays she had used before.

Neva notes that clay applications to the skin have a soothing, cleansing and healing effect. She noted that inflammation and pain would rapidly diminish with clay application. She strongly believed through experience that no conditions of toxicity were ever present with individuals who made clay a part of their daily lives.

Neva had learned that edible clay used internally would provide rapid relief from stomach irritations and bowel problems; even ulcerations. She believed that many such conditions were due to an over-acidity of the effected organs and tissues, and that clay would correct the conditions.

Neva realized that the benefits of using clay internally didn't stop with its healing capabilities. She also demonstrated that the clay used as a supplement resulted in the rapid uptake of trace minerals and micronutrients as bioavailable nutrients that many people desperately needed. Neva believed that it was the ion exchange capacity of the clay which was responsible for clay's nutritional benefits: The interchange between clay's negatively charged particles and positively charged ions, and the motion which resulted.

Neva believed that clay should be used to brush teeth, used on the face in the form of facial packs. She also believed that clay should regularly be used internally. She used clay with pets, and even with vegetation (clay added to soil). She noted that taking clay internally before and after surgery made for an excellent recovery from surgery.

In addition to the numerous uses that clay therapy practitioners use clay for, Neva used clay added in water prior to watering freshly cut flowers. She also added clay to watering tanks to help control algae. She used clay to decontaminate water and even to increase seed germination by adding clay to soil.

In her book, Neva provides an excellent thesis on the scientific origin of clay, the primitive uses of clay and a well written exploration of clay composition and trace mineral analysis. However, the author is only including information specific to the use of Terramin in this book. Interested individuals should contact California Earth Minerals for the latest edition of Neva Jensen's book. All of the "generalized" information about clays will be included in Book 3.

NASA and Terramin

Dr. Benjamin H. Ershoff, Ph.D., was hired by N.A.S.A. to find a calcium supplement that help astronauts in space with bone density loss (osteoporosis). Dr. Ershoff tested a wide variety of potential calcium supplements, including the California Earth Minerals clay deposit.

In order to determine which, if any, of the tested supplements impacted bone density, he conducted tests on male rats, hamsters, mice and miniature pigs. The animals were all fed a low calcium, low protein, and low fat diet.

The effects with the red desert clay were substantial. The results of the test showed that when 1%, 2% and 4% clay was added to the diet of the tested animals, a clinically significant increase in body weight occurred. Furthermore, the clay supplementation prevented the occurrence of pathological changes which had been observed in the bones of the control group. Clay not only increased the healthy growth rate of animals, but it also protected them from a nutrient deficient diet.

Dr. Ershoff determined that the excellent results delivered by clay were proportional to the amount of clay added to the diet. The more clay used, the better the results. He also determined that clay supplementation's protective effect was due to something other than the calcium content of the clay. He further noted that the clay contained some unknown cofactor that improved calcium utilization and/or improved bone formation.

Based on Dr. Ershoff's study, NASA began using Terramin to prevent bone deterioration in astronauts in the U.S. space program. To this day, astronauts still successfully use Terramin as a dietary supplement to prevent osteoporosis.

Another study, conducted by J.H. Quesenberry of Texas A&M University, demonstrated that California Earth Minerals Cal-MIN product was an effective bird supplement. The comparative tests were done with Texas Bentonite and Western Bentonite, along with two other clay products (including Cal-MIN). While Texas and Western bentonite are not healing grade clays, they serve as a good representation of the industrial grade bentonites commonly available worldwide.

The birds that received bentonite as a part of their diet gained more body weight and laid larger eggs. Those birds receiving the Cal-MIN supplement or taking Western bentonite laid more eggs than the control group as well. Furthermore, feed efficiency was improved for those taking Cal-MIN, and slightly improved for those taking Western bentonite.

The conclusive scientific studies done with animals translate directly to people, as well. Many individuals will notice a profound difference in health when taking Terramin internally. Anecdotal evidence suggests that even more serious cases of osteoporosis can be completely reversed within two years of supplementation; the author has personally observed such a case.

Please note that the entire NASA study has been republished, with permission, in our references section at the end of this book.

Author's Note

The importance of the California Earth "Terramin" Mineral deposit should not be neglected. Clay enthusiasts understandably tend to want to stick to the one favorite clay that they have come to trust. However, no two therapeutic clays are identical, and different clays work better for different people. Luckily, due to the nature of colloids in general, clays can often be mixed and matched, with a synergetic effect.

For internal supplementation, Terramin is equal to or superior to any other therapeutic clay available at any price. Currently, I use Terramin in all of my internal clay blends.

A few years ago I was approached by my mother when she was told she had osteoporosis. She wanted to know what clay could do for her. Terramin is not my personal first-choice clay to use for healing purposes. However, I always keep some on hand.

Terramin has very unique properties as a mineral supplement. It was the perfect choice for her condition. My mother, being a retired career medical professional, is a no nonsense, common sense type person. Terramin had the irrefutable, hard, cold science to back it up.

My mother elected to do everything. She took the medication that the doctor prescribed. She took a targeting calcium supplement, and she religiously took Terramin. Personally, I could have cared less about the prescribed medication or the other calcium supplement she took. The only thing I cared about was whether or not she continued to take the Terramin, because the only thing I cared about was her complete recovery. The medication would not accomplish this, neither would a calcium supplement.

Luckily, she did.

After two years, her bone density test came back normal. The medical doctor was so shocked that he had her come back in to his office and do the test a second time. Of course, I was not the least bit surprised.

People often ask why I choose Terramin over my own favorite healing clay. I tell them I try to be a solution oriented person; the more I develop my intuition (especially through a part time but serious study of Chi Gong), the more that I can sense different properties in clays. I tell people that the calcium bentonite I use would likely reverse osteoporosis as well; but probably not quite as good as Terramin would.

Today my entire family takes a very specific blend of clays internally. The results of using a masterful blend of clays are often quite astounding.

Using the right clays for the right jobs is something I will go into in far greater depth in Volume II of this work.

Until then, I recommend that new and old clay disciples alike start exploring the more prominent healing clays of the world, and not just the one favorite that an individual has come to trust and love.

From India with Love: Gandhi, Anjou & Pascal
Introduction

I was first contacted by someone with the *Sarvodaya International Trust* several years ago. This amazing organization is dedicated to preserving and teaching the ideas promoted by Mahatma Gandhi. The trust advised me that they were involved in a book project about clay therapy. The book, I was told, was to include Gandhi's experience with healing clays. I was asked if I could recommend a publisher for the book. Unfortunately, I didn't have any publisher contacts at the time.

In 2006, they found a publisher for their book, and the first printing of "Clay Cures, Nature's Miracle for the New Age", by Anjou Musafir and Pascal Chazot was completed and printed by Mapin Publishing.

Anjou and Pascal have an amazing perspective on healing clay therapy. They have quite a collection of truly inspiring and touching clay therapy stories, many of which are very different than the stories commonly told here in North America. Some of their clay usage methods are quite different from how many of us in the western world have used clay, and the author personally learned quite a bit by studying their text.

Pascal has an amazing perspective on naturopathy and its relationship to clay therapy. Both his and Anjou's experience with healing clay is extraordinary, in that they explore its use in a wide array of very unique and serious situations. They show in no uncertain terms that clay rightly belongs at the top of any person's "need-to-have" list.

To quote Pascal and Anjou: "Clay treatment, on the other hand, is holistic and helps the body regain its state of health and frees us from the bondage and dependencies created by organized systems."

Pascal and Anjou share an esoteric and profound truth: No matter the system, organization itself acts a form of containment or slavery. Anything holistic, by definition, is inclusive and not exclusive. Very few things in alternative medicine are actually holistic; there is a very short list of substances that are truly holistic and homeostatic.

Clay deserves to be at the top of that very short list.

The following is a short chronicle of Anjou Musafir and Pascal Chazot's experience with the art of healing with the Earth, as presented in their book "*Clay Cures*, Nature's Miracle for the New Age. It is certainly not a replacement for their book, which the author highly recommends.

Clay Cures, Nature's Miracle for a New Age

"Clay Cures" was written to fill a gap of knowledge that the authors felt existed. While clay therapy has been practiced by indigenous cultures world-wide, the modern, average day citizen of the modern world had no clear guidance… and along with a this void of natural knowledge, a certain sense of powerlessness loomed.

At the time the authors began their treatise their one year old daughter fell ill. Pascal was also sick. Their eldest daughter was ill. Pascal and Anjou diligently placed their faith in the curative powers of therapeutic clay.

At the same time, a friend of the family, a medical doctor, visited them in search of the clay cure. The doctor had diabetes. Pascal and Anjou had told him that clay could cure it. He began clay therapy, and stopped all other treatment. To the amazement of everyone, the doctor's blood sugar level was normal in fifteen days. Eventually, all of the complications associated with Diabetes were eliminated, including weight gain and gall stones. Three years later, the doctor remains in perfect health.

The authors' two year old daughter Tara suffered from Impetigo. Impetigo is a very severe and often painful skin infection. Tara's impetigo covered half of her body. Daily clay application, for one month, resulted in an inspiring and complete recovery.

Just prior to the publication of *"Clay Cures"*, floods raging in Gujarat caused major epidemics of malaria and dengue. Tara fell violently ill. She acquired a dangerous fever of 104 degrees F. that lasted for four days. On the fifth day, she seemed to be improving.

Then, she took a turn for the worse. She started hallucinating and quickly became dehydrated. She was unable to drink water. Up to this point, her parents had use clay poultices (cataplasms) on the stomach and her arm. Thinking that the fever might have affected her brain, they put a poultice on her forehead.

Within one-half hour she was resting peacefully. She woke about two hours later, asking for ice cubes. She began speaking normally. She was back to school a few short days later.

Anjou and Pascal talk about the immense pressures they have faced when using clay therapy rather than allopathic medicine. They have even been accused of experimenting on their child, which is very ironic since allopathic medicine is the new branch of medicine, and this entire branch of human experience is extremely experimental, and often tragically so.

Even in situations where modern care would have been completely and admittedly ineffective, many people would rather relinquish their personal power and responsibility to a self-proclaimed authority rather than utilize common sense, experiential science, and wisdom.

Anjou and Pascal's experience with clay therapy is nothing short of phenomenal. The experience that they share is nothing like anything experienced in North America.

"Only when we began distancing ourselves from nature did we also start to distance ourselves from the Earth's therapeutic strengths".
    -Anjou and Pascal

Mahatma Gandhi: Nature Curist

Gandhi's experience with mud therapy was the result of exposure to Dr. Kuhne's book on natural cures and Just's book called *"Return to Nature"*. He began using Kuhne's advice for hydrotherapy in the form of hip baths. He started doing cold mud poultices over the abdomen to relieve his chronic constipation.

Gandhi had a long-term problem with chronic constipation and frequent headaches. He practiced what he called a well regulated diet, and occasionally used laxatives and fruit for his digestive troubles. He started to apply the cold earthen poultices to the lower abdomen, three inches by six inches long and one-half inch thick. His body responded profoundly:

"The treatment consisted in applying to the abdomen a bandage of clean earth moistened with cold water and spread like a poultice on fine linen. This I applied at bedtime, removing it during the night or in the morning, whenever I happened to wake up. It proved a radical cure. Since then I have tried the treatment on myself and my friends and never had reason to regret it." (From Gandhi's *Nature Cure*, pp 7-8)

Gandhi also recommended using mud poultices to the head for the treatment of both headaches and fevers. He frequently used clay to treat wasp stings, scorpion bites and even typhoid fever. Gandhi reported treating seven cases of typhoid fever, and achieving seven cures.

Gandhi reportedly used a sweet smelling red earth. In certain circumstances, he would use heated clay; heated to a point to ensure sterilization of the clay. He treated his third son's broken arm with clay.

Gandhi's dedication to natural "common-sense" medicine was impressive. His disdain for modern medicine was well known. He had the following to say about the modern medical system in his book *Nature Cure*:

"Doctors have almost unhinged us. Sometimes I think that that quacks are better than highly qualified doctors... It is worth considering why we take up the profession of medicine. It is certainly not for the purpose of serving humanity. We become doctors so that we may obtain honors and riches... Doctors make a show of their knowledge and charge exorbitant fees."

Anjou and Pascal are quick to point out some staggering statistics:

"In 1973, when doctors in Israel were on strike for a month, admissions to hospitals went down by 85 per cent. The death rate dropped by 50 per cent to reach its lowest recorded level. The previous low level was 20 years before – also during a doctors' strike. During a doctors' strike in Los Angeles County in 1976 to protest against high malpractice insurance premiums, the death rate fell by nearly 20 per cent… Such strikes bring home that your *individual* longevity and individual *health* are your responsibility." (Valnet, Aromatherapie, traitement des maladies par les essences de plantes, pp. 76-77)

A most fitting way to end this section on such a historic figure is with his own words, from his book *Nature Cures*:

> "The Nature Cure man does not "sell a cure" to the patient. He teaches him the right way of living in his home, which would not only cure him of his particular ailment but also save him from falling ill in the future. The ordinary doctor or vaidya is interested mostly in the study of disease. The Nature Curist is interested more in the study of health. His real interest begins where that of the ordinary doctor ends; the eradication of the patient's ailment under nature nature cure marks only the beginning of a way of life in which there is no room for illness or disease. Nature Cure is thus a way of life."

The Accounting of Anjou Musafir

Anjou Msafir was introduced to the art of clay therapy by her future husband, Pascal. Like most individuals being introduced to healing with the Earth, Anjou was skeptical. She considered Pascal's belief in the curative properties of clay to be typical foreigner behavior, trapped in the ideas of oriental mysticism and superstition.

Anjou had witnessed Pascal use therapeutic clay to help with his recovery from Bell's Palsy. However, having not directly experienced the benefits of clay therapy, she long remained skeptical.

It was when Anjou acquired a urinary tract infection (and possibly Malaria) that she seriously attempted to use clay for the first time. Pascal had long since told her that she needed to listen to her own body's natural instincts. This time, her instincts were telling her that the medications being prescribed by her medical doctor were making her much sicker.

Anjou had become more ill as time progressed. The prescribed medications were having adverse effects. She was vomiting, could not retain water, developed rigors, started shivering uncontrollably and had a raging fever. She stopped her medications and began clay therapy.

In a state of great pain and out of desperation more than anything else, she hydrated some clay, and placed the wet clay on a dressing. She applied the dressing, by tying it, to her stomach. She described an immediate soothing and cooling sensation. Within one-half hour, she noticed a significant difference. Her pain began to ease. Within an hour, she was comfortably moving around.

Having removed the clay, three hours later the severe pain returned. It was that moment—the moment where she was absolutely certain that the clay was responsible for her earlier relief, she started to take clay seriously.

For the next several weeks, Anjou applied clay, day and night. She carried a pot of clay with her to work, along with strips of cloth to serve as dressings. She applied the clay before bed, and would change the clay if she awoke during the night when the clay had dried.

After several weeks, she was cured, although she had one relapse a year later brought on from the stress of her father falling ill. Anjou was ill for a month this time, and experienced a deep frustration with having to use clay therapy for that length of time. However, if she was not timely with the clay therapy, the agonizing pain would quickly return.

One day, after about a month's time had passed, Anjou removed the clay poultice and intuitively sensed that no further treatment was needed. Anjou was again cured. The infection and the clay therapy had given her a great gift. Anjou was now very naturally in tune with her body.

After marrying Pascal, Anjou moved to Pascal's home in the city of Ahmedabad. Pascal had a non-violence policy that did not permit the use of lethal insect repellents. Anjou was certain that she would contract malaria.

She fell ill, and utilized clay poultices on the forehead for three days while she fought off a fever and experienced severe shivering. On the fourth day she was better. She has never since contracted Malaria (it's now been over eleven years), and believes that clay therapy helped her body to develop an immunity to Malaria.

While one such reported case may simply be seen as uncommonly good fortune, the same experience was shared by Pascal and their daughter Lissa. Each of them contracted Malaria, each fought the illness off with the help of clay therapy, and none of them have since contracted this dreaded illness.

Anjou's next account involves migraine headaches. She had experienced occasional migraines since childhood, and then quite severe attacks once in college. Having become adept at using clay, she would use clay on the forehead to experience rapid relief. On one such occasion, however, her headache did not respond to clay therapy.

She asked Pascal why she was not experience relief. Pascal told her that she would need to apply clay to another part of the body; a part which she would intuitively need to discover for herself. He went on to suggest the liver. Upon applying the clay to the liver, Anjou soon began vomiting. At the same time, the pain from the headache disappeared.

The specialist doctors that she saw during her childhood thought that her migraine headaches were due to either poor eyesight or inflamed sinuses. After experiencing how her liver responded to clay, Anjou quickly ascertained that the true cause of her migraines was liver toxicity (a weak liver). She continued to apply clay poultices to the liver, which cured her chronic migraines. The only time she now experiences headaches is if she binges on food.

Anjou also reported curing a sciatica problem. By applying the clay to the lower back, she would experience relief, and eventually cured the chronic problem. She only experiences any discomfort if she over-exerts herself.

Pascal advised an individual who was often bed-ridden with sciatica pain to use clay therapy. He told the individual to apply clay along the route of the sciatica nerve. He told the individual to expect a reaction with the clay; if there was no reaction, then he advised the sufferer to change application locations to the lower back.

A few days later the individual reported experiencing great relief from the pain. She also reported that she had developed boils along her leg. The individual reported to Pascal that she also suffered from Diabetes and taking medication for the condition. Pascal told her to continue with the application due to the fact that the clay had found a successful outlet for this condition as well. A few weeks of continued clay therapy, and the individual's blood sugar was normal. She no longer needed any medication for diabetes.

Even Anjou's father used the clay cure to triumph over diabetes. Anjou reports that the earth they used was called *multani mittii* (a yellow clay). Her father would apply clay poultices to his arm day and night. It took three months, but his very serious case of diabetes (blood sugar was at 500 at one point) was test-confirmed cured at a later time when he was hospitalized in the emergency room.

One of the most amazing clay therapy stories ever recorded has to do with a great tragedy involving Anjou's father. Their story is so profound, touching and heart-wrenching, that the author of this book will not recount it. For the full story, individuals should get a copy of *Clay Cures*, and read the story as told by Anjou.

Anjou demonstrated the profound potential for clay use to bring individuals out of a trauma-induced coma. Anjou's father was admitted to the emergency room with a critical head trauma. An attending neurosurgeon stated that it would take a miracle for Anjou's father to survive 24 hours. Clay provided that miracle. Anjou applied clay directly to the forehead, changing it out often for one night.

The next day, his face looked much improved. She continued with clay therapy for a month while her father remained in a coma. Her father emerged from the coma one month after being admitted into the hospital.

Anjou's father began a miraculous recovery; one that was interrupted due to a cessation of clay applications. While her father eventually passed away at home, Ajoun now certainly had no doubt about the truly amazing abilities of clay to heal, and the ultimate mortality and fragility of life itself.

When Anjou needed a c-section during child birth, she then had eight years of clay therapy experience. She demonstrated that clay therapy, properly administered, was a choice therapy to protect and help to heal a surgical wound without infection. Her wound healed without complication, just as she knew it would.

The Accounting of Pascal Chazot

Pascal Chazot brings a very unique and valuable mélange of skills and talents to the world of clay therapy. Pascal, even from his youth, had a natural inclination for the spiritual side of life. By the time he was fifteen, he was a conscientious vegetarian. He moved from his native home in Louvroil, France, to Nepal when he was twenty years old. His experience in the Himalayas brought him into contact and communication with a spiritual yogi there; a man he called Dharma Guruju.

During this period Pascal had been studying and experimenting with a wide variety of natural medicine philosophies, including Ayurvedic medicine, and the herbal plants that the Himalayan area. He had previously learned Sanskrit at a university in Paris, and studied the Charakasamhita, an ancient Indian text on Ayurvedic medicine.

At that time, Pascal reports that he had some knowledge of clay; he used it for minor cuts, bruises and burns. He almost turned away from using clay due to one experience. He had used clay to treat a mosquito bite by applying clay and a dressing to the bite. He left the dressing on for four days, and as a result, the bite left a small scar-like mark on his skin, which remained visible for several months.

Pascal reported that in 1979, he contracted an infection that began at the corner of one nostril, and started to spread upwards. Eventually, it nearly reached his eye. Pascal elected to use clay to treat the infection. He applied clay to the effected area, and changed the clay out every two hours, after it had begun to dry out. The first application stopped the progression of the infection. By the seventh application of clay, the infection began to reduce. By the eighth application, the infection was back only to the point where it began.

Pascal reports that it was that treatment that catapulted clay to the top of his natural cure list. Clay became his first resource whenever he was faced with any health problem. To this day Pascal reports that clay is the only thing he has ever needed since that day.

Pascal reports a very unique and interesting case regarding the guru he met. Guruju was diagnosed by x-ray as having a problem with his sciatica. The sciatic nerve was severely pinched due to the erosion of a disc. Guruju had nearly collapsed with extreme pain in one leg, and had been losing weight due to his subsequent immobility.

Pascal, very aware that he was only a lay person medically, intervened in Guruju's treatment. He had Guruju use a red clay which was mined locally. Within two days after beginning clay therapy, his foot on the infected leg began to show signs of improvement.

After three of four days, Guruju reported that the pain seemed to be increasing. They finally determined that during the clay application, the pain would recede, and then increase afterward. They continued with the therapy. Within ten days, the pain was greatly diminished, and within five weeks he was completely cured. Guruji lived to the age of 98 without any further problem with the leg.

Pascal describes his experience with healing clay in the treatment of a typhoid fever case; his own daughter Lissa. A mosquito bite on her knee had become infected. She spiked a fever. She used clay locally, at the location of the bite. Subsequent blood tests revealed that she had typhoid fever.

Pascal had her continue with local clay treatments and lukewarm hipbaths. As the treatment progressed, the infected knee began to ooze out of the sore. The mouth of the wound opened, becoming deeper and wider. The day after this exteriorization her fever broke. Four days after this, she was back to normal. The inflammation of the knee took another week to heal.

Pascal states: "As a matter of fact, her typhoid was cured because of the clay applications for her knee, which became aggravated in the early stages in order to, ironically, allow rapid healing of a major disease."

In 1988, Pascal reports suffering from a case of the flu during his stay in Algeria. A flu epidemic was sweeping across the region. Most individuals who contracted the strain suffered a minimum of two weeks of fever. The flu strain resisted modern medical treatment as well as traditional medicine.

When Pascal started showing symptoms, he been applying clay non-stop, changing the clay out every two to three hours. Within thirty-six hours, he was symptom free. After one more day, his normal strength had returned.

Finally, Pascal reported that he was able to cure his newly-onset Bell's palsy in fifteen days with continuous clay therapy.

Pascal's Clays

Pascal used clays that were available locally. In India, he often used a yellow clay known as multani mitti, a variety of Bole Armeniac. This clay is also known as gule-armani in Gujarati and gernumitti in Hindu. It is an aluminum silicate.

Pascal indicated that this clay is found in the western part of India. The local people of of Multan, currently in Pakistan, have been aware of its curative powers. It is largely used for cosmetic purposes.

Interestingly, Pascal noted that one needs to be careful of the quality of the batch of clay purchased. Impurities, he noted, could adversely affect the clay's performance.

Unlike the many healing-grade clays in North America, multani mitti takes about twenty days to properly hydrate.

Pascal also noted that he sometimes used French green clay he brought from France.

He also referenced a clay called Gopichandan, which is named after a lake near Dwarka in Gujarat called Gopi, where the clay is sourced from. Pascal noted that he had difficulty in sourcing this clay due to problems with impurities in the clay they would purchase. Pascal finally found a high quality source of this clay from a villager in the city of Ambaji in Gujarat.

Geru is another clay that Pascal referenced. He described this clay as a white aluminum silicate found in Sri Lanka and China. The clay is obtained by purifying white fulspar. Pascal noted that this clay has been used in the preparation of Ayurvedic medicines. This clay is also known as a 'red clay' or red ochre. It has also been known by the name of China clay, which is a kaolinite.

Interestingly, Pascal noted that he experimented with black clay sourced in some villages in Gujarat. However, the clay did not perform satisfactorily, and he stopped using it.

Pascal's Clay Therapy

While Pascal uses clay in a similar manner in most cases as we do in North America, Pascal does have a few very unique methodologies for using clay. It is only those unique uses and treatments that will be focused on in this chapter. Pascal has an excellent usage guide in the back of his book, and readers are certainly encouraged to review his work. We will include and credit some of the more simple treatments he suggests in our own comprehensive manual on using healing clays.

Part of what makes Pascal & Anjou's work so unique in contrast to its use in North America is two-fold.

First, the wide range of conditions they have had the opportunity to treat is unprecedented in the western world. Due to both socio-economic conditions and climate differences, Pascal and Anjou have had the opportunity to put clay to the test on a level that we simply don't have in North America. Their work with infections such as malaria and typhoid fever has contributed an incredible amount of value to the modern world of healing clays, and granted us a deeper insight into the potential of clay therapy.

Second, it is apparent that in some parts of the world it is very difficult to source reliable clays. It is obvious that Pascal and Anjou have greatly contributed to making safe clay sources available. Here in the United States, we have an abundance of uncontaminated healing grade clays that can be used straight from the Earth.

Pascal's clay usage instructions are quite simple. The external dosage is simply a handful of hydrated clay (wet clay paste) applied to a clean cloth and then secured to the treatment area. Pascal rightly observed that a thin layer of clay on the skin might be good for the skin, but cannot heal. He noted that clay must be in contact with the skin. He rightly advises that ideally the clay should be removed while it is still moist, but not so wet that it sticks to the skin.

What might seem amazing to some, as an individual acclimates to clay therapy, eventually the body will start to tell an individual exactly when it is time for clay to be removed. It is in this manner that clay therapy actually induces body consciousness.

Pascal reiterated what Raymond Dextreit and Eytons' Earth have both long explained about the exact nature of clay therapy, that it acts a catalyst in the body. Its use starts a chain reaction that activates and harnesses the body's own natural healing power:

"Clay galvanizes the body into action by tapping its internal resources of energy and healing powers. Once you start to use it, be sure to continue till you are cured. Never start using clay if you are not sure of continuing. First-time users feel that as the substance has no side effects (apart from curing other illnesses), it can be employed intermittently. This is a complete misconception. Gentle as this medicine is, it is also very potent and powerful. Therefore, do not play around by just trying it now and again, or in combination with other chemical-based allopathic drugs. Start when you are thoroughly convinced and sure to persist with the treatment."

The Treatment for Asthma

Sufferers of asthma are to drink a spoonful of clay water once daily for ten days. An individual is then required to stop drinking clay for another ten days. The individual should then resume drinking clay water. This is continued for a total of one month. During this month, the individual is to apply clay cataplasm (poultices) applications to the upper arm, once daily and once nightly. The upper arm treatment should be continued until the individual is feeling better.

The Treatment for Cancer

Apply clay cataplasms to the upper arm, twice daily for a few days. If the body reacts to the clay in the form of boils, rashes or pimples, the clay therapy is having an effect. Continue applying clay to the same spot. If there is not reaction whatsoever, apply the clay to the area above where the cancer is located. Clay must be continually applied no matter how long the therapy takes. Pascal cautions that allopathic medicines and even some alternative therapies may prevent the clay from working. Clay therapy may be combined with healthy dietary changes, however, which is to include fresh vegetable juices and frugal eating habits. He notes that it is wise to starve the cancerous cells that feed on a rich diet.

The Treatment for a Coma

Pascal teaches that applications of clay are to be applied to the forehead, and changed out every two hours.

The Treatment for a Common Cold

Apply clay cataplasms to the forehead or the neck. Pascal stated that quick results can be achieved by using clay poultices on the nose. Due to the fact that application can be difficult, clay can be applied on one side of the nose over one nostril at a time.

The Treatment for Diabetes

Clay poultices are to be applied on the upper arm at night, and when possible, during the day. Continue this treatment for a month. After a month, the nighttime treatment location may be switched. Place the clay poultice over the pancreas to stimulate the organ. During the day, the treatment of the upper arm should be continued.

The Treatment for Poor Eyesight

Clay is to be applied on the back on the neck (the nape). This treatment acts on the optic nerves. Ideally, clay poultices should be applied three times each day: Once during the day, once in the evening, and again for the night. Pascal also noted that eye exercises assist the healing process.

Author's Note

The upper arm clay cataplasm treatment is one of the most fascinating treatments that I've learned from Pascal. This treatment modality has opened up a world of research possibilities, and could possibly be instrumental in unraveling some of clay's most elusive secrets.

Anjou and Pascal's book may be purchased directly by contacting the Sarvodaya International Trust, Gujarat Chapter. It may also be purchased at Amazon.com. We keep a direct purchase link at the Eytons' Earth website (*www.eytonsearth.org/clay-books.html*).

Raymond Dextreit: Naturopathic Earth Cures
Author's Note

The work of French Naturopath Raymond Dextreit, as presented in the landmark book *"Our Earth Our Cure"* (republished under the new title *"Earth Cures"*), is among the most significant natural medicine handbooks of modern times. Raymond presents a truly holistic lifestyle approach to curing illness and restoring good health. After decades of working with ill people in France, he developed a system of natural healing that was exactly opposite of the pill popping culture that began to emerge in the United States during the late 1980's and early 1990's... and by pill popping, I mean none other than *vitamin popping and powder mixing* culture that is still predominant today in many so-called health food stores.

Long before the raw food and paleolithic diet "reformists" of this new 21st century, Raymond Dextreit was teaching people about the vibrant, living force contained in foods and herbs. Raymond Dextreit knew that practicing herbology required working with processes, and that one could not get the same effect from simply taking leaves or roots, grinding them, and sticking them into very convenient and profitable (but far less effective) capsules. No, Raymond taught true herbology, and believed that the best medicine was living food. And that is exactly how Dextreit viewed clay: As a vibrant living food source.

While clay held a very prominent place within his healing system, Raymond taught that true vibrant health had to be approached holistically. My own experience and research with clay therapy began where Raymond Dextreit left off. His book became my clay bible, and without it, I would never have discovered the many uses of clay as we now use it in natural medicine.

Most of what has been published in the English language regarding clay therapy was a direct result of the French-to-English rendition of *"Earth Cures"* composed and translated into English by Michel Abehsera in 1974. Without this work, it is possible that clay therapy would never have begun its reemergence into a prominent place in the world of natural and holistic medicine.

I was very careful to work with the ideas that Raymond Dextreit presented until I actually understood them. While I do not believe that his macrobiotic vegetarian diet is for everyone, I learned to understand the value of how foods could be used to heal. I began to learn that connecting *with* the process of healing was just as important as any healing agent used.

It is the meticulous and even ruthless examination of Dextreit's ideology that I owe my own work with clay to. For example, when Dextreit wrote the words "...*very few know that the earth itself, receiving its vital energies from the sun, air, and waters, is a most powerful healing agent of physical regeneration...*" I listened very carefully. I therefore began an intense study of how energy, gasses and water work with clay. And when Abhesera used the word regeneration, I came to believe he meant to use that word in its literal sense. "Water, Earth and Sunshine" **composed as three** quickly became my primary focus in research.

In this section, I'm going to focus on giving a concise guide on how Raymond Dextreit used clay therapy in his practice as a naturopath. However, in Volume 2, Book 4, I will always include Raymond's complete protocol for everything discussed... in the event that you, the reader, would like to delve into the world of healing foods and herbology.

Earth Cures often goes out of print. When it does, I've seen used copies of the book sell for as high as $225.00 USD. I always recommend that interested individuals pick up a copy or two while they are available.

Raymond Dextreit, Earth Therapist

Raymond Dextreit came to understand that the earth itself had three different forms of life-giving, health-promoting substances: Clay, mud and sand. However, he spent far more time writing about the benefits of therapeutic healing clays than sand or mud.

In addition to utilizing the gifts of the earth, he taught that there were seven natural healing "foods" that stood far above the rest: Lemon, garlic, olive oil, sea salt, carrots, cabbage and thyme. He would often use a combination of healing foods, herbal concoctions and decoctions along with clay, to achieve what Dextreit always referred to as *a cure*.

However, no matter the remedy, clay use was always included as a part of the cure. To Raymond Dextreit, clay was both the capstone and a cornerstone for optimum health.

For internal use, Dextreit often married clay with lemon. This marriage would turn out to be nothing short of a stroke of genius.

> "Clay (together with lemon, which will be discussed later) acts on capillaries, liberating them, dissolving crystals and 'flakes'. Its natural tendency is to adsorb toxins..."

Dextreit knew and taught that microbian flora disappear when hydrated clay is present. He taught that pathogenic germs (parasitic) cannot proliferate in the presence of a clayish medium. He observed that on occasion, actual worms would be eliminated in the feces, and stated that the clay had drawn them out of organs where they had been previously lodged.

Dextreit knew that the clay action inside the body was quite complex. He believed that clay action, in the case of organic disorders, actually destroyed and eliminated unhealthy cells, and stimulated the growth of healthy replacements. He also believed that clay used internally could, and would, eliminate all noxious substances from the body.

Here it is important to note that Dextreit's medicine was a natural and thus patient medicine. He tracked case histories for years. While he always (and quite rightly) referred to his remedies as absolute cures, sometimes those cures took months, even years to render good results. Often times there are dramatic results immediately, but in other cases, it takes an extensive amount of time for the body to heal. Due to the toxic nature of our modern environments, it is even more critical to practice healthy dietary habits and learn to apply clay therapy over the long term, as a part of a lifestyle modification.

> "Everything unhealthy and emitting negative radiations is irresistibly attracted to clay (a brilliant positive pole) and becomes subject to immediate elimination."

Although Dextreit always taught how to use clay to address specific ailments, he was adamant about clay's effect on the entire organism. He knew that clay action resulted in a cleansed and enriched blood. In fact, he noted that using clay internally would result in a significant increase in red blood cell count within a few short months of use.

> "Wherever there is a deficiency, clay seems to supply the needed substance regardless of whether or not the clay itself is rich in that substance."

These are bold words, and yet Dextreit was speaking very pointedly and with great wisdom. He points out that there are cases where the body is not capable of digesting and/or using a particular substance. Therefore, supplementing with the deficient substance will have absolutely no effect, and leave individuals (and the entire medical community at large) very confused. Clay "digs deeper". Its action is corrective. It stimulates the ailing organ and helps to restore normal functions.

> "From a thermodynamic point of view we must admit that clay cannot be the sole source of energy of the phenomena it produces. Clay is effective through a dynamic presence far more significant than a mere consideration of the substances it contains. It is a catalyst rather than an agent in itself. This is possible because clay is alive – 'living earth'."

And thus Raymond Dextreit understood the clay itself mimicked all of the properties by which we define life… and years before Professor Cairns-Smith theorized that all life may have evolved in a clayish medium, and all organisms, even the very design of the single cell itself, was dependent upon clay itself.

Furthermore, Dextreit was aware that clay contained an energy that appeared to have health promoting effects:

> "Clay is radioactive to a degree (as is everything), but this radioactivity is generally imperceptible to the testing apparatus at present used in laboratories…"

Dextreit noted that this radioactive quality of clays (and other natural radiation) had scientists baffled and quite at odds with each other. With clay, the complexity of how natural radiation works with the human body gets even muddier… he knew that clay, when placed upon the body, would stimulate a deficiency or reduce toxicity (an excess of any substance, including radiation). How could the same substance act in a completely opposite manner, depending on the need? Dextreit asked many deeply insightful questions such as this, while providing very few answers. I coined the term homeostatic clay in order to highlight this characteristic that therapeutic clays possess: The clay works to restore a natural state of balance via many different mechanisms.

Dextreit discovered that in case of excess radiation exposure, clay would first enhance the radioactivity and then absorb it. He was adamant with a belief that clay was the best substance to use in cases of overexposure to atomic radiation.

Dextreit was very versed in clay's confounding ability to absorb and adsorb substances. In one experiment, he demonstrated that an egg packed in clay would lose three times more weight than an egg left out in the open. Clay literally pulls substances out of the egg itself without affecting the shell at all. He demonstrated this neat little experience to quell the skepticism associated with transdermal clay therapy, where clay placed upon the body can have a profound effect deep within the body.

> "These absorbent properties, certainly due to the micro-molecular structure of clay, explain its action – but only partially. We cannot always penetrate Nature's secrets, we must merely acknowledge and use them.
>
> There are substances which do not destroy themselves in action; they are the diastases and enzymes; clay is particularly rich in these. Some of these diastases, the 'oxidase', have the power of

fixing free oxygen, which explains the purifying and enriching action of clay in the blood."

Dextreit again grants us great insight into the properties of clay. Dextreit taught that clay action was primarily catalytic: Changes occur in the presence of clay, without clay changing at all. Following his wisdom and guidance, I learned that it is very wise to watch what changes do occur when using clay. Clay, by virtue of how the body responds to its use, can reveal many things that can be used to help the body regain an optimum level of health.

> "The knowledge of these properties would be insufficient to explain clay's active power if we did not know that clay is a powerful agent of stimulation, transformation and transmission of energy. As every filing which comes from a magnet keeps its properties, every piece of clay retains a considerable amount of energy from that large and powerful magnetic entity which is our planet earth… We have extraordinary energy resources which normally remain dormant—clay awakens them."

I do not believe that Dextreit was overly familiar with crystal sciences. Even so, he knew that clay had the transducing properties of fine crystals. Clay transduces light to sound and sound to light, and does this—quite bafflingly— for the benefit of the organism. Whether by sympathetic resonance, whether by the activation of high spin elements, or by some other unknown mechanism, clay has an anti-entropy effect with living organisms.

In his book, Dextreit gives a brief but concise history of clay use by modern man, all of which will be included as a natural part of Volume II. However, one thing stands out that should be mentioned here.

Dextreit commented that scientists had long been trying to duplicate the therapeutic properties of natural mineral water (which is far simpler than clay). Experiment after experiment has failed, even though the scientists involved became very certain that they had duplicated the chemical makeup of the water being contrasted.

> "Observation of nature convinces one that duplication of its properties, through chemical or physical means is impossible. Chemistry and physics cannot rebuild life… "

> "…Clay is a living cure."

Finally, Dextreit knew that an individual would need to find clay that had a sympathetic relationship with the individual. One type of clay might work well for one person, but not for another. While any therapeutic clay would have some effect, he recommended that individuals try a variety of clays to find those that acted in synergy with the individual.

Dextreit believed that clay should be subjected to sun, air and rainwater before use. The more proper weathering (non-toxic) a clay undergoes, the more active a clay will become. Today, rain water is likely to contain at least some undesirable contaminants in most major metropolitan areas. Natural waters can be used, and clays can generally be safely sun-dried or sun-activated as long as the environment is not overly polluted with gasses in the air. Dextreit hypothesized that clay particles act as condensers capable of freeing withheld energy at the appeal of an opposite pole. He thought that perhaps this could explain how clay can fix oxygen in water. He advised people to expose clay to the sun just prior to use.

Raymond Dextreit on Using Clay Internally

Dextreit made many interesting observations about clay used internally. I use clay a bit differently than he recommends, primarily due to the effects from an increasingly toxic world. However, Dextreit's wisdom should certainly always be considered when learning how to best use clay internally.

Dextreit believed that clay modified itself depending on how it was prepared. He noticed differences between adding dry clay to water, or adding water to dry clay. He also believed that clay modified itself according to the method used. Every method of use has a very different physiological affect. This fact cannot be stressed enough. The effect will be different when bathing in clay compared to using a clay poultice; the effect will be different when taking clay internally compared to applying a clay poultice.

Dextreit taught that when clay is taken internally in the early morning before breakfast, it has a tendency to obstruct the bowels, but has a completely different effect if taken at night before bed. Conversely, Dextreit taught that if an individual needed to combat stomach pains experienced after eating, then clay must be taken prior to the meal.

Dextreit taught that clay should be used internally, daily, for the first three weeks. After the first three weeks, he recommended that the individual break for one week. After the first break, individuals should continue taking clay internally, one week on, and one week off. The standard adult dose should be one teaspoonful of clay added to one-half glass of water. For best results, he taught that the clay should be prepared the night before use.

> "Clay does remarkable work in restoring deficient organs and organic functions. It does not accomplish this by supplying the missing elements, but by aiding the organism to be able to fix and assimilate those elements where previously it was failing. These catalytic substances need only be present in infinitesimal doses. Therefore, it is un-necessary to absorb large quantities of clay."

This helps to explain why, for example, a normal calcium supplement has little to no impact on conditions such as osteoporosis, while a quality clay supplement can, over time, have a drastic impact. It also helps to explain that clay supplementation, on one hand, has been seen to increase muscle mass, hair and nail growth, while on the other hand, has been observed to reduce unhealthy and unnatural weight gain.

Dextreit also knew that there were individuals who would need to start taking clay internally very slowly to allow the individual to acclimate to clay use. For people who could not tolerate clay use very well, he suggested that they start off by adding smaller amounts of clay to a glass of water, and only drinking the clayish water. Such an individual will acclimate to clay use slowly, and eventually be able to well tolerate standard doses.

For those with problems taking clay, Dextreit also advised that small clay balls could be made. He advised people to suck on the balls and let the clay slowly dissolve in-mouth. Clay could be combined with an aromatic infusion for children (such as mint or eucalyptus) or the balls can be prepared with a concoction of senna or rhubarb (for adults with constipation issues).

There are a few high quality clays, Dextreit notes, that naturally contain a petroleum-like taste. He notes that this does not alter the clay properties, but enhances the clay. Dextreit believed that the petroleum taste was due to clay contact with natural naphtha.

Dextreit cautioned individuals who regularly had high blood pressure to limit clay use during periods where the blood pressure was high. He taught that individuals with constipation should take small doses of clay throughout the day, in between meals, and drink plenty of water. He advised against using mineral oil internally while using clay, although only as a precaution as there has never been a case of oil mixing with clay and hardening while still in-body.

Dextreit even recommended that babies take a teaspoonful of clayish water before three feedings every day.

Raymond Dextreit on Using Clay Externally

Raymond Dextreit always believed that people should have a large amount of pre-prepared clay on hand. He advised that clay could possibly be stored in plastic in powder or raw form, but he highly recommend that hydrated clay be stored in wood, ceramic or glass.

Dextreit recommended a very specific method for clay hydration. He believed that individuals should not mix clay at all, but rather, add boiled water to clay powder spread evenly at the bottom of a basin or tub. He advised people to pour the water over the clay until the water was about one-half inch above the clay. Then he advised people to just let it sit without touching it while the clay went through its process of hydration. This is extremely wise advice.

Some companies and clay users recommend that individuals take clay and water, place them in a blender, and mix. Others recommend that clay and water be endlessly stirred until a smooth consistency is reached. While hand mixing clay in an emergency may be ok, it is still advisable to use the patient hydration method for best results whenever possible. In volume two, I will demonstrate a similar method, whereby large amounts of hydrated clay can be made effortlessly.

> "...When it is stirred up, it becomes sticky and difficult to handle. It loses its porosity becoming smooth and, in consequence, impermeable. Its possibilities of absorption are very much reduced... handle it as little as possible."

> "...The prepared clay has to be a smooth, very homogenous paste and not very concentrated – just enough to avoid falling apart. Whenever possible, place the container in the sun, covering it with a gauze to avoid impurities."

Dextreit had a very deep insight into clay therapy that is the result of an astute observational ability and extensive personal experience with clay. He taught that clay should be used cold, tepid, or hot, depending upon the situation at hand. If an individual was feverish or if clay was to be used over an over-active or naturally warm organ, then he recommended that cold clay always be used. If the clay did not warm up after application, then the cold poultice was to be discontinued. If the clay poultice became too warm or hot, then the clay needed to be removed right away and a new cold clay poultice was to be used in place (this may occur after five to ten minutes of the clay having been applied to the body).

For deficiencies in the body or organs, Dextreit recommended clay be used either tepid or warmed. Treatment over the liver, gallbladder, kidneys, etc., should be done with warmed clay.

> "The guiding principle is that 'every action is immediately followed by a reaction'. Thus, if we use the poultice on a feverish, angry or congested part, we have to refreshen it; but, if used with the goal of strengthening or revitalizing, we have to warm it. Applied on a weak or feeble organism or organ, it is possible to make cold applications of cold water, air, or mud, but the overheating, which is the goal of this application, must follow rapidly.
>
> "For fever or congestion, where the cold treatment may be compared with the system of water circulation for cooling car engines, overheating is dangerous and must be avoided."

Dextreit was quick to point out that there were always exceptions to the rules. There are times when the body needs to be warmed slowly, and times where clay may need to be removed before the treatment has been completed or even left on longer than usual.

He stated that in some cases, clay therapy would at first weaken a patient. Dextreit advises that in such a case, use smaller poultices, placing them in different positions on the body. He then recommended to gradually increase the size of the poultice and the duration of each treatment.

Dextreit also knew that clay did not necessarily need to be applied directly to the affected area; clay acts upon the entire organism. He noted that while clay can be applied directly on the effect gum and tooth of an abscess, that he believed it was actually more effective to place a large poultice on the cheek.

To heat clay without interfering in the clay's properties, Dextreit taught that a double-boiler method worked best. He advised to never allow clay to come into direct contact with a heat source. To use the double-boiler method, simply fill a pot with some water (half the height of the next container containing the actual clay). Then, place the container that houses the clay in the first container, and add a low flame. Dextreit notes that in some cases, radiant warmth can be used to heat clay as well. Finally, Dextreit advised individuals to heat only enough clay for the current poultice, because it is far easier than heating a lot of clay!

Dextreit also used clay compresses. He taught that in order to prepare a compress, one should simply add some water to a clay magma until it is runny. Then, a clean, thin dressing should be soaked in the clay water, and then the compress applied to the area where it is needed.

When teaching people how to use poultices, Dextreit was very clear that using clay as an ointment would yield very poor results. He insisted clay poultices needed be at least ¼" thick, and often times as much as 1 inch thick. A four inch by eight inch poultice, as an example, is what Dextreit would use to treat a single boil.

He cautioned people about mixing clay with other substances. For example, he rightly noted that if an individual mixed wheat bran or flaxen flour in gauze, that it would severely dampen the clay action.

Dextreit noted that if necessary, a piece of gauze could be placed between the skin and the clay. However, he made it clear that the best method for clay application is directly on the skin, even in cases of wounds or serious ulcerations. In addition, clay applied directly to the body helps to determine the duration of the treatment.

> "Clay applied in direct contact can do this because, after producing its effects, it falls off as does ripe fruit off the tree."

He noted that on an abscess or boil, the clay would usually naturally detach after about twenty to thirty minutes. Once the clay was detached, its action is finished.

Dextreit would use a standard wound dressing type of application: Covered with a clean white cloth or dressing. He noted that dressings could be modified to suit any individual need. However, he was always quick to point out that it was important to secure the dressing without compressing the clay onto the body. Securing a dressing around the area treated is usually the most efficient method (corner taping the edges, using T-dressings, corner wrapping with an ace-type bandage, etc.)

Dextreit sometimes recommend that a cabbage dressing be used to cover a clay poultice. He noticed that this would slow down the drying of the clay, allowing for longer treatment applications (such as overnight treatments). In particular, he noted that this was effective for conditions such as varicose ulcers.

Dextreit wrote an entire subchapter in his book about rhythms of application, documenting how to know how often to use clay, how long to use it, etc. The basic ideology is that every clay treatment protocol must be adjusted to the temperament and tolerance of each individual being treated.

The artful skill of working with clay in this manner comes with practice and careful observation. It is far to easy to over think things. If the body well tolerates clay, then more frequent treatments can be done. If clay use fatigues the body, then this is a sign it is working well, but usage needs to be adjusted to give the body time to catch up to the clay action. Treating ulcers and the like often requires steady treatment that can persist throughout the day and night. The same can be said with wounds. However, the standard daily "dose" of clay poultice therapy is once daily, applied for an hour (but first start with a 20 minute treatment, and increase time gradually).

Dextreit noted that clay applied to the adnominal area should be done well apart from eating (2 hours), to avoid interfering in the body's digestive process. He also noted that applications to the bladder or ovaries should be applied warm to help avoid a converse reaction.

Many writers tout clay as a miracle substance without side effects. However, Dextreit was far more experienced than they. He noted that sometimes ulcers will enlarge before the dead flesh of the periphery will fall off, and blood and pus can appear. Many, many exteriorizations are possible with clay use, and they are usually a sign that clay action will ultimately provide a cure.

He noted that even violent reactions could occur. In such a case, he advised that it was wise to take action to temper the exteriorizations. If the reaction is too great, Dextreit recommended that clay therapy be suspended until the reactions pass, but that clay therapy should always be resumed.

In cases with serious illness, clay treatment can literally exhaust an individual. Steps must be taken to strengthen the individual, including, if necessary, a temporary pausing of clay application. This is certainly much more critical when clay poultices are used over the body's organs. Dextreit emphasized that Clay application externally would invoke a cleansing reaction in the body, and that any toxic substances being mobilized in the body would begin to move toward the clay application. Clay action can even cause serious pain if the clay is treating something extremely serious in the body, such as deep-seated cancer.

However, Dextreit is also quick to point out that more often than not, clay quickly starts to act to soothe the body and reduce pain.

Dextreit is among those serious clay practitioners who believed that once clay therapy is started, it should not be abandoned. He believed, via extensive observation and decades of experience, that clay used with the body would start a chain reaction which would affect the entire organism. No matter how long it took, individuals should follow through.

The author would like to interject a small note here, stating that Dextreit's words should be headed with all seriousness. I've seen it time and time again where people stop using clay therapy as soon as the first good signs appear. In each case, clay therapy was halted prior to achieving the vital health that it can produce. The outcome was usually an eventual serious relapse.

Dextreit taught that clay should not be applied to more than one area at a time. If more than one area of the body needed direct treatment, then the next area of the body should be done at least an hour after the previous area treatment has been completed.

Dextreit was clear that if clay, having been applied for five to ten minutes, caused a cooling effect in or on the body, that it must be removed immediately. Also, if clay warmed quickly when applied to a heated, over-active, feverish part of the body, then the clay needed to be immediately changed out just before it warmed up, and immediately replaced with cool clay.

Dextreit was clear that the use of clay by an expectant mother was very advantageous to the health of the fetus, when combined with a healthy diet. He stated that poultices could be applied to the stomach if a child was situated poorly, applied to the lumbar to help with discomfort, and to the abdomen after childbirth to help prevent infection.

Finally, Dextreit recommended that clay be discarded after use.

The author will cover many of Dextreit's complete cure protocols in Volume II of this work. However, it will be impossible to reproduce his entire body of work. His natural medicine handbook, currently entitled "Earth Cures", is an excellent addition to any bookshelf.

Other Clay Therapeutic Adepts
Independent Researchers and Clay Practitioners
Line de Courssou & Thierry Brunet

Line de Courssou from France spent one year in a remote village in Africa treating an "incurable" condition known as Buruli ulcerations. This flesh eating bacterial infection had long thwarted any clinical treatment, experimental or otherwise. For decades, researchers from around the world had gone to Africa in an attempt to understand Buruli ulcerations, and find a cure. After more than forty years, the disease thwarted every attempt at a cure.

It wasn't until Line de Courssou brought clay to the remote African village of Zouan-Hounien that the afflicted had any real hope at all. Line quickly discovered that therapeutic clay was capable of eliminating mycobacterium ulcerans, the pathogenic organism responsible for the flesh eating disease.

Line de Courssou discovered that the clay would eliminate the infection, protect the treatment site from further infection, and assist healthy tissue growth. She documented case history after case history of successful treatment. The Buruli Buster Project, compiled and published online by Line's son, Thierry Brunet, currently houses over 2000 images documenting the Buruli ulcerations, treatment, and subsequent recoveries from the disease.

Thierry Brunet eventually became deeply fascinated with clay therapy due to the astounding results achieved in Africa by his mother. Clay seemed to defy logic. Thierry, a highly accomplished engineer, set out to study and start to unravel the mysteries behind clay's most impressive action.

Line de Courssou used two types of clay in her African relief project. She utilized a French illite, which is mica, and a French montmorillonite, a smectite. Thierry began researching all clays known to have therapeutic value, and he flew all over the world to meet with people he thought could help him understand how clay worked. He also began studying the Buruli ulcer condition, and clay's effect on both the diseased and healthy tissue.

Thierry eventually did what no other research team could previously do: He uncovered the exact cause of the Buruli ulceration. Thierry discovered, and then proved, that a water-born insect called Lethocerus was a carrier of mycobacterium ulcerans and that its bite would transmit the organism. While this insect is relatively rare, even in Africa, Thierry also chillingly discovered that the insect could survive in North America.

Thierry went on to develop numerous theories and explanations for clay action. One of his more astounding ideas is an understanding that therapeutic clays act as highly specialized naturally-engineered nanocrystal vacuum cleaners.

In March of 2002, Thierry went on to give an amazing presentation before the World Health Organization in Geneva. While the WHO was impressed with the data and the presentation, no other follow up work was to be funded.

Thierry also went on to use clay baths to cure his own mercury Thermisol poisoning. He documented the results of using clay therapy by taking a Melisa test before taking clay baths and afterward.

Other Therapeutic Adepts

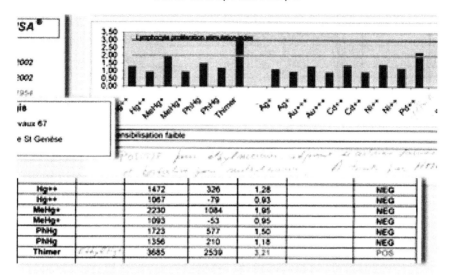

The Melissa Test (before): Elevated levels of Thimer

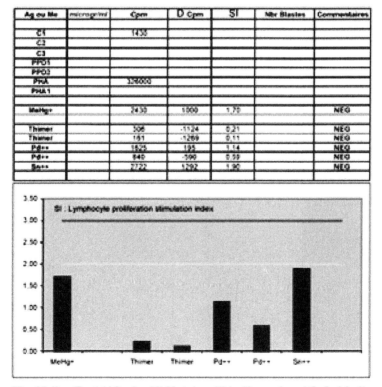

The Melisa Test (After): All Metals within Normal and Safe Limits

Thierry went on to completely reverse all of the neurological symptoms associated with heavy metal toxicity. To this day Thierry remains one the most advanced minds studying clay therapeutics, and an avid clay disciple and clay enthusiast.

Victor Earl Irons & Sodium Bentonite

V.E. Irons developed the first internal-use clay supplement for a commercial market in the United States. For use as a detoxifcant, Irons provided a super hydrated sodium bentonite, and sold it as a part of an internal cleansing and detoxification program.

Irons came to believe that good health began-- and ended-- in the large intestines. He became interested in natural cures and remedies after being told that there was no cure for a degenerative condition he'd been diagnosed with: Ankylosing spondylosis. Rather than accept the medical doctors' grim long term prognosis, he began studying natural medicine.

Specifically, he studied the work of Dr. J. H. Tilden and Dr. John Harvey Kellogg (inventor of the corn flakes brand cereal). Dr. Kellogg taught that no less than 90% of all disease conditions began in the colon, due to its improper function. Dr. Tilden believed in colonics, cleansing diets, and a raw food lifestyle.

Irons eventually started doing cleansing fasts and colonics. Within fourteen months he cured himself of his "untreatable" degenerative condition. His success with his own cure led him to dedicate his life to natural remedies, and he went on to lecture about natural nutrition for twelve years. In 1956, Irons refused to plead guilty to federal charges regarding health claims, and defiantly served six years in a federal prison, where he evidently plotted long and hard against the FDA.

Irons had refused a judge's order to recant statements such as the following: "Nearly everyone in this country is suffering from malnutrition or in danger of such suffering because of demineralization and depletion of soils and the refining and processing of foods."

After serving his time in prison, he continued to dedicate his life to health education, and helped to found the National Health Federation, which he used as a lobbying club to strike back against the FDA. He was instrumental in getting the Proxmire Vitamin Bill unanimously passed through Congress, which prohibited the FDA from banning the use of vitamins and minerals as drugs.

Eventually, V. E. Irons was publicly recognized as a national hero by President Ronald Reagan for his significant contributions to the science of longevity. He is also widely recognized as a pioneer by countless of health professionals.

> "During the course of his life, V.E. Irons perfected a system of self-detoxification based on fasting and colonic cleansing that this writer regards as one of the most important contributions to modern medicine and world health in the 20th century." – Daniel Reid in the dedication to his book "The Tao of Detox"

The V.E. Irons seven day bowl cleansing program remains to this day a vital and valuable program for vibrant health. Thousands upon thousands of people have learned the incredible value of detoxifying and cleansing diets, of which hydrated sodium bentonite plays a dominant role.

> "Bowel problems can cause nutritional deficiency, regardless of how good your diet is or how many vitamins you take." - V.E. Irons.

To this day, V.E. Irons original formulas are used. More information about V.E. Irons programs can be found by visiting the following website: (*http://www.detoxifynow.com/vitratox-greenlife.htm#16*).

The works of the early pioneers of the 20th century are still being practiced by many health professionals today, including Dr. Schulze and Dr. Richard Anderson, who both teach colon cleansing and detoxification programs with the help of high quality sodium bentonite.

G. Michael King and the Sacred Clays of Oregon

G. Michael King, a life enrichment counselor and herbalist, creator of the "Heart Balance Herbal Rejuvenation" line of products, is one of the few health advocates in North America that promotes the use of acidic, sedimentary clays as valuable health-promoting substances.

These clays, which King markets under the brand names of Pyro Clay and Ormalite, are quite different from most of the other clays used around the world. Pyro clay is acidic rather than alkaline; amphorous rather than highly structured. According to independent analysis done on the clay, Pyro clay may actually be a rectorite clay, which is smectite that has been naturally altered due to weathering. In this case, the clay "weathering" was likely caused by prolonged and extreme subterranean geothermal activity. It is rich with sulphur and an abundance (some might say an overabundance) of inorganic minerals. Such clays have not been widely scientifically studied for use for human health. That said, the region of Crater Lake has long been held as sacred land by the Natives of North America, long before modern civilization emerged.

There is likely much more freely available silica in clays such as the Pyro clay, due to the weathering of the original smectite. Such clays are usually more active energetically, although in a far less unified way (independent activity of single crystals rather than generating a collective electromagnetic field).

Michael King takes a more metaphysical, holistic approach to clay use, and teaches the use of clay therapy both for physical rejuvenation and for spiritual well being. He is also a strong advocate for using soil-enriching clays for agriculture and gardening.

Furthermore, although it has not been widely studied, Pyro Clay is very similar to an acidic, sedimentary clay that was studied in a Mexico health clinic. The medical doctors in Mexico used clay to successfully treat a wide variety of severe illnesses often considered untreatable by allopathic medicine. In particular, the clay was used to successfully treat chronic conditions associated with late stage AIDS. The clay was used both externally and internally.

Acidic, amphorous, sedimentary clays may have beneficial properties not shared by other, more traditional, clays. Conversely, the therapeutic action may also be limited by the same properties that cause such clays to stand out. Pyro clay makes a very interesting addition to the world of therapeutic earths.

Individuals with severe and terminal illness may be the ones who could gain the most from using clay such as Pyro clay, both internally and externally. Late stage AIDS patients, individuals with terminal and untreatable cancer are among those who may find help from taking such a clay internally, bathing in it, and applying clay poultices to the affected organs.

Furthermore, individuals interested in ancient alchemy and M-state elements would likely benefit from a thorough exploration into the rather mystical clays of Crater Lake, Oregon.

Siberian Healing Clays

Mined out of Siberia, Russia offers the world two unique healing clays: Rapan Blue and Yellow clays mined from the Siberian Dead Sea. According to research done on the Rapan clays, the biological activity of the Rapan is up to 5 times greater than that of the Dead Sea mud/clays of the Middle East. These sedimentary clays are similar in activity to Pyro clay, even though the clay structure is not the same.

All clays such as the Rapan line of products can greatly complement the use of the evolutionary, alkaline therapeutic clays used for clay therapy. However, neither type of clay should be discarded for the other. Rather, individuals studying pelotherapy should learn how to incorporate both into any natural health regime.

Resources

Purchasing Therapeutic Clay

Purchasing Therapeutic Clay in the United States

www.greenclays.com – Founded by the late Cano Graham and Eytons' Earth founder Jason Eaton, this internet-based wholesale clay company provides the green calcium bentonite/montmorillonite used by Cano and studied by Eytons' Earth. Also available are the newly developed "second generation" *Tecopia Essentia* clay blends which combine some of the finest North American therapeutic clays together in order to harness the unique properties of each clay used.

www.californiaearthminerals.com – California Earth Minerals markets their red desert clay as the ION-MIN clay mineral supplement, including Terramin.

www.pascalite.com – Pascalite clay, the pale calcium bentonite from the Wyoming Big Horn Mountains.

www.redmondclay.com – Redmond Clay from Utah, therapeutic grade sodium bentonite clay provided by the same company that markets award winning Real Salt.

www.pyroclay.com – "Sacred" Pyro clay is a very unique amphorous clay mined in the pristine Crater Lake area in Oregon.

http://www.veirons.com/products_line_detoxificant.html - V. Earl Iron's sodium bentonite detoxificant (referenced in our research documents section)

www.naturalrussia.com – Source for the Russian / Siberian Rapan clay and salt products.

www.herbhealer.com – Dr. Schulz website (listed for his colon cleansing program).

Purchasing Therapeutic Clay in Australia

www.echolife.com.au – Echolife Australia distributes the green calcium bentonite/montmorillonite studied by Cano Graham and Eytons' Earth.

Purchasing Therapeutic Clay in Canada

www.spasensation.ca – Spa Sensation distributes the green calcium bentonite/montmorillonite studied by Cano Graham and Eytons' Earth, as well as clay blends for supplements, wraps and baths.

For Further Research

www.eytonsearth.org – The fascinating world of healing clays online.

www.westonaprice.org – The Weston Price Foundation.

For Further Reading
Sources and Recommendations

1. "*Earth Cures*", by Raymond Dextreit, currently out of print
2. "*The Clay Cure, Natural Healing from the Earth*", by Ran Knishinsky
3. "*Clay Cures*", by Anjou Musafir
4. "*More Precious than Gold*", by Ray
5. "*The Clay Disciples*", by Cano Graham
6. "*Restoring Your Digestive Health*", by Jordan S. Rubin and Dr. Joseph Brasco, M.D.
7. "*The Wellness Project*", by Roy Mankovitz
8. "*The Healing Power of Hydro-thermally Produced Living Clay*", by Neva Jensen
9. "*Nutrition and Physical Degeneration*", by Weston A. Price, DDS

Credits and Acknowledgments

The author would like to offer special thanks to the following people, for invaluable assistance in putting together this two book set: *My favorite clay scientist* – who wishes to remain anonymous… for lending his expertise on clay mineralogy and the science of clays.

Thierry Brunet, Buruli Busters – for helping to set such a high standard for the study of clay therapeutics.

Ray Kong and Jim Brown, California Earth Minerals – for providing me with everything I needed for the chapter on Terramin, including the use of the NASA sponsored study.

Neal and Darryl Boshardt, Redmond Clay – for providing me with the materials used in the chapter on Redmond Clay.

Cano Graham, The Clay Disciples – for showing up at just the right time to reignite my active interest in promoting clay therapy.

The Eytons' Earth Yahoo Group – …and all that I've learned over the years from the fabulous group of clay disciples online.

Stephen Quinto, Natural Immunogenics – for helping me study the effects of oligodynamic silver combined with healing grade clay.

Book II Part B:
Science and Research

Introduction

This section contains some of the most interesting and revealing documents ever to be compiled about the use of clay for health. It includes a few simple articles and some landmark scientific studies that demonstrate beyond a doubt the profound effects clay use can have on health.

The author is deeply indebted to each and every source for permission to use the work in this book. Without their support, book two would not have been possible.

Although the upcoming books three and four (Volume II) will present far more practical information on using clays and the science behind therapeutic clays, it is pertinent to point out some important facts that Book two has presented, in order to dispel some prevalent myths about healing clays. I feel that it is imperative that the general public be made aware of certain undisputable truths.

On Which Clays to Use

First, the quality of any clay cannot be determined by the dominant anion (calcium, sodium, magnesium, etc.). It is a myth that only calcium bentonites have value. Sodium bentonites and calcium bentonites, as well as micas and amphorous clays all have unique properties that can make them invaluable for use.

Particle characterization alone is not a definitive indicator of the quality of any clay. Whether the crystal is highly structured, severely fragmented by weathering, or highly specialized (such as clays like French illite), different clays have unique value *because* of their differences.

Mineral content alone is not an indicator of the quality of any given clay. Some clays known for therapeutic value are incredibly (comparatively) clean, while others are incredibly rich with both inorganic and organic matter (such as Pascalite). Some are rich in minerals but devoid of organic compounds.

The pH of any clay is not a valid indicator of the quality of the clay. There are incredible alkaline therapeutic clays and incredible acidic clays. Some of the best clays for internal use are closer to neutral.

The safety of any clay for human use cannot be determined by a Material Safety Data Sheet. A mineral analysis needs to be examined and compared to actual human use (or animal use) results. Consumers should also be aware that there are falsified mineral analysis reports being used to market clay in the United States. Remember that all natural smectites are aluminosilicates.

All of the available scientific data that can be used to contrast clays is only beginning to provide us with a glimpse into what makes each therapeutic clay such a special gift of nature. Data should not be used to hold one clay above another; such an abuse of science cannot be tolerated if we are to serve the public's highest interests.

In fact, readers should be advised that there are very few individuals in the world that study more than one clay, and therefore, very few individuals in the world that are even remotely qualified to form an opinion about any clay other than the one having been studied by the individual.

However, there are highly committed and individuals of incredible integrity involved in the world of therapeutic clays. These individuals and companies are always given fair recognition at the Eytons' Earth Project Website (*www.eytonsearth.org*).

How, then, should an individual choose what clays to use? Personal experimentation and personal experience are excellent teachers. Based on my own experience, here is what I suggest:

First, those people interested in clay therapy should acquire a high quality, base healing clay in bulk. There may come a time when an individual may need to use four, five, even six lbs of clay for one person's healing treatment. Buying in bulk is more affordable. A base healing clay should work good as an edible clay, for clay baths, poultices, compresses and general skin care.

A family interested in studying clay therapy should always have at least forty to fifty pounds of good, all purpose clay on hand at all times; at least ten pounds prehydrated, stored correctly, and ready to use in the event of an emergency. I use a <u>green desert calcium bentonite</u>, but other knowledgeable individuals have their own favorite base clay that they rely on for clay therapeutics.

Next, it is wise to accentuate your favorite all purpose healing clay with specialty clays. Individuals shouldn't be afraid to experiment, provided that the sources one acquires the clay from is reputable. It is important that clay be used internally on a regular basis. A high quality edible clay, which may be a bit more expensive, is worth its weight in gold.

Additionally, clays like green French illite are excellent to have on hand. A good sodium bentonite for internal use and bath use is excellent, as well. A good acidic, sedimentary clay can be invaluable. There are several high quality North American calcium bentonite deposits to explore as well. Clays from Morocco make a nice addition to a cosmetic clay collection. There are also some very interesting Russian sedimentary clays that have gained recognition for their therapeutic properties.

Regardless of which clays a new disciple finds, nothing beats personal experience. Clays which sit unused cannot do much healing! It is my hope that the documents that follow will act to encourage people to use therapeutic grade clays on a daily basis, as a part of an increasingly healthy lifestyle.

Oligodynamic Silver & Smectite Time Kill Study

Initially Conducted in April of 2002

This study documents the results of a high quality colloidal silver product combined with natural clay (smectite) and tested against staphylococcus aureus. The results of the study indicate that the addition of colloidal silver improves the antibacterial properties of a high quality, natural calcium-based smectite against gram positive bacteria (the direct effect that clay has on gram positive bacteria is negligible compared with its effect against other types of pathogens). Conversely, the effectiveness of the silver was reduced.

The study was commissioned by Jason R. Eaton of Eytons' Earth (*www.eytonsearth.org*) and completed by Stephen Quinto, founder of Natural Immunogenics Corporation.

Hydrated Clay

Partially Hydrated Raw Clay

The antibacterial efficacy of Bentonite -- combined with Sovereign Silver (solution A), and without Sovereign Silver (solution B) -- was evaluated in this experiment. In a series of dilutions such as are used by this lab in comparing other antibacterial 'products', esp.

colloidal silvers, both were challenged equally by known pathogens. The clay material used was a pre-prepared mixture [received from Jason R. Eaton]. This smectite clay (0.1g) was combined with 1 mL of SS to create solution A; similarly (0.1g) the clay was combined with 1 mL of nanopure water to create solution B.

Typical YT media was poured into sterile polystyrene plates and allowed to dry overnight. A 3mm scrape of both wild type Staphylococcus aureus (S1) and MRSA Staph (S2) were placed separately into 1250 l of nanopure water to achieve an optical density (O.D.590) of 0.135. From these cultures two standard 10:1 dilution series were performed.

Both dilution series were then inoculated, one with solution A, and the other with solution B, and exposed to them for a period of 3 minutes on the one hand and 7 minutes on the other. In the first experiment 10µl of solution A were added to the culture (S1 and S2 dilutions) for 3 minutes; similarly, this was repeated with solution B. In the second experiment 10µl of each solution was added to the respective Staph dilutions and exposed to them for 7 minutes.

After the elapsed time, a 10µl spot of cells and solution was placed onto the YT media. A positive control plate of only S1 and S2 was made, as was a negative to ensure no contamination (picture not included-no contamination). The plates were placed in a 37 C incubator overnight and the results can be seen below.

Results:

As can be seen from the relative performance of the two formulations, solution A outperformed solution B in both trials, at 3 and 7 minutes. Nonetheless, while solution B (clay alone) showed some antibacterial activity, it was significantly inferior to that of the combined product (solution B). It should be noted, too, that the antibacterial efficacy of solution A is somewhat less than we have come to expect from SS alone (as in similar assays) leading one to hypothesize that some other property is thereby gained in the compromise, surely having to do with the value added by the clay.

Results of Inhibition by Sol A (Sovereign Silver and Clay) & Sol B (Clay) @ 3 Mins.

	S1 (Wild Staph)	S2 (MRSA Staph)
Positive		
Solution A		
Solution B		

Results of Inhibition by Sol A (Sovereign Silver and Clay) & Sol B (Clay) @ 7 Mins.

	S1 (Wild Staph)	S2 (MRSA Staph)
Positive		
Solution A		
Solution B		

Similar laboratory studies were conducted with bentonite by Dr. Howard E. Lind, M.S., BS, Ph.D. of Lind Laboratories, Brookline, Mass., with a slightly different slant. Dr. Lind was interested in studying the effects of bentonite used internally as a stomach and large intestine detoxifying agent. The dilution used was 150 ml of bentonite to 1 ml bacterial solution. The bacterial studies were conducted on Serratia Marcescene, E Coli, and Staphylococcus Aureus. The time periods where measurements were taken were every 30 minutes for 90 minutes.

In his studies, Staph responded the slowest, with only an average of a 33% reduction in bacterial counts through the trial period. The other bacteria studied responded significantly better, with the minimum reduction percentage being 85%. Dr. Lind continued on to show a 100% reduction of Proteus Mirabilis.

To further his experiments, Dr. Lind studied a mixture of P. Mirabilis, E. Coli, and S. Aureus, and demonstrated conclusively bentonite's property of selective sorption. The bentonite virtually eliminated all bacteria except the Staph.

Why in various experiments does bentonite respond slowly to Staph? The simple answer is that staph is a gram positive bacterium, and clay colloids have a negatively charged surface area. However, it should be clearly noted that a 33% reduction in population counts, if this were to occur in the body, is still clinically significant.

The great infection fighting properties of natural clays have little to do with the antibacterial effect of bentonite. This is something that key researchers have neglected to realize. Most experimentation has been centered around studying clay applications as an intestinal detoxifying agent.

In the body, the clay particles, unless they collect on intestinal walls, etc., are very limited in possible action compared to an undiluted product as used externally. Externally used, the bentonite as a hydrated magma can actually pull an infection out of the body, as the preparation creates a subtle but strong electromagnetic field, which, in an effect that is not fully understood, also stimulates the body's own natural defenses at the treatment site.

Another key element that can throw off studies conducted with clay is the type of product used. We also submitted a fully processed bentonite (according to our supplier, an FDA grade internal clay, rendered white through over-processing) to Natural Immunogenics along with the samples of natural bentonite. The "high grade" clay turned out to be virtually useless for our study purposes!

The true pioneer of the westernized use of sodium bentonite internally was V. Earl Irons. V.E. Irons, Inc. has always paid very special attention to the balance between the purity of a product and loss of effect through processing. In fact, V.E. Irons set the standards for USP grade bentonite that much of the (wiser) natural supplement community has followed for decades.

All of this said, we were very pleased with the results that compared the clay solution with the clay and colloidal silver mixture.

Clay and colloidal silver share very little beyond that fact that each can exist as a colloid. A high quality clay is excellent against some viri, an extremely wide variety of bacteria, and body inflammations and deficiencies; far more so than colloidal silver.

Colloidal silver always requires direct contact for effectiveness. It attaches to cell walls and has a direct effect on cells, including cellular respiration.

The two are nearly opposite substances. The bentonite particles are formed by a complex crystal structure and carry a negative charge, while the silver ions (dissolved) carry a positive charge. Any colloidal silver aggregates (particulate silver) have a simple structure (chemically) and the particles maintain a slight zeta potential.

What we needed to understand is what, if anything, happens with the charged silver particles and the silver ions upon being combined with clay. A properly hydrated clay is comprised of negatively charged particles with a self-sustaining electromagnetic field; in fact, there may be numerous charge layers formed. We had little doubt that the negatively charged particles would coexist in such a solution with little consequence. But what about the silver ions? Would the charge of the Ag+ be great enough to effect a chemical reaction? Or would the silver ions be held via sorption on the wide particle surface area of the bentonite, ready to be exchanged with the body when conditions provided? How extensive would agglomeration be?

Through our "real world" experiments it was easy to see that the sorptive properties of the clay were not affected. In fact, although we have no explanation for observations, the silver in the clay apparently allowed the bentonite to overcome the rejection of some boils and certainly lesions that we had noticed for years through the use of bentonite alone. The effect on efficacy, with our limited experience, was pointed and dramatic as compared to either colloidal silver or clay used alone (after all, the silver must penetrate the skin and actually reach the underlying infection in order to be effective).

Our experience told us what these new lab results confirmed: The colloidal silver is not significantly degraded by addition to a quality bentonite. While it is true that Sovereign Silver is about 10-15% MORE effective against staph on direct contact than when combined with the clay preparation, the other properties of bentonite, and their possible combined action when used on the body, more than makes up for this minimal loss of efficacy, especially in circumstances where the silver is, for whatever reason, not directly reaching the infection.

It will be nearly impossible for us to scientifically prove that clay has the potential to exchange substances with the body. But this effect is one reason why one should pay careful attention to substances used in combination with clays.

The reader may be interested to know that follow-up work was done on this same clay by researchers at Arizona State University. The author, through Thierry Brunet, gave ASU a sample to study, and the direct anti-microbial property of the clay was confirmed by the microbiologists.

Hydrated Bentonite Studies: Dr. Howard E. Lind
Sodium Bentonite, V.E. Irons

Three IN VITRO (in the laboratory) experiments (reviewed below) were conducted by Dr. Howard E. Lind, M.S., BS, Ph.D. Dr. Lind is president of Lind Laboratories, Brookline, Mass. He was born in Providence, R.I., 1913; received his Bachelor of Science from the University of RI, 1934 and was assistant in Bacteriology there 1934 - 1935; Master of Public Health, Mass. Institute of Technology 1937; attended Saint Louis University 1939 - 1940; Senior Bacteriologist at Chicago Branch Laboratory, State Health Dept., Illinois 1940 - 1943; Bacteriologist at Dow Chemical Co., 1945 - 1946; Research Director at Sias Memorial Laboratory of Brooks Hospital, Brookline, Mass., 1946 to date.

EXPERIMENT I

(Reported Feb. 7, 1961)

PURPOSE:

To demonstrate in vitro sorptive (to condense and hold upon its surface) powers of an aqueous solution of bentonite.

PROCEDURE:

One hundred fifty milliliters of the Bentonite preparation were placed in a 250 ml. beaker which contained a plastic coated magnetic agitator. One ml. of a 24 hour broth culture of serratia marcescene was added to the bentonite preparation and the beaker placed on a magnetic agitator. One ml. of a 24 hour broth culture of serratia marcescene was added to the bentonite preparation and the beaker placed on a magnetic stirrer. In order to avoid the heat of the magnetic stirrer the beaker was placed approximately 1/4 inch above the base. After five minutes of stirring, 1 ml. of bentonite suspension was removed for culturing.

A brass-coated mesh cylinder containing alkaline pellets was lowered into the bentonite-bacteria mixture and allowed to remain for thirty minutes. The cylinder with its surrounding jell was removed, washed with water, filled with new pellets and again placed in the bentonite-bacteria solution. This was repeated at 30 minute intervals for 90 minutes. This experiment was repeated several times to show that the phenomenon was genuine and reproducible.

RESULTS

The two trials below indicate the quantitative extremes of bacteria population change.

CHANGES IN BACTERIAL COUNTS OF SERRATIA MARCESCENS IN PRESENCE OF BENTONITE

	Trial 1		Trial 2	
	Bacterial count/ml.	Reduction %*	Bacterial count/ml.	Reduction %
Initial	4,095,000		5,760,000	
30 minutes	3,675,000	10.257 %	4,260,000	26.042 %
60 minutes	2,495,000	32.109 %	2,660,000	37.559 %
90 minutes	620,000	75.150 %	27,500	98.967 %
(% reduction)	(85 %)		(99 + %)	

These two trials representing the extremes of a series of runs show a minimum reduction of 85% and a maximum reduction of 99% of the bacteria in 90 minutes. Results indicate that approximately 25% of the bentonite preparation was able to remove 85% to 99% of the organisms.

SUMMARY:
The research results indicated that by the in vitro method it has been possible to demonstrate that the bentonite preparation Vit-Ra-Tox #16 (et al.) is able to remove bacteria by sorption. It was definitely established

that the bacteria were not inactivated but were removed by sorption.

EXPERIMENT II

(Reported March 10, 1961)

PROBLEM:

To demonstrate in vivo sorption powers of a bentonite preparation against two organisms, Escherichia coli (a gram-negative organism) and Staphylococcus Aureus (a gram-positive organism).

PROCEDURE:

Essentially the same as in Experiment I, reported above, but modified by using a four-hour culture instead of the 24-hour culture of Experiment I. This was to avoid excessive clumping of the organisms.

RESULTS

CHANGES IN BACTERIA COUNTS OF ESCHERICHIA COLI IN THE PRESENCE OF BENTONITE

	Trial 1		Trial 2	
	Bacterial count/ml.	Reduction %*	Bacterial count/ml.	Reduction %*
Initial	1,170,000		10,500,000	
30 minutes	410,000	64.940%	6,100,000	41.905%
60 minutes	0	100.00%	5,200,000	14.755%
90 minutes	0	-	900,000	82.693%
% reduction	(100 %)		(91 %)	

The above two trials show that the E. coli were reduced 100% and 91% respectively after 60 to 90 minutes using only about 20% of the bentonite preparation. This compares favorably with the removal of the serratia marcescents in Experiment I above.

CHANGES IN BACTERIAL COUNTS OF STApHYLOCOCCUS AUREUS IN THE PRESENCE OF BENTONITE

	Trial 1		Trial 2		Trial 3	
	Bacterial count/ml.	Reduction %*	Bacterial count/ml.	Reduction %*	Bacterial count/ml.	Reduction %*
Initial	780,000		230,000		490,000	
30 minutes	740,000	5.129%	160,000	30.435%	290,000	40.816%
60 minutes	810,000	-8.642%	100,000	37.500%	290,000	-0-
90 minutes	620,000	23.547%	140,000	-28.572%	300,000	-3.333%
(% reduction)	(21%)		(39%)		(40%)	

With S. Aureus (a gram-positive organism), in Trials 1, 2, 3, it was shown that the numbers of S. Aureus were reduced 21%, 39%, and 40% respectively, or an average of 33%. Results of these trials indicate that 20-30% of the bentonite was able to remove 33% of the organisms.

SUMMARY:

The research indicated that by the technique employed, it has been possible to confirm the previous conclusion that the bentonite preparation can remove significant numbers of certain gram-negative bacteria, while it appears to be only one-third as effective as to a gram-positive organism, S. Aureus.

EXPERIMENT III

(Reported May 8, 1961)

PURPOSE:

To demonstrate in vitro sorptive powers of a bentonite preparation against A. Proteus mirabilis, a gram-negative organism which can cause diarrhea, and B. its selective sorptive value in a mixture of 3 organisms, namely Proteus mirabilis (gram-negative), Escherichia coli (gram-negative) and Staphylococcus aureus (gram-positive).

PROCEDURE:

Essentially the same as that used in Experiment I and II above, using the 4-hour culture used in Experiment II instead of the 24-hour one of Experiment I, and lowering the concentration of each organism.

RESULTS

A. CHANGES IN BACTERIAL COUNTS OF PROTEUS MIRABILIS IN THE PRESENCE OF BENTONITE

	Trial 1		Trial 2	
	Bacterial count/ml.	Reduction %*	Bacterial count/ml.	Reduction %*
Initial	155,000		240,000	
30 minutes	45,000	70.968%	70,000	70.834%
60 minutes	15,000	66.667%	20,000	71.429%
90 minutes	1,000	93.333%	-0-	-
120 minutes	-0-	-	-0-	-
% reduction	(100%)		(100%)	

In trials #1 and #2, it was shown that the numbers of Proteus mirabilis were reduced 100% after 90 to 120 minutes in the concentration of organisms employed by 15% of the volume of bentonite.

B. CHANGES IN BACTERIAL COUNTS OF A MIXTURE OF P. MIRABILIS, E. COLI, AND S. AUREUS

	Trial 3		Trial 4	
	Bacterial count/ml.	Reduction % *	Bacterial count/ml.	Reduction %*
Proteus mirabilis				
Initial	34,000		90,000	
30 minutes	18,000	47.059%	20,000	77.778%
60 minutes	2,000	88.889%	10,000	50.000%
90 minutes	1,000	50.000%	0	-
Escherichia				

coli				
Initial	18,000		10,000	
30 minutes	14,000	22.223%	10,000	-0-
60 minutes	8,000	42.857%	1,000	90.000%
90 minutes	3,000	62.500%	0	-
Staphylococcus aureus				
Initial	2,000		3,000	
30 minutes	2,000	-0-	2,000	33.334%
60 minutes	3,000	- 33.334%	3,000	- 33.334%
90 minutes	0	-	0	-

In trials #3 and #4 it was indicated that approximately 15% of the bentonite preparation removed from 95-100% of Proteus mirabilis organism, 83-100% of the E. coli organisms and 100% of the S. aureus organism in the concentrations employed. In other words there appeared to be selective sorption when the quantity of organism concentration was much less than the high concentration used in previous tests.

COMMENTS

With lower concentrations of mixed organisms there appears to be selective sorption. However, when the population of mixed organisms is over 100,000 and the concentration of bentonite remains the same as when individual organisms were used, there was apparently little or no selective sorption by the technique employed. Thus it may be that selectivity of mixed organisms above 100,000 will require the use of a much larger quantity of bentonite than that used for sorption of single organisms or for sorption of mixed organisms under 100,000 population.

While the bentonite is working to remove the undesirable bacteria it could also remove an equal number of desirable bacteria, but when one realizes the large difference in the relative population of the bacteria this may not present a problem. In a normal healthy individual the population of desirable bacteria can run from 100,000 to 100,000,000 per cubic centimeter while the undesirable will generally run only 1/10 of one percent to 1% (.001 to .01) of that number. However, when the population of undesirable bacteria gets up to 2% or 3%, the individual may be in real trouble and may perhaps have cramps or serious diarrhea. To illustrate, assume a desirable population of 50,000 organisms with 1% undesirable or 500,000, assuming that the undesirable population increases to 2% or 1,000,000 and by increasing the quantity of bentonite suppose we removed 500,000 of each within 2 hours, we then would get:

Desirable 50,000,000 - but, Undesirable 1,000,000
Removed 500,000 - removed 500,000
Balance 49,500,000 - we now have 500,000

…or a reduction of only 1% which should be rapidly replaced with or a reduction of 50% in this category, bringing the population back to a more normal state, where it should stay if conditions of normal good health prevail.

Note: In this summary Dr. Lind stated, "It also appears that if one wishes to accurately determine that a specific organism will be removed or sorpted from the gut by bentonite, one must set up "in vivo" experiments in animals. This would involve oral administration of the specific organism in question and following its path through the gut in the presence of a bentonite preparation." The clinical work done by Dr. Damrau's group seems to have already demonstrated this "in vivo" (in the body) within the scope of the matters under investigation. His research results in the treatment of diarrhea in humans indicated as 97% satisfactory treatment rate, and had the dosage been raised as per Dr. Lind's procedures, the results might have been even more impressive.

Pascalite Article

Pascalite, Inc.
P.O. Box 104   329 Lawson
Worland WY 82401
ph 307 347 3872   fax 307 347 2346

From "Nature's own laboratory in Wyoming's Big Horn Mountains" comes a wonderful healing clay called Pascalite. Tests and experiments have revealed many almost unbelievable cures.

The valley near the top of the Big Horn Mountains, South Paint Rock Valley, was for a vast period of time a favorite camping ground and arrow-chipping ground for various Indian tribes - the Crows, Arapahoes, Shoshones, Blackfeet and Sioux. They knew about and used Pascalite, which they called "Ee-Wah-Kee" ("The-Mud-That-Heals").

Some tribes even offered it for bartering purposes at the various rendezvous, such as the Green River Rendezvous, where trappers, traders and Indians all congregated once a year to trade furs.

Pascalite was unknown to the white man until Emile Pascal, a trapper, found it by accident about 1930. He accidentally got his badly chapped hands coated with Pascalite. His hands improved, and with continued use of the clay, healed. Pascal filed mining claims on it, and his friends began using it as his urging.

Ray is president of Pascalite, Inc. now and has many interesting stories to tell. He recalls a story he found in an old newspaper: "Chief Washakie of the Shoshone tribe, on his last buffalo hunt, about 1888, had a white newspaperman with him. After the party had hunted over the Owl Creek Mountains in Wyoming, traveling north from the Wind River Reservation to the Greybull River at the foot of the Big Horn Mountains, the newsman got very sick. Chief Washaie ordered his medicine man to cure him. The medicine man muttered some incantations over him, rubbed his abdomen and chest with some herb, then gave him some of the white powder from the mountains in water to drink. After ingesting this decoction (Pascalite), the man felt soothed and shortly fell into a sleep which lasted several hours. When he awoke, he was completely well".

Ray also recalls:

> "Back in the 'golden days' of our mining venture - in the 1930's -
> we had the entire mountain (that section of it containing Pascalite)

to ourselves. It was our kingdom in which we were for the most part the only subjects. Few people ever came down into that deep valley - it was off the beaten trail; the road was rocky, rough, and on occasion impassable... And this was as close to Shangri La as civilized man could come in the 20th century.

"Nature was indulgent toward us; we had the icy pure water from the spring-fed little lake (which we had stocked with cutthroat trout), and we had abundant fuel in the dead pine, quaking aspen, and red spruce within a few yards of us. We had wild raspberries and gooseberries. We had 'uncontaminated' sun... And we had the Pascalite.

"We has a 50-gallon iron barrel fastened to one of the buildings for an outdoor shower. We would fill it by hose and let the sun warm it; it was always available along with the Pascalite to make a thick paste to be smeared over our scratched or bruised limbs, then rinsed off with the needle-sharp finger of water, still cold enough to bring forth a gasp, and a resulting feeling of well-being that bordered on euphoria!"

Ray explains how he came into the picture when, as an unemployed coal miner in the 1930's he sought for and found a job as the mine foreman for Labbe Products, which was the company formed to market the product - then called "Life Mud". The company had acquired a processing plant in Worland and a factory in Casper. It manufactured toothpaste, hair pomade, rectal suppositories, ointment, poultice and soap.

The company (faced with accumulated debts and public indifference) failed, Ray bought a half interest in the mine claims from Emile Pascal for a nominal sum plus his agreement to do the assessment and other mining work, file labor proofs, etc.

"During the fifties I tried vainly to get large drug and cosmetic companies interested in the material we renamed Pascalite (after Pascal). We finally leased it to a mining man, but after one year he was unable to meet the advance royalty payment and we canceled his lease.

"Meanwhile, people who became interested used the product and reported their results. We were gradually building up a file on its uses with sometimes dramatic results being reported."

An outstanding case history is that of Carl Largent, a teenage boy in Ten Sleep, Wyoming at the foot of the Big Horns, who had scratched his leg accidentally. It became infected and gangrenous. His doctor want to amputate it, saying this was the only way to save his life, but Carl's father would not permit it; instead he packed it with a thick Pascalite paste and the leg promptly healed and was as good as ever in three weeks.

Finally in 1970 Ray was able to get an article published in a national publication called "Beyond," and he began to get requests from all over for the product. It was sent out to them with no claims made and the signed understanding that it was being obtained and used at their own risk and for research purposes only. Other magazines picked up his story, and the demand continued.

"We do not make any claims for Pascalite," explains Ray, "nor do we prescribe it or offer it as an agent for any treatment. But results of experimental usage of Pascalite, as done by the U.S. Testing Company of Hoboken, New Jersey, private testing companies, medical doctors, and users who, acknowledging that no claims were made for it, willingly used it at their own risks, cannot be ignored. I have documentary support of all cases in my files."

Ray shares the results of some of those cases and test with us:

Germicidal test show Pascalite to be sterile; and further, that it possesses the physical ability to occlude and precipitate cultural media. A solution of 2 ounces of powdered Pascalite in one gallon of water used to wash two walls of a hospital room showed a sterile culture 4 days after washing. The other walls, washed by the conventional method, showed daily contamination.

A patient taking 2 no. 00 capsules of powder by mouth four times a day removed all symptoms of an active ulcer and hyperacidity in 7 days.

A wet pack applied to corns and calluses on and between the toes was left on 3 days, then changed and left on 3 more days. All symptoms were relieved, and the corns had disappeared.

Eczema, treated by 'everything' for 10 years, responded within 2 days to treatment by Pascalite, an in 1 week the hands were normal.

Used as a water-and-Pascalite pack on the face and arms of an explosion-burn victim, it relieved the pain almost immediately and these areas did not blister. The hands, given conventional treatment, did blister.

Used in powder form, it has cleared diaper rash overnight.

Three individuals stated under oath that topical use of Pascalite paste had removed all symptoms of hemorrhoid in 2 to 4 nightly applications. Many other have reported similar results in its use for piles, rectal fissures and related conditions.

Kit Nelson of Scottsdale, Arizona explains how Pascalite cured her 22-year old daughter of a serious case of chicken pox: "she was very ill and covered from head to toe with pox which nearly drove her crazy because of the itching and irritation. In desperation she mixed Pascalite with water to a thin consistency and applied it to her body. In a matter of hours (!) the healing set in and she had complete rest and relief. Her recovery was fast and her skin remained lovely - the pox left no scars, which was a miracle."

Nell Coates of Amboy, Washington, explained in her letter of [sic.] how Pascalite cured her psoriasis: Her doctors said there was "no know cure for it and gave me a list of things to purchase." After getting home and thinking about it, she decided it was too expensive for something that wouldn't work anyway. Instead she ordered a pound of Pascalite, mixed it with water to make a thick paste and applied this to the spots. When it dried, she washed it off with warm water, applied peroxide with a cotton ball, rinsed this off and held a 250 watt light close enough that the heat dried it. At night she applied the past and wrapped her legs in plastic and let it dry more gradually. She began this treatment in May of 1970 and continued through to August - by then she didn't have even a scar left."

A case of anemia due to anorexia nervosa was reported by a doctor in New York: "As this is an emotional disorder, it is difficult to establish any biochemical effect with regard to Pascalite. Nevertheless, after 2 weeks of 3 No. 00 caps per day, the blood serum of this patient had returned to normal."

A woman suffering from cataracts and threatened loss of sight was advised by a psychic to use water filtered through Pascalite as eye drops, combining this treatment with Pascalite paste on the eyelids. The psychic did not know of Pascalite by name, referring to it as a "white clay in the Big Horn Mountains in Wyoming, ' and it was some time before the patient was able to get an address and secure the white clay, Pascalite. She reports the treatment was effective, the cataracts dissolving. Two other persons have also reported similar results.

A woman who was taking 3 No. 00 capsules of Pascalite daily, reported that a place on her scalp damaged several years previously by a hair preparation was now growing new hair by using Pascalite applied directly to the scalp.

A sufferer from an advanced stage of pyorrhea was told by her dentist that she should have all her teeth extracted. She began to use cotton pads soaked in a Pascalite-and-water solution, applying them between gums and cheeks at night. Her dentist later found the pyorrhea gone; and now, 10 years later, her teeth and gums are in better condition than originally.

A Cleveland, Ohio doctor who has repeatedly ordered Pascalite, states that he has found it aids in eliminating arthritis, that it reduces cholesterol, dissolves gallbladder and kidney stones, and neutralized metabolic waste.

A man suffering from a case of penile Herpes Simplex first used the expensive cream prescribed by his doctor, but to no avail; the infection spread. He turned to a mixture of Pascalite and honey and within 3 days the swelling had disappeared and within an additional week "blister, cratering, necrosis, and suppuration had healed over with fresh pink flesh." When it appeared again the following year, he "nipped it in the bud by using mere tap water added to the Pascalite and within 7 days it was all healed, and the original blisters never spread as before, and the amount of pain was this time almost negligible. The skin is healthy, pink and unscarred."

Some animal testing and usage was done by some vets with gratifying results. Several cattlemen in the Worland area have been using Pascalite for the treatment of scours in their herds. Two large tablespoonful placed well down into the back of their pried-open mouths, repeated a second day, was the average treatment used to bring about complete relief from all symptoms. They reported a 100% success during the 2 years they have been using this treatment. One of these cattlemen states he used the same treatment for pneumonia in one of his cows with complete success.

"The list of often-dramatic benefits from the use of Pascalite is so long and varied that it might well cause skepticism in the minds of the uninitiated. The surface has been barely scratched herein; and documentary support of all statements exists in our files."

In addition to its other abilities, Pascalite has been shown to be an anesthetic. Many users have reported almost immediate cessation of pain following its application in paste form to the areas.

"In our mining operations we have discovered that dead animals, buried in the tailings of the mine which contained a minor amount of Pascalite, did not decompose, but eventually became mummified.

HOW DOES PASCALITE DO IT?

To help explain some of the abilities possessed by Pascalite, Ray quotes the report by Dr. Walter Bennett, Ph.D., Epistemologist and Research Scientist, who spent several months during 1975 in a very sophisticated examination of Pascalite. He reports:

"The presence of protein in this material gives evidence of yet undisclosed amino acids. The fact that amounts are small, and that even the requirements are for minute quantities, in no way diminishes their great importance. Suffice it to say, we may be flirting with the outskirts of some carinolytic exposure."

"Microbiological analysis reveals the interesting fact that the raw material is completely sterile as pertains to any bacteria. However, it contains the spores of at least 6 different types of fungi."

"When used as a media of raw material it inhibits the growth of representative pathogens such as staphylococcus, streptococcus, salmonella, escherichia coli, and pseudomonas aeruginosa."

"Only 2 of the fungi of the several found in the sample have been identified at this time; namely Actinomyces and Penicillium. Each of these fungi is responsible for production of its own class of antibiotics."

Ray explains he offers Pascalite as a mineral and protein supplement which under a federal law of April 13, 1976, removes such supplements from the drug classification.

However, since the Pascalite mine exists of [sic.] Forest Service land, the government decided it had the right to dispute all the claims made about Pascalite on the grounds that there were no valuable minerals in that stratum.

When the case finally came to court, the government presented their one witness, a geologist, to state his opinion that there were no minerals in Pascalite. In response, Pascalite presented a number of witnesses, including a medical doctor who came from Oklahoma to testify to the great value as a healing agent for *"fiddleback spider" bites - no cure for which had ever had ever been developed previously.* This same doctor also testified that Pascalite was the best know to her for *burns, and was 'very, very good' for the treatment of varicose ulcers, acne, and other related conditions.* Other witnesses from outside the Worland area were glad to come and testify, including 2 veterinarians and one dentist.

Last summer, the government finally agreed to dismiss the case provided all the buildings were removed - one small dwelling house and 2 storage buildings. Ray explains "we felt this was probably the easiest solution, rather than dragging the matter out for an indeterminate time. The Forest Service is permitting us to proceed to develop and market; however, we cannot at this time do any strip mining, but must go underground."

Dr. Bennett summarizes regarding Pascalite:

> "Considering the mineral composition and the soluble forms available, this natural mineral is certified as a valuable food supplement and has extraordinary qualities as related to nutrition and health.
>
> "All analyses and testing confirms that there is no contradiction to human health when this material is consumed in moderation."

(Dr. Walter Bennett has more than thirty years experience in scientific research, consulting and teaching as a graduate professor. He holds four academic degrees in science with testimonial qualifications as a Doctor of Philosophy.)

REDMOND CLAY: A HIGH AFFINITY SORBENT OF AFLATOXIN B, AND CHOLERA TOXIN

Dr. Kim L O'Neill and Joshua D. Stubblefield
Department of Microbiology
Brigham Young University
September 5, 2000

Submitted to
Milo Bosshardt
Redmond Minerals Inc.
Redmond, Utah

LIST OF FIGURES

Figure

1. Romanian Baby with Chronic Diarrhea
2. Healthy Romanian Baby
3. Action of Cholera Toxin
4. O.D. Values of Veratox ELISA
5. O.D. Values of Cholera Toxin ELISA
6, The Human Gastrointestinal Tract
7. Epithelium Cell of the Small Intestine

LIST OF TABLES

Table

1. Veratox Calibration
2. Oral Rehydration Solution Electrolyte Concentrations
3. Biochemical Assay of Bentonite

ABSTRACT

Studies of the pathophysiology involved in the human gastrointestinal tract show that two types of diarrhea exist: osmotic and secretory. Osmotic diarrhea is caused by the presence of poorly absorbed luminol osmols in the lumen of the gut. Secretory diarrhea is usually caused by bacterial toxins or viral agents, which promote the secretion of an excess of water and electrolytes. These infections become dangerous due to dehydration, which can often lead to death if left untreated. Clays, such as bentonite, may reverse the dehydration caused by secretory diarrhea by replenishing lost electrolytes and adsorbing bacterial toxins; thereby promoting water reabsorption.

Enzyme-linked immunosorbent assays (ELISA) were conducted to measure the efficacy of hydrated sodium bentonite in binding aflatoxin B_1 (AFB_1) and cholera toxin (CT) from solution. Using 5 ml of a 44 g/ml aqueous solution of AFB_1, and 1-2 g of sodium bentonite, adsorption abilities ranged from 99.9990% to 99.9995%. Values of 20,000 ppb were brought within concentrations safe for human consumption (<20ppb) (14, 23). Using a 0.1 ml diluted aqueous solution of CT and 1-2 g of sodium bentonite, adsorption values were similar to those of bentonite with AFB_1. These results implicate a possible use of hydrated sodium bentonite in the preventative management of bacterial enterotoxin induced secretory diarrhea; however, its efficacy in protecting against these should be verified further by in vivo testing.

INTRODUCTION

Severe dehydration due to acute diarrhea causes more than 5 million deaths per year worldwide (12, 34). Children and the elderly are the most susceptible to this dehydration because of underdeveloped, or decreased immune function. The World Health Organization (WHO) defines acute diarrhea as three or more liquid stools within 24 hours and chronic, or persistent, diarrhea as acute diarrhea that lasts at least fourteen days (12). "The WHO estimates that 3-20% of acute diarrheal episodes in children under 5 years of age in developing countries become persistent (12). This statistic is alarming, considering every child under five years of age in these developing countries, on average, has 2-3 episodes of diarrhea per year (2, 12). Chronic diarrhea can lead to other serious problems besides mortality, such as malnutrition, dehydration, and morbidity. In Columbia, a scientific paper reported that chronic diarrhea can cause a negative effect on a child's growth in the first three years of life. This study estimated that a child's growth is stunted between 2.5 and 10 cm, resulting from a loss of nutrients essential to promote growth hormones (12).

The Dystrophic Center in Romania starkly portrays the problems that diarrhea can cause in children. This orphanage contains about one hundred children ranging from a few months to three years of age. Due to cramped quarters, and the lack of sanitation, all of these children suffer from chronic diarrhea. The causes of diarrhea vary from malabsorbtion to intestinal infection. Because of these diarrheal problems, three year old children in the orphanage only have the body size and development of an average healthy Romanian one year old. (Figures 1 and 2 provide a graphical representation of the serious health detriments of chronic diarrhea.)

Apart from the problems suffered by the children and elderly in developing countries, 20-50% of adult travelers that visit these developing countries often suffer from this same diarrhea, commonly known as "travelers' diarrhea" or "Montezuma's revenge.- (7). The effects of this ailment include discomfort, lost travel time, and impaired health. Because of the seriousness of chronic diarrhea, a search for more efficient antidiarrheals has increased greatly over the past twenty years. Currently, the only generally accepted treatment for acute diarrhea is not an antidiarrheal but an oral rehydration solution. The purpose behind the rehydration solution is to replenish the fluids and electrolytes lost during an episode of secretory diarrhea. Oral rehydration solutions do not decrease the duration or severity of diarrhea, but only prevent the severe dehydration that can lead to death.

The search for an antidiarrheal to accompany oral rehydration therapy has spanned a variety of drugs that target different aspects of diarrhea, such as antimicrobial and antimotility agents. Besides the high cost, most of these drugs have dangerous side effects, and therefore are not generally accepted. Antimotility agents, such as opiates and loperamide target slowing the passage of fluid through the intestinal tract, allowing time for the colon to reabsorb water. However, opiates cause drowsiness, respiratory depression, hypotension, nausea, and addiction; furthermore, Loperamide causes abdominal distension. There are many antimicrobial agents, all of which have some side-effects. These side-effects range from intestinal irritation and hemorrhages to accumulation of salicylate in the blood stream.

Apart from dangerous side-effects, there is also a concern for the cost and availability of these drugs. In 1996, the WHO reviewed a large majority of antimotility drugs, antimicrobial drugs, and adsorbents; and concluded that they should not be implemented as treatments for diarrhea (13). The WHO determined that Oral Rehydration Therapy (ORT) was sufficient; and only in cases of dysentary, and severe cholera should an antimicrobial be used until scientific information supports a safe and effective antidiarrheal (13).

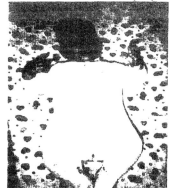

Figure 1: A two and a half year old Romanian baby with chronic diarrhea

Figure 2: A one year old healthy Romanian baby

This standpoint was taken because all but the adsorbents demonstrated dangerous side-effects and would be expensive to incorporate. Adsorbents were most likely disapproved because of the lack of consistent scientific evidence in vivo to support them.

Adsorbents such as kaolin and smectite have been tested in double-blind placebo studies as treatments for diarrhea. The results. however, have been deemed inconclusive by the WHO. The WHO currently does not support sorbents as an effective treatment for diarrhea on these grounds. We suggest that inconclusive data in the double-blind studies may be due to a lack of consideration made as to the source of diarrhea among the subjects in the studies. We hypothesize that sorbents such as bentonite would be more effective in treating a toxin-induced secretory diarrhea and not so effective with a case of osmotic diarrhea caused by malabsorption. Most studies that test sorbents as a treatment for diarrhea have targeted decreasing the motility of the lumen. We propose that the emphasis should be on the sorbents' ability to bind and remove toxins produced by enterotoxigenic bacteria. In a case of malabsorption. sorbents would only increase the osmotic load of the lumen and may result in a greater loss of fluids.

According to scientists Berschneider and Powell,"the need for a safe, effective antidiarrhoeal agent is clear", and the search for such an agent continues. It should have the following characteristics: 'a high degree of activity, oral effectiveness, target its action on the intestine without systemic absorption or systemic effect, have no effect on a normally functioning gut and have a mechanism which is well understood (12). Our study was to determine through in vitro tests whether the adsorbent Redmond Clay fits this description.

Redmond Clay (activated sodium bentonite) has been shown to be one of the best swelling clays (adsorbents) (38). Swelling clays contain a large array of electrolytes that can function as cation and anion exchangers. We propose that this quality allows bentonite to bind harmful toxins and prevent them from causing damage. A wide variety of toxins exist in nature and cause illnesses ranging from severe diarrhea to cancer. We chose to test Redmond Clay against Aflatoxin B_1 (AFB_1) and cholera toxin, which are two of the most dangerous toxins in nature. Aflatoxins are toxic, carcinogenic, mutagenic, and teratogenic in animals including humans (8, 15). We chose to test the clay with aflatoxin first because of the availability of a simple ELISA to test for the presence of AFB_1 in solution. (Additional information on aflatoxin may be of interest and is provided in Appendix A.)

Cholera toxin is produced by the bacterial strain Vibrio cholerae. Cholera toxin, as well as many other enterotoxins, causes severe secretory diarrhea. Vibrio cholerae binds to the mucosal lining of the small intestine. Once bound, the toxin is synthesized and released into the lumen of the gut. The toxin is made up of two subunits. The B subunit's main function is to bind to the GM, receptor on an epithelial cell of the intestinal lining (12, 34). The A subunit enters the epithelial cell and activates the adenylate cyclase on the basolateral membrane. The adenylate cyclase in turn creates cAMP, which completely blocked by the B subunit. (Fig. 3) (Background information on the physiology of the gastrointestinal tract and the pathophysiology of diarrhea can be found in Appendix B.) We hypothesize that activated bentonite in the lumen of the small intestine, can prevent cholera toxin and other enterotoxins from binding to their receptors. The inability to bind to their receptor would neutralize the damaging effects of the toxins. We propose that if our study shows Redmond Clay can remove a significant amount of cholera toxin from solution in vitro, it may function as an effective antidiarrheal treatment in vivo.

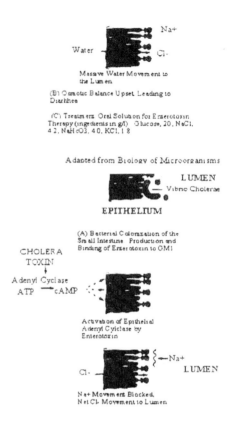

Affinity of Redmond Clay

MATERIALS AND METHODS

Materials

The sodium bentonite, Redmond Clay, was provided by Redmond Minerals Inc. (Redmond, UT). Aflatoxin B, purity >99%, Cholera toxin, Anti-rabbit IgG peroxidase conjugate antibody, and Anti-cholera toxin antibody were all purchased from Sigma Chemicals (St. Louis, MO). An AFB, specific ELISA kit, Veratox Quantitative Aflatoxin Single Test (AST), was obtained from NEOGEN Corporation (Lansing, MI).

Sorption of APB

A 70% methanol stock solution containing 1 mg unlabeled AFB, was prepared to give a working solution of 4ug AFB,/ml(20,000ppb). For each ELISA, 5 ml of stock solution was aliquoted into four 15ml tubes. Two of these tubes were labeled and set apart as controls for the ELISA. The other two were labeled "w/bentonite." Total incubation time for the samples was 1 hour at 25°C. All tubes were vortexed at the beginning of incubation and at 15 min. intervals throughout the incubation period. The sorption was terminated after 1 hr. by centrifugation for 10min. at 1,500 rpm. 10041 of the supernatants were decanted and added to the proper microwells of the ELISA.

The Veratox AST was conducted according to NEOGEN guidelines. The test is a competitive ELISA between AFB, and a conjugate to the anti-aflatoxin B, antibody. One control consisted of an internal standard of 20ppb of AFB, solution provided by NEOGEN. A negative control was also used. The test is quantitative for concentrations of 5-350ppb of AFB,. The optical densities are measured with a 650nm filter in a microwell plate reader. The results are then compared to a set calibration curve determined by

Std. ppb	Calc. O.D.
0	2.102
5	1.833
10	1.554
20	1.150
50	0.693
100	0.427
300	0.200
500	0.170

Table 1: Calibration Curve for Veratox

NEOGEN. (Table 1) The ELISA was repeated twice using 2 mg of bentonite. A third ELISA was run using 1 mg of bentonite.

Sorption of Cholera Toxin

A 50% PBS diluted stock solution was prepared with cholera toxin. 12 ml of a .1 ml dilution was added to two 15 ml test tubes. Two negative controls were also run with 12 ml of PBS. 1 g of sodium bentonite was added to one of test solution and to one of the controls. The other test solution and control were left untreated. The tubes were left to incubate at 22-25°C for 1 hr. and were vortexed at the beginning of the incubation period and at 15 min. intervals. The samples were then centrifuged at 1,500 rpm for 10 min. 100 ul of supernatant from each tube was aliquoted into their respective wells. The microwell was left to incubate for 24 hrs.

After 24 hrs., the wells were emptied and washed twice with 300 ul of a PBS solution with 0.5% tween20. The wells were then flushed a third time with PBS alone. 300 ul of block solution (PBS with 3% FBS) was then aliquoted to each of the wells and left to incubate for another 24hrs. Afterwards, the same washing procedures as above were performed.

A 100 ul of 1:10,000 PBS diluted solution of anti-cholera toxin antibody was added to each well and incubated for 2 hrs. The same washing procedures were followed and 1000 of a 1:7,000 PBS diluted solution of anti-rabbit IgG labeled with horseradish peroxidase was added to each well. The microwell plate was left to incubate for 2hrs. and then washed. 100 ul of 3,3",5,5"- Tetramethylbenzidine (TMB) was then added to each well and left to react for 30min. The optical density (OD) was then measured with a 450 nm filter. Results were compared with controls.

RESULTS

The AFB, ELISA results showed that the bentonite removed approximately 20,000 ppb of aflatoxin, bringing the levels within ranges set as safe for human consumption (20 ppb: All food except milk). The optical densities showed that the 4 ug AFB, solution had levels well beyond the ranges measured by the ELISA. The samples with bentonite had levels of aflatoxin lower than the 2O ppb control. (Fig. 4) The graph shows that the sample of aflatoxin treated with bentonite had approximately the same O.D. as the control sample with only 2O ppb. of AFB. The O.D. value for the sample not treated with bentonite was very low.

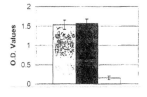

Figure 4: O.D. Values of Veratox ELISA

This means that there was a very large concentration of AFB, in proportion to the antibody conjugate. Therefore the two samples began with the same concentration of AFB, but the sample treated with bentonite had

The cholera toxin ELISA worked a bit differently than the Veratox AST ELISA. Instead of being a competitive ELISA, it simply measured for the presence of cholera toxin. The larger the concentration of cholera toxin present resulted in a larger O.D. This is the reverse of what occurred with the Veratox AST ELISA. The cholera toxin results showed that the O.D. of the negative controls and the cholera toxin sample with bentonite were of about equal value. They both had a reasonably low O.D. Even though the control did not have any cholera toxin present it had a very small O.D. which is common to occur. It is customary to set the O.D. of the control as the negative point (no cholera toxin). Therefore the sample treated with bentonite tested negative for the presence of cholera toxin. The bentonite effectively bound the toxin and removed it from solution during centrifugation. The positive control of cholera toxin not treated with bentonite had a significantly higher O.D. which means -that it tested positive for the presence of cholera toxin. (Fig. 5) We did not determine a concentration value of how much cholera toxin was removed from the sample treated with bentonite, but we can assume that almost all of the toxin was removed from solution. These results are exciting, because we know that the toxins in both tests were bound and not just inactivated by the bentonite. We know this because we used polyclonal antibodies in both of the ELISA's. Polyclonal antibodies recognize several epitopes on the toxin. Therefore if the toxin was mutated at one epitope by a mutation, it's other epitopes would still be recognized by the antibody and counted as present in solution. Our results, however, showed that the toxins were completely removed from solution. It is therefore an effective binder of AFB, and cholera toxin in vitro, and may be an effective anti-toxin with all toxins.

DISCUSSION

Redmond Minerals Inc. approached our lab on the premise that they had a clay (Redmond Clay) that they and many personal testimonies claimed to cure diarrhea. Our lab agreed to look at the clay's attributes and test it for a possible mechanism by which it might cure diarrhea. We first tested the Redmond Clay for any antimicrobial qualities. We ran tests with several bacterial strains, but the clay showed no inhibition on their growth. Our second approach on the matter was to test the clay for any immune enhancement attributes. We tested the clay with macrophage response and immune function. None of our tests. however, were statistically significant to conclude that it enhance immune response.

After thorough research in the literature on the topic, we hypothesized that the clay may not be affecting the bacteria directly; but rather, it may be affecting the toxins that the enterotoxigenic bacterial strains produce. Many studies have shown that sorbents such as Redmond Clay have the ability to adsorb dangerous toxins such as carcinogenic aflatoxin (29, 30, 31), killer yeast toxins in wines (26), T-2 toxin (6). staphylococcal enterotoxin A (20). and E-coli enterotoxins (5, 6, 19). Successful in vivo studies have been conducted with cholestyramine (4, 28) and even one with smectite, conducted on egyptian children (18. 27). This last study found that 48 hrs. after treatment, "19 patients (42%) of the group receiving smectite were free of diarrhea, while this was true of only 6 patients (13%) receiving placebo."(27).

In our study we first tested Redmond Clay-with AFB, to see if this theory is plausible. Our results show that Redmond Clay did effectively bind AFB, and removed it from solution. These positive results encouraged us to devise an ELISA for cholera toxin. We could use this ELISA to test Redmond Clay against an actual enterotoxin. After determining the proper concentrations of antibodies for the ELISA, the results gave proof that Redmond Clay does in fact bind cholera toxin in solution and may do likewise with other enterotoxins.

In addition the positive results of our study, we also analyzed the biochemical make-up of sodium bentonite and found an interesting possibility. A biochemical assay of sodium bentonite shows that it contains the proper electrolytes at the same concentrations of the average oral rehydration solution. (Table 2)

Bentonite lacks only a glucose-glutamine additive that would make it function properly as a rehydration treatment for children suffering from acute diarrhea. (The biochemical assay of sodium bentonite and background on oral rehydration therapy can be consulted in Appendix C.) Implementing bentonite as an oral rehydration solution would be somewhat unnecessary unless it offered some other aspect in the fight against secretory diarrhea. Sodium bentonite's ability to sequester toxins in solution may be that other aspect. If sodium bentonite can perform this function within the lumen of the small intestine, it is possible that it may perform the roles of an oral rehydration solution and an antidiarrheal.

CONCLUSION

Before a new antidiarrheal can be permitted into the health institutions of the world it should be endorsed by the World Health Organization. History shows that the WHO will not accept any new treatment for secretory diarrhea unless it is cost effective and safe. Redmond Clay does not have to be engineered but is rather a natural resource. It could be modified for glucose content and taste for a minimal amount. As for its safety, the FDA has labeled activated bentonite as GRAS, meaning Generally Regarded As Safe.

The antidiarrheal must also be proven scientifically first through in vitro studies and then through in vivo studies.

Berschneider and Powell set forth basic qualifications of such an antidiarrheal: it must have "a high degree of activity, oral effectiveness, target its action on the intestine without systemic absorption or systemic effect, have no effect on a normally functioning gut and have a mechanism which is well understood." We believe that after further studies Redmond Clay may be proven to fit each of these categories.

Redmond Clay has demonstrated a potential for a high degree of activity through its high affinity to cholera toxin. Should the activated bentonite bind enterotoxins just as successfully in vivo, it would be very effective. The central concern that must be answered through in vivo trials is whether activated bentonite can sequester enterotoxin after they have bound to a receptor. Should the bentonite have a higher affinity for the toxin than the receptor, it may be concluded that it definitely has a high degree of activity.

Solution	Sodium mmol/L	Potassium mmol/L	Chloride mmol/L	Glucose * mmol/L
WHO solution	90	20	80	111 (20)
Rehydralyte	75	20	65	139 (25)
Pedialyte	45	20	35	139 (25)
Resol	50	20	50	111 (20)
Ricelyte	50	25	45	(30)
Gatorade	23.5	<1	17	(40)
Bentonite**	90	25	25	------

Figures in parenthesis represent grams of carbohydrate

Table 2 - Composition of Oral Replacement Solutions for the Treatment of Diarrhea

Activated bentonite is oral effective because it is easily swallowed and kept down. Although Redmond Clay does not have a completely unpleasant taste, some may show reserve in taking it orally. It may be possible to modify the taste or take the solution with food without hindering its action. Because Redmond Clay is taken orally, its action is targeted to the lumen of intestine. As previously addressed, the solution of activated bentonite is constituted of mainly electrolytes and trace metals which are necessary for the diet and essential as a part of oral rehydration therapy during acute diarrhea. Many scientists have voiced a concern that clay based sorbents may cause granuloma in the intestine. Granuloma is the build up of macrophages which can be detrimental to self cells. Only further trials will show if this will be a side-effect of the treatment.

As for the final qualification set forth by Berschneider and Powell. the mechanism by which sodium bentonite may function as an antidiarrheal has been shown with the presented research. Activated bentonite should not be used to treat osmotic diarrhea because its mechanism is through binding the enterotoxins that cause secretory diarrhea. A sorbent should be used to target the source of the problem and not used to slow motility. The effect of allowing more time for water to be reabsorbed will be offset by the increase in luminal osmolarity. Our study only endorses the possible use of Redmond Clay as a treatment for enterotoxigenically induced secretory diarrhea.

We conclude that our study on Redmond Clay's action against the mycotoxin. AFB, and the enterotoxin, cholera toxin, was successful. In solution, Redmond Clay does effectively bind these toxins. These toxins can then be removed from the solution through centrifugation. We propose that this action may make Redmond Clay an effective antidiarrheal against secretory diarrhea. Its biochemical make up lends it to be an effective oral rehydration solution as well. Should Redmond Clay function as both an antitoxin and oral rehydration solution in vivo, not only would it be a cost effective replacement of the current ORS, but it also has an excellent shelf life. We have not found or know of any other functions that Redmond Clay might have as a treatment for diarrhea. We hope that our research may prove useful to others that may continue this work.

APPENDIX A

Aflatoxin is considered a Group I carcinogen in humans by the International Agency for Research on Cancer (IARC). In the human liver, aflatoxin is activated by cytochrome p450 into an 8,9-epoxide that readily forms DNA adducts (8). Binding of this reactive intermediate to DNA results in disruption of transcription. leading to abnormal cell proliferation and the formation of tumors. In certain parts of the world, levels of aflatoxins in food produced for human consumption are monitored because aflatoxin is a product of grain mold, Aspergillus flavzis. commonly found in animal feed. It is estimated that one quarter of the world's food crop may be affected with mycotoxins (16).

Detoxification of aflatoxin-contaminated foods and feed is a current problem in agriculture. The ingestion of aflatoxins can lead to an illness known as aflatoxicosis in animals. The symptoms of aflatoxicosis are: decreased carbohydrate. lipid, nucleic acid, and protein metabolism, reduced growth rate of young animals, and impaired immunological responsiveness (8, 16, 23). These problems leave the animal susceptible to additional infections which may lead to death.

Dairy cows often suffer from aflatoxicosis when levels of aflatoxins in their feed is high. Besides the previously mentioned symptoms, aflatoxicosis results in high counts of aflatoxins in their milk. Dairy cows convert from .25% to 4.8% of the aflatoxins in the feed to afltatoxin M, in the milk (15). This poses a problem for dairy farmers when their milk productions does not meet FDA standards for aflatoxin levels in the milk. Treatment with antibiotics may cure the aflatoxicosis but it will also be toxic to the normal flora of the lumen which will contribute to high cell counts in the milk, The most recent form of treatment, to keep supplementary feed under $5\mu g/kg$ of aflatoxin. is the addition of sorbents in contaminated feeds to bind the aflatoxins. This will prevent aflatoxicosis while keeping the somatic cell counts of the milk low (34). In vitro studies have shown that activated carbons (10) and hydrated sodium calcium aluminosilicates (22) are capable of binding AFB, in aqueous solution. In vivo tests on weanling piglets (30, 31) and broiler chickens (29) show that treatment with bentonite may prevent aflatoxicosis.

APPENDIX B

General Intestinal Physiology

All of the vitamins, carbohydrates, fat, proteins, electrolytes, and trace minerals essential to the human body's cellular and organ functions are obtained from ingested foods. "Knowledge of the normal physiology of the transport of water and electrolytes across the gastrointestinal tract is an essential prerequisite for understanding of the pathophysiology of electrolyte disturbances resulting from diarrheal disorders." (11). In this section, a basic description of electrolytes and fluid transport involved in the digestion process will be given to provide a background understanding as to why diarrhea occurs and how it might be prevented or cured by bentonite.

As food enters the mouth, it is broken down into smaller pieces by enzymes. The food travels down the esophagus until it reaches the stomach, where enzymes and acids are secreted from its walls. Once in the stomach, all of the ingested food is liquefied. This liquefaction is necessary for absorption through the walls of the intestines. Upon leaving the stomach, this liquid food first travels to the duodenum, the first part of the small intestine. "9-10 liters of fluid enter the duodenum daily...2 liters are dietary...7-8 liters are from secretions." (21). Absorption of the dietary nutrients begins in the duodenum and continues as this fluid travels to the large intestine, called the colon. (Fig. 6)

Most of the electrolytes (sodium and potassium) are absorbed into the lining of the small intestine. To the naked eye the lining of the intestine looks like a fleshy shag carpet. Upon

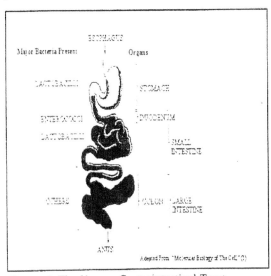

Figure 6: The Human Gastrointestinal Tract

microscope examination of a single section of that "carpet" it would appear to be packed with small bumps called villi.

Examination of one individual villi would reveal trillions of cells with more finger-like bumps called microvilli. The sum of the surface area created by all of these bumps is equal to about 200 square meters, an area larger than the size of a football field. This extensive surface area becomes important in allowing maximum absorption of essential body nutrients.

At the tips of the villi are the cells (tip cells) involved in absorption, while the cells at the base of the villi (crypt cells) primarily function as secretory cells (11). Sodium and potassium (Na^+ and K^+ respectively), can enter the bloodstream either through "tight" junctions between these cells or through the tip of cells themselves. It is important to note that whenever Na^+ and K^+ are transported across these cells, water is brought with them, into the circulatory system. The reverse of this statement is true as well. Whenever Na^+ and K^+ are secreted out of the crypt cells into the lumen, water is brought with them. It is necessary that more water is absorbed than secreted, in order to prevent dehydration. Many scientists have conceded that when glucose, a basic sugar, is present, the tip cells will allow the junction to open up even larger, thus increasing permeability (3, 7, 12, 32). (Fig. 7)

To enter the bloodstream and from there to be taken to the various parts of the body, Na+ and K+ must pass through the basolateral membrane of the cells, which requires energy. This action is important because Na+ and K— are used for nerve impulses in the body. Three pathways exist in the body for sodium to obtain the energy necessary to pass through the basolateral membrane and into the bloodstream. One. uncoupled absorption of Na+i two, co-transport of Na+ and CI-: and three, Na+ coupled to absorption of organic solutes (sugars and amino acids). The first pathway does not play a large role in diarrhea. so it will not be detailed. It is a simple exchange between lK+ and Na+ in and out of the lumen. The second pathway is the common method of diffusion. Na-- and CI- coupled together can create enough energy to pass through the basolateral membrane into the bloodstream. In the third pathway, energy is derived from sugars such as glucose (as previously mentioned) and amino acids. This pathway occurs through the "tight" junctions. This third pathway plays a very important role in Oral Rehydration Therapy because it is the only transport mechanism that continues to function during secretory diarrhea. More details on this subject are covered in the following section.

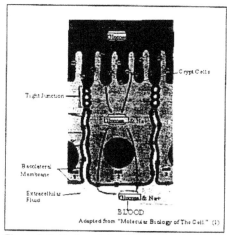

Figure 7: Epithelium Cell of the Small Intestine

The electrolytes and water that are not absorbed in the small intestine are passed into the colon. Here, 80% of the water from the fluid passing into the colon is absorbed along with 90% of the remaining electrolytes (12). "Normally 1-1.5 liters [of fluid] enters the colon. The colon absorbs all but 200 mL [of that]... [in cases of diarrhea] the maximum colonic absorptive capacity [is] 4-6 liters." (21). This mass absorption of water turns the remaining waste back into solid form that is later excreted from the body as fecal matter. "Normal stool output is approximately 100 to 200 g/day." (2, 21). Most cases of diarrhea occur because the amount of fluid exceeds the maximum absorptive capacity of the colon. The fluid that is not absorbed is excreted as watery stool. Therefore, an antidiarrheal should target on preventing secretion of electrolytes, which will in turn prevent large volumes of water from being secreted and causing secretory diarrhea.

PATHOpHYSIOLOGY OF DIARRHEA

The symptoms involved in diarrhea include an increase in frequency and volume of watery stools. Diarrhea can be classified as osmotic or secretory. Osmotic diarrhea is the result of a decrease in water absorption in the colon. Secretory diarrhea, on the other hand, results from an increased secretion of fluid into the intestinal tract (21). These two forms of diarrhea differ widely in their causes, signs and symptoms. The following portion details the differences between these two classifications of diarrhea.

OSMOTIC DIARRHEA

Osmotic diarrhea is typically caused by non-infectious condition, The major condition leading to osmotic diarrhea is malabsorption. Malabsorption is the inability of certain ingested carbohydrates to be absorbed by the microvilli (11. 12, 21, 32). When these water-soluble carbohydrates reach the colon they are fermented by colonic bacteria into luminol osmols, which not only can not be absorbed but also prevent reabsorption of water by the colon, resulting in watery stools (11, 12, 21).

Several types of molecules in food can lead to osmotic diarrhea. One example is glucose-galactose (dissacharide). This molecule will not be absorbed due to a defect in transport mechanisms or if the intestinal microvillus membrane is damaged (11). Another example of an unabsorbable carbohydrate is lactose. The body can not absorb lactose. Lactobacillus, a bacteria that is part of the normal intestinal flora, produces lactase, an enzyme capable of breaking down lactose into an absorbable form. Thus, if lactobacillus is absent, a person will be unable to absorb lactose which causes lactose intolerance. Thus, lactose intolerance causes osmotic diarrhea, abdominal distention, abdominal pain, and excessive gas (32).

Laxatives are another cause of osmotic diarrhea. When a person is suffering from constipation or is unable to defecate, a laxative is taken to loosen up their stools. Laxatives are made up of nonabsorbable inorganic components that are fermented by bacteria in the colon.

When these components are fermented, they become luminol osmols which means they prevent reabsorption of most of the water. The extra water in the lumen is what induces a looser stool or diarrhea, depending on the strength of the laxative. Because water is only prevented from being absorbed and no water is secreted, osmotic diarrhea is always small in volume (<1 liter/day) (21). Children that suffer from malabsorption may experience severe weight loss and dehydration if their diets are not adjusted. The carbohydrates, essential to growth, that are not being absorbed must be substituted by a similar carbohydrate that can be absorbed. Fructose, a simple sugar often found in fruit, is the suggested substitute for glucose and sucrose for malabsorption caused by glucose-galactose. Lactose can be replaced by Soy milk, or lactase pills can be taken. The most common sign that diarrhea is osmotic is discontinuance of symptoms upon fasting (21, 32). Without ingesting carbohydrates that create an osmotic load, watery stool will not continue.

SECRETORY DIARRHEA

Infectious bacterial enterotoxins are the most common cause of secretory diarrhea (12). Bacterial enterotoxins cause an increased secretion of Chloride (Cl-) and Na+ in the crypt cells of the mucosal membrane (12). As previously mentioned, when Na+ is transported across the mucosal membrane into the intestinal lumen water also enters the intestinal lumen. This increase of fluid in the intestinal tract can become too large for the colon to reabsorb, resulting in large stool volume (>1 liter/day) (21). Other causes of secretory diarrhea include viral agents, tumor hormones and neurotransmitters. There are three ion secretion mechanisms: One, cyclic adenosine monophosphate (cAMP); two, Cyclic guanosine monophosphate (cGMP); and three, calcium (Ca+-r) (11, 12, 32). All three of these mechanisms function almost identically by phosphorylating mucosal membrane proteins via protein kinases.

This phosphorylation results in a conformational change in the mucosal membrane proteins. This change in conformation prevents neutral NaCl absorption (the second sodium transport mechanism) and stimulates secretion of Cl-, which takes Na+ and water along with it. The Na+ absorption by means of the glucose carrier mechanism continues to function (12, 32). This provides a method of replenishing electrolyte and water losses by means of oral rehydration solutions.

APPENDIX C

ORAL REHYDRATION THERAPY

In the mid 1970's. Oral Rehydration Therapy (ORT) was the most revolutionary advance in the treatment of acute diarrhea and today it remains the cornerstone (7). The WHO has stated that ORT is "potentially the most important medical advance this century [20th century]." (12). It took an understanding of the physiologic concepts of water and electrolyte transport for researchers to find a solution to remedy the loss of fluids and electrolytes. The key is in the fact that although bacterial enterotoxins shut down the NaCl co-transport absorption pathway. the sodium and glucose paired pathway remains functional.

Supplementing the diet of a child suffering from secretory diarrhea with only electrolyte salts (NaCl, KCl and MgCl) would not do much for the child's increasing dehydration. It was found that adding electrolyte salts to a solution of water and glucose would make a solution that would function amazingly in replenishing the lost fluids and electrolytes in that child. The WHO has even gone as far to say that ORT is sufficient treatment for the majority of episodes of acute diarrhea (13). The WHO estimates that 90-95% of patients with acute diarrhea can be successfully treated with ORT alone, including those with travellers' diarrhea (7, 12, 25).

ORT, however, is not very beneficial for children with osmotic diarrhea caused by malabsorption. Because malabsorption diarrhea is caused by the inability to digest sugars such as glucose, a solution of glucose-based oral rehydration solution would only enhance the problem. If a child that suffers from malabsorption is diagnosed with secretory diarrhea. ORT may induce an osmotic diarrhea (11, 12). It is suggested that sucrose or amino acids can replace glucose, but the result is not nearly as effective. If the case is severe, intravenous therapy could be implemented without any problems. Intravenous therapy is when fluids and electrolytes are put directly into the blood system, without the patient having to orally take anything.

A concern that many scientists had about the WHO accepted ORT was its high concentration of sodium. Too much sodium in the human system can result in hypernatremia. This fear has subsided with further studies that have shown the concentration to be harmless (11, 25). The cost of such prepared solutions is cheaper than medications but still can be burdensome for poor families with several children.

BIOCHEMICAL ASSAY OF SODIUM BENTONITE

Note: Aluminum and Silicon are also part of the elemental content Bentonite, but they are bonded in a compound called Aluminosilicate which
is the basis of the clay. All trace minerals attach themselves to this compound
which constitutes the clay.

Analyte	mg/L units in Bentonite
Antimony	0.84
Arsenic	0.05
Barium	98.6
Beryllium	0.13
Bismuth	0.57
Boron	2.3
Bromine	0.68
Cadmium	0.019
Calcium	1130
Carbon	3000
Cerium	6.55
Cesium	0.089
Chloride	990
Chromium	0.75
Cobalt	0.3
Copper	4.21
Dysprosium	0.39
Erbium	1.2
Europium	less than 0.1

Flouride	1.5
Gadolinium	0.62
Gallium	0.59
Germanium	7.3
Gold	less than 0.1
Hafnium	less than 0.33
Homium	less than 0.4
Indium	0.23
Iodine	4.1
Iridium	less than 0.5
Iron	550
Lanthanum	5.29
Lead	0.97
Lithium	26
Lutetium	less than 0.3
Magnesium	1080
Manganese	28.9
Mercury	less than 0.005

Molybdenum	less than 0.5
Neodymium	8.22
Nickel	0.52
Niobium	less than 0.3
Osmium	less than 0.2
Palladium	less than 0.3
Phosphorus	4.95
Platinum	less than 0.3
Potassium	990
Praseodynium	0.57
Rhenium	1.45
Rhodium	less than 0.5
Rubidium	12
Ruthenaim	less than 0.2
Samarium	0.26
Scandium	0.33
Selenium	0.11
Silver	0.26
Sodium	2070
Strontium	5062
Sulfur	275
Tantalum	less than 0.2

Redmond Clay BYU Study

Tellurium	less than 0.2
Terbium	less than 0.2
Thallium	60.3
Thorium	1.57
Thulium	less than 0.3
Tin	0.25
Titanium	215
Tungsten	1.95
Vanadium	12.2
Ytterbium	0.19
Yttrium	2.1
Zinc	2.9
Zirconium	859

Adapted From: "The Contents of Bentonite Clay" (33)
Table 3: Biochemical Assay of Bentonite Clay

BIBLIOGRPAHY

WORKS CITED

1. Albers, B., et al., Molecular Bioloav of The Cell. 3r° ed. New York: Garland Publishing Inc., 1994.

2. Aranda-Michel. J. and R. A. Giannella. "Acute Diarrhea: A Practical Review," The American Journal of Medicine. 106 (June 1999), 670-676.

3. Beaugerie, L., et al., "Effects of An Isotonic Oral Rehydration Solution. Enriched with Glutamine, on Fluid and Sodium Adsorption in Patients with A Short-bowel," Alimentary Pharmacology Therapy. 11 (1997) 741-746.

4. Berant, M., Y. Wagner. N. Cohen, "Cholestryamin in the management of infantile diarrhea," J. Pediat., vol.88 no. 1 (1976) 153-154.

5. Brouillard. M.Y. and J.G. Rateau. "Adsorption of bacterial enterotoxins by smectite and kaolin clays. In vitro study in cell culture and in the newborn mouse." Gastroenterol. Clin. Biol., 13 (1989) 1824.

6. Carson. M.S. and T.K. Smith, "Role of Bentonite in Prevention of T-2 Toxicosis in rats," Journal of Animal Science, vol.57 no.6 (1983) 1498-1505.

7. De Las Casas. C., J. Adachi, and H. Dupont. "Review Article: Traveller's Diarrhoea," Alimentary Pharmacology Therapy, 13 (1999) 1373-1378.

8. Ellis, W.O., et al., "Aflatoxins in Food: Occurrence. Biosynthesis. Effects on Organisms, Detection, and Methods of Control." Critical Reviews in Food Science and Nutrition. vol.30 no.3 (1991) 545550.

9. Fioramonti, J., M.T. Droy-Lefaix, L. Bueno, "Chances in Gastro-Intestinal Motility Induced by Cholera Toxin and Experimental

Osmotic Diarrhosea in Doss: Effects of Treatment with an Argillaceous Compound." Digestion, 36 (1987) 230-237.

10. Galvano. F.. et al., "Activated Carbons: in Vitro Affinity for Aflatoxin B, and Relation of Adsorption Ability to Physiochemical Parameter," Journal of Food Protection, vol.59 no.5 (1996) 545-550.

11. Ghishan. F.K.. "The Transport of Electrolytes in the Gut and the Use of Oral Rehydration Solutions," Pediatric Clinics of North America. vol.35 no.1 (February1988) 35-49.

12. Gracey, M. and V. Burke. eds., Pediatric Gastroenteroloev and Hepatoloev, 3d ed. Boston: Blackwell Scientific Publications. 1993.

13. Haak, H. and M.E. Claeson. "Regulatory Actions to Enhance Appropiate Drug Use: The Case of Antidiarrhoeal Drugs," Social Science Medicine, vol.42 no.7 (1996) 1011-1019.

14. Hamilton, P.B.. "Determining Safe Levels of Mycotoxins." Journal of Food Protection, vol.47 no.7 (July 1984) 570-575.

15. Harvey, R.B., et al., "Effects on aflatoxin M, residues in milk by addition of hydrated sodium calcium aluminosilicate to aflatoxin-contaminated diets of dairy cows," Am. J. Vet. Res., vol.52 no.9 (Sept. 1991) 1556-1559.

16. Lindemann, M.D., et al., "Potential Ameliorators of Aflatoxicosis in Weanling/ Growing Swine," Journal of Animal Science. 71 (1993) 171-178.

17. Madigan, M.T., J.M. Martinko. and J. Parker,Biology of Microorganisms, 8th ed. New Jersey: Prentice Hall, Inc., 1998.

18. Madkour, A.A.. et al.. "Smectite in Acute Diarrhea in Children: A Double-Blind Placebo-Controlled Clinical Trial," Journal of Pediatric Gastroenterology and Nutrition. 17 (1993) 176-181.

19. Mullan, N.A., et al., "The Ability of Cholestyramine Resin and Other Adsorbents to Bind Escherichia coli Enterotoxins,- Journal of Medical Microbiology, 12 (1979) 487-496.

20. Nagaki. M., et al.," Clearance and Tissue Distribution of Staphylococcal Enterotoxin A in the rat and potential use of adsorbents for removal from plasma." Journal of Medical Microbiology, 38 (1993) 354-359.

21. "Pathophysiology of Diarrheal 1988." *http://bio-3.bsd.uchicago.edul-cpoweb/ta/pathophysiology of diarrhea.html*

22. Phillips, T.D.. et al., "Hydrated Sodium Calcium Aluminosilicate: A High \ ffinity Sorbent for Aflatoxin," Poultry Science. 67 (1988) 243-247.

23. Pier, A.C., J.L. Richard, and S.J. Cvsewski, "Implications of Mycotoxins in Animal Disease," J. Am. Vet. Med. Assoc.. 176 (Apr. 1980) 719-723.

24. Pierce, N. and 0. Fontaine, "Does Smectite Have Antidiarrheal Activity," Journal of Pediatric Gastroenterology and Nutrtion. yol.19 no.2 (1994) 505-506.

25. Pizarro, D., "Oral Rehydration in Infants in Developing Countries," Drugs, vol.36 suppl.4 (1988) 3947.

26. Radler, F. and M. Schmitt, "Killer Toxins of Yeasts: Inhibitors of Fermentation and Their Adsorption.- Journal of Food Protection, vol.50 no.3 (March 1987) 251-254.

27. Rhoad, M.J., "Earth, Wind, and Fiber: Is There a Drug to Treat Acute Diarrhea?," Journal of Pediatric Gastroenterology and Nutrtion. vol.19 no.2 (1994) 251-254.

28. Rowe, G.G., "Control of Diarrhea by Cholestyramine Administration," The American Journal of the Medical Sciences, 255 (Feb. 1968) 84-88.

29. Santurio, J.M., et al., "Effect of Sodium Bentonite on the Performance and Blood Variables of Broiler Chickens Intoxicated with Aflatoxins," British Poultry Science, 40 (1999) 115-119.

30. Schell, T.C., et al., "Effectiveness of Different Types of Clay for Reducing the Detrimental Effects of Aflatoxin-Contaminated Diets on Performance and Serum Profiles of Weanling Pigs," Journal of Animal Science, 71 (1993) 1226-1231.

WORKS ALSO CONSULTED

1. Abely, M., "Effect of Cholera Toxin on Glutamine Metabolism and Transport in Rabbit Ileum," Am. J. Physiol. Gastrointest. Liver Physiol. 278 (2000) G789-G796.

2. Ericsson. C.D., et al., "Bismuth Subsalicylate Inhibits Activity of Crude Toxins of Eschericia coli and cholerae." The Journal of Infectious Diseases, vol.136 no.5 (November 1977) 693-696.

3. Harvey, R.B., et al., "Effects of Treatment of Growing Swine with Aflatoxin and T-2 Toxin," Am. J. Vet. Res., vol.51 no.10 (October 1990) 1688-1693.

4. Jones. F.T, W.H. Hagler, and P.B. Hamilton. "Association of Low Levels of Aflatoxin in Feed with Productivity Loses in Commercial Broiler Operations," Poultry Science. 61 (1982) 861-868.

5. Nath, S.K., et al., "Emergence of Na+-Glucose Cotransport in an Epithelial Secretory Cell Line Sensitive to Cholera Toxin." Am. J. Physiol. Gastorintest. (1989) G335-G341.

6. Said, H.M., et al., "Transport Characteristics of Glutamine in Human Intestinal Brush-Border Membrane Vesicles." Am. J. Physiol. Gastrointest., (1989) G240-G245.

7. Silva, A.C., et al., "Efficacy of a Glutamine-Based Oral Rehydration Solution on the Electrolytes and Water Absorption in a Rabbit Model of Secretory Diarrhea Induced by Cholera Toxin," Journal of Pediatric Gastroenterology and Nutrition. 26 (1998)

513-519.

8. "Today's Drugs," British Medical Journal,, ed. British Medical Association, 4 (December 1969) 606607.

9. Veldman, A., *et al.,* "Carry-Over of Aflatoxin from Cows' Food to Milk." Anim. Prod., 55 (1992) 163168.

Terramin NASA Study by Dr. Benjamin Ershoff, Ph.D.

FINAL REPORT ON CONTRACT NUMBER NAS 9-3905

"pHYSIOLOGIC EFFECTS OF DIETARY CLAY SUPPLEMENTS"

Principal Investigator: Benjamin H. Ershoff, Ph.D. Co-Investigator: Gurwant S. Bajwa, D.V.M., Ph.D.

Institution: Institute for Biological Research 5345 West 102nd Street Los Angeles, California. 90045

Period Covered: 1 December, 1964 through June 15,1965

Submitted to: NASA Manned Spacecraft Center General Research Procurement Office, 2101 Webster-Seabrook Road, Houston, Texas. 77058

Please note: The plate images of all of the figures referred to in this study have not been reprinted due to image quality issues. The original plate images, however, are on file with the original study documents.

FOREWARD

The investigations described in this report were carried out during the period of 1 December 1964 to 15 June 1965. The research was supported by Contract No. NAS 9-3905 with NASA Manned Spacecraft Center, Procurement & Contracts Division, General Research Procurement Branch, Houston, Texas. The technical initiator and monitor of the project was Dr. Paul A. LaChance. The technical assistance of Mr. K. S. Dhindsa, L. Slaughter and L. Galpern of the Institute for Biological Research is gratefully acknowledged. Animal experimentation was done in accordance with the Principles of Laboratory Animal Care as established by the National Society for Medical Research.

Introduction

An extensive literature is available which has recently been reviewed by Cooper (1) indicating that the eating of clay has been observed in many peoples and animals in all parts of the world since antiquity. Many of the early writers considered clay-eating a manifestation of perverted appetite and responsible for a wide variety of physical ailments, debility and disease. Christopherson (2) and Mathieu (3) considered the principal danger of earth-eating or clay-eating to be that of swallowing the ova or embryos of intestinal parasites that may be present in these materials. Other writers have reported that clay eating was apparently without deleterious effects and may even have contributed toward well-being and health. Blair (4) described the widespread use of kanwa (earth from a "lick" near Lake Chad) for animals and humans in Nigeria. Long journeys were made to the lick to obtain a tribal supply of this earth, and it was then issued as rations to cattle and humans. Blair noted that from parturition to weaning the nursing mothers received a double ration, the infants being given lumps to suck from eighteen months onward. Lasch (5) reported that earth-eating was widespread in parts of Central Europe, particularly among women and children, and reported a number of the common superstitions concerning it: namely that it stops vomiting in pregnancy, is a remedy for constipation, serves as a specific against syphilis, secures a good posture in the foetus - causes it to "stand up", and the old superstition that it insures fine progeny. French (6) mentions that licking and eating of earth at certain recognized spots by domesticated animals has been such common feature of native animal husbandry in many parts of Africa that it is regarded as natural and even essential to health and fertility of livestock. If no edible earths are available locally it is customary to trek animals at regular intervals to areas where the above spots are located or to bring supplies of such soil to the animals. Foster (7) reported that earth or clay eating and other forms of pica in animals are indicative of a dietary deficiency. He noted that pica is prevalent among humans in widely scattered races, being commonest in pregnancy, lactation and the growth period when demands upon nutrition are greatest. From the analogy of natural and experimental cases of pica among animals, he suggested tentatively that the underlying factor in human pica lies in a deficiency in the inorganic constituents of the diet.

That earth or clay-eating is not merely of historical interest is indicated by some very recent references to it. In 1942 Dickens and Ford (8) made a survey of Negro school children in rural Mississippi. Their findings showed that of 207 children, 26% of the boys and 25% of the girls had eaten dirt or clay in the two-week period immediately preceding. A significant relationship was found between dirt and clay eating and the type of food taken, the dirt and clay-eaters being those who had fewer iron-rich foods. In 1952 deCastro (9) reported that in Bahia, a city of northeastern Brazil, nearly 40% of the school children were found to be suffering from anemia. When a supplement containing iron was added to their diet, the anemia rate dropped in four months to only 3%, confirming the fact that a deficiency was the cause of the disease. In places where this evil is most intense, one finds the strange phenomenon of geophagy or geomania, "the habit of eating earth". This custom, according to deCastro, represents a state of specific hunger. He states that "An analysis of the clays that are eaten as foods in Brazil confirms the fact observed by Cobert in Tunisia, and Batz in the Congo - they are for the most part clays which contain high proportions of iron salts. There are indications, however, that the beneficial effects of earth or clay eating may be due, at least in part, to factors other than their iron content. Thus Sydenstricker (10) observed that the eating of Kaolin was very common among pellagrins and that "Certain veins of clay were greatly esteemed; they carved it into sticks and ate it like candy". Of possible pertinence to the above is the report by Cooper (1) that "Keepers in the Baltimore Zoo routinely supply to the kangaroos three to four pounds of red clay per week as a dietary supplement. In discussing this with the administrative and veterinary staff of the Zoo they said it is common knowledge among zoo keepers that kangaroos in captivity are liable to develop lesions in the mouth which are more or less comparable to canine black tongue. When this condition in the kangaroo is discovered very early, it can be treated successfully by the administration of the B-complex (untreated, it is rapidly fatal), but it can be avoided entirely by supplying red clay to the animals regularly". Additional data indicating the beneficial effects of clay supplementation have recently been obtained by Ershoff and Bajwa (12) who found that certain batches of clay when incorporated at levels of 2% to 4'% in the diet largely counteracted the adverse effects of feeding a low calcium, low protein, low fat, cariogenic ration similar to diet 256 of McClure (13) on the weight increment, caries experience, and bone pathology of rats. The following experiments were undertaken to obtain further data on the effects of dietary clay supplements on the immature rat, hamster, mouse and miniature pig.

Experimental: Procedure and results

Experiment No. 1: Comparative effects of clay supplement "A" on the increment in body weight and the microscopic appearance of the long bones of immature male rats, hamsters, mice and miniature pigs fed a low calcium, low protein, low fat, non-heat processed, wheat flour-containing ration similar to diet 256 of McClure.

The basal ration used in these studies consisted of non-heat processed wheat flour, 80%; cerelose, 18%; and Dessicated Liver N.F., 2%; To each kg. of the above were added 5,000 U.S.P. units of vitamin A, 500 U.S.P. units of vitamin D2 and 100 mg. of alpha-tocopherol acetate. Diet Al was the unsupplemented basal ration indicated above; diets A2, A3, and A4 were similar but were supplemented with clay sample "A"1 at levels of 1%, 2%, and 4% of the ration respectively. The latter was incorporated in the diet in place of an equal amount of cerelose.

a. Studies with rats.

Sixty male rats of the Long-Evans strain were selected at an average body weight of 43.5 gm (range 37 to 53 gm) and were divided into four comparable groups of 15 rats each. Animals were placed in metal cages with raised screen bottoms (3 rats per cage) and the four groups were provided with diets Al to A4 respectively and distilled water ad libitum. The rats were weighed once weekly during the course of the experiment. Animals were sacrificed after eight weeks of feeding, The hind legs were placed in 10% neutral formalin for fixation, decalcified in 10% nitric acid in 10% formalin, washed with saturated lithium carbonate, dehydrated and infiltrated in the routine manner, imbedded in paraffin, and sections prepared at 7μ in thickness and stained with hematoxylin and eosin.

In agreement with previous findings (13) the ingestion of a clay supplement significantly improved the weight increment and the microscopic appearance of the long bones of immature rats fed a low calcium, low protein, low fat, non-heat-processed, wheat flour-containing ration similar to diet 256 of McClure. The increment in body weight was proportional to the level of clay supplement fed. The average weight increments in rats in the various groups after 2, 4, 6, and 8 weeks of feeding are summarized in Table 1.

Table 1

Effects of graded levels of clay supplement "A" on the weight increment of immature male rats fed a low calcium, low protein, low fat, non-heat-processed, wheat flour-containing ration (15 animals per group).

Dietary Group	Initial body wt (gm.)	Gain in body wt. after the following weeks of feeding (gm.)			
Basal ration (diet A1)	43.5	26.1	52.5	65.0	80.0
Basal ration + 1% clay supplement "A" (diet A2)	43.5	29.3	64.2	92.3	121.2
Basal ration + 2% clay supplement "A" (diet A3)	43.5	36.0	83.6	125.5	166.7
Basal ration + 4% clay supplement "A" (diet A4)	43.4	39.7	92.2	144.2	187.7

The bones of rats on the unsupplemented basal ration diet (diet 1A) showed gross and microscopic changes typical of rickets. Grossly the tibia and femur were bent, enlarged at the epiphyseal ends and knobby in appearance due to healed spontaneous fractures. Their marrow cavity was much widened. The articular surfaces had an uneven and somewhat flattened appearance due to under-developed and deficient supporting epiphyseal trabecular bone. Spontaneous fractures observed regularly were healed and were accompanied by moderate to marked chondromatosis and periosteal thickening. Pathologic changes occurred in all areas of the bones and were marked by severe cancellous degeneration of the cortical bone (Fig. 1), defective and deficient modelling of the spongiosa bone in the metaphysis (Fig. 4), abnormal bone regeneration, osteoid replacement and deficient mineralization of the formed bone, generalized osteoblastic hyperplasia, marked decrease in the hematopoietic marrow (Fig. 4,7), compensatory thickening and hyperplasia of the periosteum, and generalized congestion of the marrow. The cortical cancellous changes were regularly more severe along the convex aspect of the tibial and femoral shaft (Fig. 1). The epiphyseal plate was considerably thickened due to lack of ossification of its columns. The bone growth was usually so defective that the entire metaphysis was seen as a mere network of osteoid and hyperplastic osteoblasts (Fig. 4). These changes often extended deep into the diaphysis involving the entire shaft. The marrow everywhere was sparse in hematopoietic tissue and consisted mainly of fatty tissue and engorged capillaries (Fig. 7).

In contrast, the bones of rats fed the basal ration supplemented with 4% clay supplement "A" (diet A4) were normal in appearance with well developed compact cortical bone (Fig.2), a normal looking epiphyseal plate supported by normally modelled spongiosa bone (Fig. 5), and active hematopoietic marrow (Fig 8).

The cortical bone was virtually equal in thickness in the convex and concave side of the shaft of the femur. A significant improvement in the appearance of the femur and tibia both grossly and microscopically over that of rats fed the basal ration (diet Al) was also observed in rats fed the basal ration plus 1% and 2% clay supplement "A" (diets A2 and A3) respectively). The bone in the latter groups was not as well developed and modelled however, as that of rats fed clay supplement "A" at a 4% level (diet A4). Minimal rachitic changes were present in rats fed clay supplement "A" at a 1% level (diet A2)(Fig. 3 and 6) but not at the 2% level of supplementation (diet A3). The hematopoietic tissue although well developed in rats fed diets A2 and A3 compared to that of rats fed the unsupplemented basal ration (diet Al), was less abundant than that of rats fed the 4% clay supplement (diet A4)(Fig 8 and 9). No spontaneous fractures were observed in any of the rats fed clay supplement "A" at any level of feeding.

b. Studies with hamsters.

Sixty male hamsters were selected at an average body weight of 41.3 gm (range 36 to 49 gm) and were divided into four comparable groups of 15 animals each. Animals were placed in metal cages with raised screen bottoms (3 hamsters per cage) and the four groups were provided with diets Al to A4 respectively and distilled water ad libitum. The hamsters were weighed once weekly during the course of the experiment. Animals were sacrificed after 8 weeks of feeding. Histological sections of the hind legs were prepared by the same procedure as was employed in the rat experiments (section a, above). In agreement with findings in the rat experiments the ingestion of clay supplement "A" significantly improved the weight increment and the microscopic appearance of the long bones of immature male hamsters fed the low calcium, low protein, low fat, non-heat-processed, wheat flour-containing ration similar to diet 256 of McClure. In contrast to findings in rats, however, clay supplement "A" at a 1% level of supplementation (diet A2) did not differ significantly from the 2% and 4% levels of supplementation (diets A3 and A4, respectively) insofar as effects on increment in body weight were concerned. The average weight increments of hamsters in the various groups after 2,4,6, and 8 weeks of feeding are summarized in Table 2.

Table 2

Effects of graded levels of clay supplement "A" on the weight increment of immature male hamsters fed a low calcium, low protein, low fat, non-heat processed, wheat flour-containing ration (15 animals per group).

Dietary Group	Initial body wt (gm.)	Gain in body wt. after the following weeks of feeding (gm.)			
Basal ration (diet A1)	41.3	20.5	30.3	36.1	35.6
Basal ration + 1% clay supplement "A" (diet A2)	41.3	20.3	39.2	51.7	59.0
Basal ration + 2% clay supplement "A" (diet A3)	41.3	25.3	42.6	53.7	60.8
Basal ration + 4% clay supplement "A" (diet A4)	41.2	21.2	39.4	53.6	62.8

The bones of hamsters on the unsupplemented basal ration (diet A1) exhibited gross and microscopic changes typical of rickets but less marked than those of rats fed a similar diet. Normal modelling of the bone was generally preserved excepting moderate enlargement of the epiphyseal ends. The bones were smaller than normal and had some irregularity of their articular surfaces due to malformed and underdeveloped supporting trabecular bone. The major effects noted were on the hematopoietic marrow which was replaced in large part by fatty tissue (Fig. 10 and 16). The cortical bone was thin and porous and exhibited moderate chondromatosis and thickening and hyperplasia of the periosteum along the anterior and convex aspect of the shaft (Fig. 10). There was marked disruption of the normal architecture of the spongiosa bone due to defective growth and modelling of its supporting epiphyseal processes. The metaphysis was transformed into a network of thin, malformed and irregular trabeculae, hyperplastic osteoblasts and severely engorged blood vessels (Fig. 13). These changes were contiguous with similar lesions in the diaphysis. The trabeculae here and in the metaphysis were composed of thin osseous bone, persistent chondroblasts and abundant osteoid surrounded by multiple layers of proliferating osteoblasts (Fig. 13). The osteoclastic activity appeared to be either minimal or completely absent. The bony cortex along the posterior or concave aspect of the shaft although thin and less cancellous contained prominently widened canals. Slight to moderate periosteal thickening and hyperplasia were also present. (Fig. 10)

In contrast, the bones of hamsters fed the basal ration supplemented with 1% clay supplement "A" (diet A2) had only minimal rachitic changes and a near normal appearance. A marked increase in hematopoietic tissue was apparent throughout. Bone growth and modelling of the spongiosa bone were only slightly abnormal and the supporting epiphyseal processes had assumed a normal downward growth pattern and thickness. There was marked reduction of osteoplastic activity adjacent to the trabeculaewhich showed well developed bone and only a slight amount of osteoid. The epiphyseal plate had deeper penetrating blood capillaries and essentially normal thickness. The spongiosa bone contained abundant hematopoietic tissue. There was marked reduction of periosteal thickening except along the cancellous cortex of the anterior or convex part of the midshaft. Supplementation with 4% clay supplement "A" (diet A4) promoted bone growth and development to the fullest extent. The bones of hamsters in the latter group showed normal modelling, thick, well developed cortical bone (Fig. 11), abundant hematopoietic tissue (Fig. 11 and 17), normal bone growth (Fig. 14), and well developed trabecular bone (Fig. 14). The bones of hamsters fed the basal ration supplemented with 2% clay supplement "A" (diet A3) were devoid of rachitic changes and were normal in appearance but were less developed than those of hamsters fed the 4% clay supplement (diet A4)(Fig. 12, 15 and 18).

c. Studies with Mice.

Sixty male mice of the Swiss Webster strain were selected at an average body weight of 12.7 gm.(range 10.6 to 14.2 gm) and were divided into four comparable groups of 15 animals each. Animals were placed in metal cages with raised screen bottoms (5 mice per cage) and the four groups were provided with diets Al to A4 respectively and distilled water ad libitum. The mice were weighed once weekly during the course of the experiment. Animals were sacrificed after 8 weeks of feeding. Histologic sections of the hind legs were prepared by the same procedure as was employed in the rat experiment (section a, bove) . Findings indicate that clay supplement "A" at all levels of feeding resulted in a significantly greater weight increment than occurred in mice fed the unsupplemented basal ration (diet Al). The growth promoting effects of the clay supplement were particularly marked during the first 4 weeks of feeding. As in the case of hamsters (section b above) the weight increment of mice fed the basal ration + 1% clay supplement "A" (diet A2) did not differ significantly from that of mice fed the 2% or 4% clay supplements (diets A3 and A4 respectively). The average weight increments of mice in the various groups after 2,4,6, and 8 weeks of feeding are summarized in Table 3.

Table 3

Effects of graded levels of clay supplement "A" on the weight increment of immature male mice fed a low calcium, low protein, low fat, non-heat-processed, wheat flour-containing ration.

Dietary Group (15 animals per group)	Initial body wt (gm.)	Gain in body wt. after the following weeks of feeding (gm.)			
Basal ration (diet A1)	12.7	4.5	5.4 (13)	7.2 (13)	8.5 (13)
Basal ration + 1% clay supplement "A" (diet A2)	12.7	9.6	14.1	17.0	17.1
Basal ration + 2% clay supplement "A" (diet A3)	12.7	7.5	11.7	13.9	15.4
Basal ration + 4% clay supplement "A" (diet A4)	12.6	10.7	13.7	15.3	15.8

The values in parenthesis indicate the number of animals which survived and on which data are based, when less than the original number per group.

Among the various species of animals used in this study, mice fed the unsupplemented basal ration (diet AI) showed the least changes in respect to the microscopic appearance of the bone. Only mild rachitic changes were present as evidenced by a slightly defective bone growth pattern (Fig. 21). Otherwise, in respect to the cortical and trabecular bone, hematopoietic tissue and modelling, the bones were well developed and normal in appearance (Fig. 19). The addition of 1% clay supplement "A" to the basal ration prevented the early rachitic growth defect and promoted bone development. Higher levels of clay supplementation (diets A3 and A4) promoted bone development in excess of that obtained on diet A2, the effects being proportional to the amount of clay added (Fig. 20 and 22).

d. **Studies with miniature pigs.**

Eight male miniature pigs[3] were selected at an average body weight of 26.7 lb. (range 23 to 31 lbs.) and were divided into two comparable groups of 4 animals each. Animals were placed in wooden pens (4' in width, 6' in length, and 42" in height), containing 2 pigs per pen. The pens had solid wooden bottoms covered with wood shavings which were changed daily. One group was fed the unsupplemented basal ration (diet Al); the other, the basal ration + 2% clay supplement "A" (diet A3). The diets were mixed with distilled water immediately before feeding into a semi-liquid mash. These diets as well as an additional supply of distilled water were provided ad libitum daily. The pigs were weighed at 2 week intervals during the course of the experiment. Animals were sacrificed after 12 weeks of feeding. One hind limb of each pig was removed at the hip joint at the time of sacrifice and x-ray pictures taken for examination. Histological sections of the other leg were prepared at the proximal end of the tibia for microscopic examination. In contrast to findings in rats, hamsters and mice, miniature pigs fed clay supplement "A" at a 2% level in the ration (diet A3) did not exhibit an increment in body weight significantly greater than that obtained on the unsupplemented basal ration (diet Al). The average weight increments of miniature pigs on the test diets during the 12 week experimental period are summarized in Table 4.

Table 4

Effects of clay supplement "A" when fed at a 2% level in the ration on the weight increment of immature male pigs fed a low calcium, low protein, low fat, non-heat processed, wheat flour-containing ration (4 animals per group)

Dietary Group (15 animals per group)	Initial body wt (gm.)	Gain in body wt. after the following weeks of feeding (lbs.)					
Weeks of Feeding		2	4	6	8	10	12
Basal ration (diet A1)	27.1	3.8	9.8	14.1	19.3	24.3	28.5
Basal ration + 2% clay supplement "A" (diet A3)	26.3	3.8	8.2	13.1	18.7	26.2	30.3

The miniature pigs on the unsupplemented basal ration (diet A1) exhibited gross findings suggestive of early rickets. Both the tibia and femur had enlarged joints due to widened epiphyseal ends and exhibited decreased density in the x-ray film. The femoral neck was shortened and the head increased in diameter (Fig. 23 and 24). Histologically, the tibial shaft showed demineralization, absorption and increase in osteoid as evidence of early osteoporotic changes (fig. 25). The cortical and trabecular bone was thin throughout. Bone growth was defective resulting in malformed spongiosa bone, especially its supporting epiphyseal processes (Fig. 27). The spongiosa bone showed marked compensatory fibroblastic proliferation, a defective trabecular modelling, marked congestion and scant hematopoietic tissue and engorged blood vessels (Fig. 29). In contrast to the above miniature pigs fed the basal ration + 2% clay supplement "A" (diet A3) had bones with only slight rachitic alterations. On x-ray examination they were denser, more normally modelled and more developed than those of pigs fed the unsupplemented basal ration (diet I)(Figs. 23 and 24). The trabecular bone was thicker and more compact but not fully developed

(Fig. 26). The epiphyseal trabecular and spongiosa bone were more developed and normally modelled (Fig. 28). Bone growth was more normal as shown by deeper capillary penetration, moderate ossification, reduced thickness, and more normally modelled supporting spongiosa processes of the eiphyseal plate (Fig.30). The marrow contained a moderate amount of hematopoietic tissue and near normal vasculature (Fig 30).

Experiment No. 2: Comparative effects of calcium carbonate and clay supplement "A" on the increment in body weight and the microscopic appearance of the long bones of immature male rats fed different types of low calcium diets.

Four basal low-calcium were employed in the present experiment: Diets Al, B1, Cl, and DI: Diet Al was identical to the unsupplemented basal ration used in Experiment No. I and was a low calcium, low protein, low fat, non-heat-processed, wheat flour-containing ration similar to diet 256 of McClure. Diet B1 was similar to diet Al but rye flour was incorporated in the ration in place of the non-heat-processed wheat flour. The composition of diet B1 was: Rye flour, 80%; cerelose, 18%; and Desiccated Liver N.F., 2%. To each kg. of the above were added 5,000 U.S.P. units of vitamin A, 500 U.S.P. units of vitamin D2, and 100 mg_ of alpha-tocopherol acetate. Diet Cl was a highly purified, calcium-deficient ration *containing* casein as the source of dietary protein. It consisted of: Vitamin-Free Test Casein[4], 18%; cottonseed oil, 5%;calcium-free salt mixture[5] 3%; and sucrose, 74%. To each kg. of the above were added the following vitamins: thiamine hydrochloride, 4 mg; riboflavin, 4 mg.; pyridoxine hydrochloride, 4 mg; calcium pantothenate, 40 mg; nicotinic acid, 100 mg.; ascorbic acid, 200 mg.; biotin, 1 mg.; folic acid, 2 mg.; para-aminobenzoic acid, 200 mg.; inositol, 400 mg.; vitamin B_{12}, 100 µg; 2-methyl-1, 4-napthoquinone, 5 mg; choline chloride, 2 gm; vitamin A, 5,000 U.S.P. units; vitamin D2, 500 U.S.P. units; and alpha-tocopherol acetate 100 mg. The vitamins were added in place of an equal amount of sucrose. Diet D1 was similar to diet Cl but contained methioninesupplemented soy protein in place of casein as the source of dietary protein. It consisted of Soya Assay Protein[4], 18%; cottonseed oil, 5%; calcium-free salt mixture,[5] 3%;ail-methionine, 0.375% and sucrose 73.625%. To each kg. of the above were added the same vitamin supplements as were added to diet Cl. The vitamin supplements and dl-methionine were added in place of an equal amount of sucrose.

a. Comparative effects of calcium carbonate and graded levels of clay supplement "A" on the increment in body weight and the microscopic appearance of the long bones of immature male rats fed a low calcium, low protein, low fat, non-heat-processed, wheat flour-containing ration similar to diet 256 of McClure.

Sixty-six male rats of the Long-Evans strain averaging 43.5 gm. in body weight (range 37-53 gm.) were employed in the present experiment. Animals were divided into 5 groups, 4 of which consisted of 15 animals each; the 5th group of 6 rats. One group of 15 rats was fed the unsupplemented basal ration (diet Al). Three additional groups of 15 rats each were fed the above basal ration supplemented with 1%, 2% and 4% clay supplement "A" (diets A2, A3, A4 respectively). The above 4 groups were the same animals that were reported on under section "A" of Experiment No. 1. The 5th group was fed diet AS which consisted of the above basal ration plus 3 gm. $CaCO_3$ per kg. of diet which was added in place of an equal amount of cerelose. This amount of $CaCO_3$ contained the same amount of calcium present in the clay supplement "A" incorporated in a kg. of diet A4. Animals were placed in metal cages with raised screen bottoms (3 rats per cage) and were provided with the test diets and distilled water ad libitum. The rats were weighed once weekly during the course of the experiment. Animals were sacrificed after 8 weeks of feeding and histological sections of the hind legs prepared as described under section a, experiment 1. Findings indicate that whereas clay supplement "A" at levels of 1%, 2% and 4% of the ration (diets A2, A3 and A4 respectively) resulted in a significant increment in body weight over that obtained on the unsupplemented basal ration (diet Al),the $CaCO_3$ supplement (diet A5) was ineffective in promoting an increment in body weight. The average weight increments of rats in the various groups after 2, 4, 6, and 8 weeks of feeding are summarized in Table 5.

Table 5

Dietary Group	No. of rats	Initial	Gain in body wt. after the following weeks of feeding (gm.)			
Weeks of Feeding			2	4	6	8
Basal ration (diet A1)	15	43.5	26.1	52.5	65.0	80.0
Basal ration + 1% clay supplement "A" (diet A2)	15	43.5	29.3	64.2	92.3	121.2
Basal ration + 2% clay supplement "A" (diet A3)	15	43.5	36.0	83.6	125.5	166.7
Basal ration + 4% clay supplement "A" (diet A4)	15	43.3	39.7	92.2	144.2	187.7
Basal ration + 2% clay supplement "A" (diet A5)	6	43.6	27.8	43.6	63.0	73.8

The microscopic appearance of rats fed diets A1, A2, A3 and A4 was previously reported under section a, experiment 1 (Fig. 1 to 9). Supplementation with $CaCO_3$ (diet A5) resulted in a moderate improvement in the appearance of bone (Fig. 31, 32, and 33) over that of rats fed the unsupplemented basal ration (diet A1). Rats fed the $CaCO_3$ supplement had bones which were similar in appearance to those of rats fed the 1% clay supplement (diet A2). $CACO_3$ supplementation, however, resulted in no improvement in the appearance of hematopoietic tissue over that of rats fed the unsupplemented basal ration in contrast to the well developed hematopoietic tissue in rats fed the 1% clay supplement (diet A2) (Fig. 9 and 33).

b. Comparative elects of calcium carbonate and graded levels of clay supplement "A" on the increment in body weight and the microscopic appearance of the long bones of immature male rats fed a low calcium, low protein, low fat, rye flour containing ration.

Fifty-four male rats of the Long-Evans strain averaging 41.7 gm. in body weight (range 36 to 50 gm) were employed in the present experiment. Animals were divided into 5 groups, 4 of which consisted of 12 animals each; the 5th group of 6 rats. One group of 12 rats was fed the unsupplemented basal ration (diet B1). Three additional groups of 12 rats each were fed the above basal ration supplemented with 1%, 2% and 4% clay supplement "A" (diets B2, B3 and B4 respectively). The 5th group was fed diet B5 which consisted of the above basal ration plus 3 gm. $CaCO_3$ per kg. of diet which was added in place of an equal amount of cerelose. This amount of $CaCO_3$ contained the same amount of calcium present in the clay supplement "A" incorporated in a kg. of diet B4. Animals were placed in metal cages with raised screen bottoms (3 rats per cage) and were provided with the test diets and distilled water ad libitum. The rats were weighed once weekly during the course of the experiment. Animals were sacrificed after 3 weeks of feeding and histological sections of the hind legs prepared as described under section a, experiment 1, above. Findings indicate that the ingestion of clay supplement "A" significantly improved the weight increment and the microscopic appearance of the long bones of immature male rats fed a low calcium, low protein, low fat, rye flour-containing ration. The increment in body weight was proportional to the level of clay supplement fed. In contrast to the effects obtained with clay supplement "A", $CaCO_3$ when fed at a level of 3 gm. per kg. of diet was without activity in promoting an increment in body weight. On the contrary, the weight increment of rats fed the $CaCO_3$ supplement was less *than that of rats fed the* unsupplemented basal ration (diet 31). The average weight increments of rats fed diets BI-B5 after 2, 4, 6, and 8 weeks of. feeding are summarized in Table 6.

Table 6

Comparative effects of calcium carbonate and graded levels of clay supplement "A" on the increment in body weight of immature male rats fed a low calcium, low protein, low fat, rye flour-containing ration.

Dietary Group	No. of rats	Initial Gain in body wt. after the following weeks of feeding (gm.)			
Weeks of Feeding		2	4	6	8
Basal ration (diet B1)	12	41.7	24.0	42.1	55.7	78.9
Basal ration + 1% clay supplement "A" (diet B2)	12	41.6	23.7	54.7	81.7	107.3
Basal ration + 2% clay supplement "A" (diet B3)	12	41.7	31.2	71.1	110.3	144.9
Basal ration + 4% clay supplement "A" (diet B4)	12	41.7	38.3	81.3	130.6	164.4
Basal ration + 2% Basal ration + 3 gm CaCO3 per kg. of diet (diet B5)	6	41.6	24.7	38.7	48.2	54.7

The bones of rats on the unsupplemented basal ration (diet B1) showed gross and microscopic changes typical of rickets. Grossly the tibia and femur were bent, malformed and enlarged at their epiphyseal ends. Their articular surfaces were uneven and somewhat flattened in appearance due to thin articular cartilage supported by thin and underdeveloped epiphyseal trabecular bone. Spontaneous fractures were common giving the bone a knobby appearance. The lesions were generalized and characterized by marked thinning, porosity, demineralization and increased ostcoid of the cortical bone, especially along the anterior or convex aspect of the shaft (Fig. 34), widening and thickening of the epiphyseal, defective and deficient bone growth (fig 38), and defective modelling of the trabeculae and epiphyseal processes of the spongiosa bone (Fig. 38). The marrow was deficient in hematopoietic tissue and was replaced by fatty tissue (Fig. 42). The hematopoietic tissue of rats fed diet B1, however, was more abundant than that of rats fed diet Al (Fig. 7 and 42). The above changes were essentially similar to but less severe than those observed in rats fed the unsupplemented basal ration (diet Al) (Fig. 1, 4, and 7).

In contrast to the above the bones of rats fed the basal ration supplemented with 4% clay supplement "A" (diet B4) had fully and well developed bones with compact and mineralized cortical bone (Fig. 35), normal appearing spongiosa, epiphyseal trabecular bone and hematopoietic marrow (Fig. 39 and 43); A significant improvement in the appearance of the femur and tibia both grossly and microscopically over that of rats fed the basal ration (diet B1) was also observed in rats fed the basal ration plus 1% and 2% clay supplement "A" (diets B2 and B3 respectively)(Fig.36,40, and 44).The bone in the latter groups was not as well developed and modelled as that of rats fed clay supplement "A" at a 4% level (diet B4) and some rachitic changes were present in these groups, particularly in rats fed the 1% clay supplement (diet B2). No spontaneous fractures were observed, however, in any of the rats fed clay supplement "A" and all animals fed rations containing this supplement (Diets B2, B3 and B4) had bone marrows with abundant hematopoietic tissue. Rats fed the $CaCO_3$ supplement (diet B5) had bones which were similar in microscopic appearance to that of rats fed the 2% clay supplement (diet B3) (Fig.36,37,40,41,44, and 45). Little if any improvement was observed however, in the amount of hemato-poietic tissue in rats fed diet B5 over that of rats fed the basal ration (diet B1) C. Comparative effects of calcium carbonate and graded levels of clay supplement "A" on the increment in body weight and the microscopic appearance of the long bones of immature male rats fed a purified, calcium-deficient ration containing casein as the source of dietary protein.

Fifty-four male rats of the Long-Evans strain averaging 41.8 gm in body weight (range 36 to 50 gm) were employed in the present experiment. Animals were divided into 5 groups, 4 of which consisted of 12 animals each; the 5th group of 6 rats. One group of 12 rats was fed the unsupplemented basal ration (diet Cl). Three additional groups of 12 rats each were fed the basal ration supplemented with 1%, 2% and 4% clay supplement "A" (diets C2, C3 and C4, respectively). The 5th group was fed diet C5 which consisted of the above basal ration plus 3 gm. $CaCO_3$ per kg. of diet which was added in place of an equal amount of sucrose. This amount of CaCO3 contained the same amount of calcium present in the clay supplement "A" incorporated in a kg. of diet C4. Animals were placed in metal cages with raised screen bottoms (3 rats per cage) and were provided with the test diets and distilled water ad libitum. The rats were weighed once weekly during the course of the experiment. During the 5th week of feeding a number of animals fed the unsupplemented basal ration (diet CI) lost weight and during the ensuing 2 weeks 7 of the 12 rats in this group died. The experiment was accordingly terminated and animals sacrificed after 7 weeks of feeding. Histological sections of the hind legs were prepared as described under section a, experiment 1. Findings indicate that the ingestion of clay supplement "A" significantly improved the weight increment And the microscopic appearance of the long bones of immature male rats fed a purified, calcium-deficient ration containing casein as the source of dietary protein. The increment in body weight was proportional to the level of clay supplement fed.

In contrast to the effects obtained on diet A1 and diet B5, CaCO3 when fed at a level of 3 gm. per kg. of diet also promoted a significant increment in body weight over that obtained on the unsupplemented basal ration (diet Cl) although less than that obtained with 4% clay supplement "A" (diet C4). The average weight increments of rats fed diets C1-C5 after 2,4,6, and 7 weeks of feeding are summarized in Table 7.

Table 7

Comparative effects of calcium carbonate and graded levels of clay supplement "A" on the increment in body weight of immature male rats fed a purified, calcium-deficient ration containing casein as the source of dietary protein.

Dietary Group	No. of rats	Initial Gain in body wt. after the following weeks of feeding (gm.)			
Weeks of Feeding		2	4	6	7
Basal ration (diet C1)	12	41.8	53.6	79.5	73.4 (9)	82.2 (5)
Basal ration + 1% clay supplement "A" (diet C2)	12	41.8	56.0	101.8	126.0	137.4
Basal ration + 2% clay supplement "A" (diet C3)	12	41.8	58.8	122.7	176.5	195.5
Basal ration + 4% clay supplement "A" (diet C4)	12	41.7	66.0	144.7	210.4	231.7
Basal ration + 3 gm CaCO3 per kg. of diet (diet C5)	6	41.8	58.2	123.2	180.5	200.7

The values in parenthesis indicate the number of animals which survived and on which data are based when less than the original number per group. The bones of rats on the unsupplemented basal ration (diet Cl) showed severe rachitic changes. The femur and tibia were markedly bent and deformed with epiphyseal ends about twice the normal size.

The bones had a knobby appearance due to multiple spontaneous fractures. The articular surfaces were dented and prominently flattened. Microscopically these bones were so malformed that the metaphysis and diaphysis were indistinguishable in appearance consisting of a network of trabecular osteoid, hyperplastic osteoblasts and severely congested vessels. The cortical and trabecular bane throughout were reduced to a thin lamina of osteoid surrounded by layers of hyperplastic osteoblasts (Fig. 46). The epiphyseal plate was 2 to 3 times normal width and was devoid of penetrating capillaries. The epiphyseal supporting processes of the spongiosa were poorly developed (Fig. 50). The marrow cavity was absent and was largely replaced by a network of osteoid tissue with the hematopoietic tissue severely decreased (Fig. 50). Moderate to severe chondromatosis were noted adjacent to the fractured bone. The blood vessels were generally enlarged and had a cavernous appearance. The periosteum was increased in thickness and hyperplastic. In contrast to the above, rats fed the basal ration plus 4% clay supplement "A" (diet C4) had well developed bones with thick and mineralized cortical and trabecular bone (Fig. 47); normal bone growth and modelling of the pongiosa bone and supporting epiphyseal processes (Fig. 51) and abundant hematopoietic tissue (Fig. 47). No spontaneous fractures were observed in any of the rats in this group. A significant improvement in the appearance of the femur and tibia both grossly and microscopically over that of rats fed the basal ration (diet CI) was also observed in rats fed the basal ration plus 1% and 2% clay supplement "A" (diets C2 and C3 resp,) (Fig.48 and 52). The bones in the latter groups were not as well developed and modelled as that of rats fed clay supplement at a 4% level (diet C4) and a number of rachitic changes were present in these groups, particularly in rats fed the 1% clay supplement (diet C2). Spontaneous fractures were also observed in a number of rats fed the 1% and 2% clay supplements. Rats fed the $CaCO_3$ supplement (diet C5) also showed a *significant* improvement in the appearance of the femur and tibia both grossly and microscopically (Fig 49 and 53) over that of rats fed the basal ration (diet Cl) but were less well developed than those fed the 4% clay supplement (diet C4). No fractures were observed in any of rats in this group. The bones of rats fed diet C5 were intermediate in appearance between those of rats fed the 2% and 4% clay supplements (diets C3 and C4 respectively).

d. **Comparative effects of calcium carbonate and graded levels of clay supplement "A" on the increment in body weight and the**

microscopic appearance of the long bones of immature male rats fed a purified, calcium-deficient ration *containing* methionine-supplemented soy protein as the source of dietary protein.

Fifty-four male rats of the Long-Evans strain averaging 41.9 grams in body weight (range 36 to 51 gm) were employed in the present experiment. Animals were divided into 5 groups, 4 of which consisted of 12 animals each; the 5th group of 6 rats. One group of 12 rats was fed the unsupplemented basal ration (diet Dl). Three additional groups of 12 rats each were fed the basal ration supplemented with 1%, 2%, and 4% clay supplement "A" (diets D2, D3, and D4 respectively). The 5th group was fed diet D5 which consisted of the above basal ration plus 3 gm. $CaCO_3$ per kg. of diet which was added in place of an equal amount of sucrose. This amount of $CaCO_3$ contained the same amount of calcium present in the clay supplement "A" encorporated in a kg. of diet C4. Animals were placed in metal cages with raised screen bottoms (3 rats per cage) and were provided with test diets and distilled water ad libitum. The rats were weighed once weekly during the course of the experiment. During the 5th week of feeding as was the case in rats fed diet Cl a number of animals fed the unsupplemented basal ration (diet Dl) lost weight and during the ensuing 2 weeks 6 of the 12 rats in this group died. The experiment was terminated after 7 weeks of feeding, animals sacrificed, and histological sections of the hind legs prepared as described under section a, experiment 1. Findings indicate that the ingestion of clay supplement "A" significantly improved the weight increment and the microscopic appearance of the long bones of immature male rats fed a purified, calcium-deficient ration containing methionine-supplemented soy protein as the source of dietary protein. The increment in body weight was proportional to the level of clay supplement fed. $CaCO_3$ when fed at a level of 3 gm. per 1g. of diet promoted an increment in body weight comparable to that obtained with 4% clay supplement "A". The average weight increments of rats fed diets D1-D5 after 2, 4, 6, and 7 weeks of feeding are summarized in Table 8.

Table 8

Comparative effects of calcium carbonate and graded levels of clay supplement "A" on the increment in body weight of immature male rats fed a purified, calcium-deficient ration containing methionine-supplemented soy protein as the source of dietary protein. The values in parenthesis indicate the number of animals which survived and on which data are based when less than the original number per group.

Dietary Group	No. of rats	Initial Gain in body wt. after the following weeks of feeding (gm.)			
Weeks of Feeding		2	4	6	7
Basal ration (diet D1)	12	41.9	60.0	89.6 (11)	90.9 (10)	82.3 (6)
Basal ration + 1% clay supplement "A" (diet D2)	12	41.9	47.8	109.3	148.7	162.4
Basal ration + 2% clay supplement "A" (diet D3)	12	41.8	56.7	130.2	193.3	211.4
Basal ration + 4% clay supplement "A" (diet D4)	12	41.8	66.7	145.3	219.9	244.4
Basal ration + 3 gm CaCO3 per kg. of diet (diet D5)	6	41.9	56.2	141.7	217.2	241.7

Histologically the bones of rats fed the basal ration (diet Dl) although rachitic were significantly better developed than those of rats fed the purified basal ration (diet Cl). The cortical bone was less porous; it was wider and more mineralized than that of rats on the latter diet (Fig. 54). The epiphyseal plate was decreased in width and thickness and was supported by better formed spongiosa bone (Fig. 57). The marrow contained more hematopoietic tissue and was less congested (Fig. 54). Spontaneous fractures were observed however, in all rats fed the basal ration (diet Dl). In general, rats fed the latter ration were comparable both grossly and in microscopic appearance to those fed diet Al. Rats fed the basal ration plus 4% clay supplement "A" (diet D4) were normal in appearance with well developed compact bone (Fig.

55 and 58). A significant improvement in the appearance of the femur and tibia both grossly and microscopically over that of rats fed the basal ration (diet Dl) was also observed in rats fed the basal ration plus 1% and 2% clay supplement "A" (diets D2 and D3 respectively). The bone in the latter groups was not as well developed and modelled, however, as that of rats fed clay supplement "A" at a 4% level (diet D4). Minimal rachitic changes were present in rats fed clay supplement "A" at a 1% level (diet D2) but not at the 2% level of supplementation (diet D3). The hematopoietic tissue although well developed in rats fed diets D2 and D3 compared to that of rats fed the unsupplemented ration (Dl) was less abundant than that of rats fed the 4% clay supplement (diet D4). No spontaneous fractures were observed in any of the rats fed clay supplement "A" at any level of feeding. Rats fed the $CaCO_3$ supplement (diet D5) also showed a significant improvement in the appearance of the femur and tibia both grossly and microscopically (Fig. 56 and 59) over that of rats fed the basal ration (diet Dl) but were less well developed than those fed the 4% clay supplement (diet D4). No fractures were observed in any of the rats fed diet D5. These animals were intermediate in appearance between those fed the 2% and 4% clay supplements (diet D3 and D4, respectively).

Experiment No. 3: Comparative effects of clay sample "A" and other clay and soil samples on the weight increment of immature male rats fed a low calcium, low protein, low fat, non-heat-processed, wheat flour containing ration similar to diet 256 of McClure.

One hundred and four male rats of the Long-Evans strain were selected at an average boyly weight of 44.2 gm (range 39 to 52 gm) and were divided into 13 comparable groups of & animals each. One group was fed the unsupplemented basal ration (diet Al) ; the others were fed a similar ration plus the various supplements indicated in Table S. The test supplements were incorporated in the diets in place of an equal amount of acielose. Animals were placed in metal cages with raised screen bottoms and were provided the various diets and distilled water ad libitum. Rats were weighed once weekly during the course of the experiment. Data were obtained on the average weight increment of rats in the various groups over a 6 week period. Results are summarized in Table 9.

Table 9

Comparative effects of clay sample "A" and other clay and soil samples on the weight increment of immature male rats fed a low calcium, low protein, low fat, non-heat-processed wheat flour-containing ration similar to diet 256 of McClure (8 animals per group).*

Dietary Group	Initial Body wt. gm.	Gain in body weight after the following weeks of feeding (gm.).		
		2	4	6
Basal ration (diet Al)	44.6	22.8	48.5	62.0
Basal ration + following supplements:				
2% clay supplement "A"	44.0	34.6	74.1	109.6
2% clay supplement "B"	44.0	30.0	68.4	101.1
2% clay supplement "C"	44.1	26.7	63.7	96.2
2% clay supplement "D"	44.0	28.8	63.4	95.6
2% clay supplement "A"	44.0	29.0	60.0	90.9
2% clay supplement "F"	44.0	23.9	51.1	72.5
2% bentonite	44.6	27.8	63	96.1
2% kaolin	44.4	24.4	47.5	84.7
2% ditch bank dirt	44.0	22.8	43.8	67.8

2% top soil	44.2	21.8	46.3	62.2
2% beach sand	44.1	21.2	41.0	57.8
2% silica	44.2	22.4	46.5	63.8

*All clay samples employed in this experiment were ground to a particle size that passed through a # 12 screen. Clay sample "A" was the same material used in experiments No. 1 and 2. It was pinkish tan clay obtained from a deposit near Brawley, California. Clay sample "B" was a grayish-white clay obtained from the Coyote Mountain area 35 miles west of Brawley. Clay sample "C" was a brownish clay obtained approximately 200 yards east of clay sample "A". Clay sample "D" was a tan colored clay obtained approximately 1/2 mile south of clay sample "A". Clay sample "E" was a pinkish tan clay obtained approximately 3/4ths of a mile south east of clay sample "A". Clay sample "F" was a pinkish tan clay obtained from an area approximately 5 miles south of clay sample "A". The ditch bank dirt was obtained from an area near Brawley, California. The top soil was obtained from grounds adjacent to the Institute for Biological Research at its former location in Culver City, Calif. The beach sand was obtained from Santa Monica, California.

Findings indicate that the various clays differed significantly in growth-promoting activity. The most active material tested was clay sample "A" which promoted a highly significant increment in body weight over that obtained on the unsupplemented basal ration (diet A1) whereas clay sample "F" and kaolin were virtually devoid of growth promoting activity. It is of interest that clay samples "C", "D", and "E" which were obtained within one mile of the clay sample "A" deposit were consistently less active than clay sample "A" in growth-promoting activity. No correlation was observed between the color of the clay and its effect on the increment in body weight. Clay sample "B" which was only slightly less active than clay sample "A" was grayish white in color in contrast to the pinkish tan appearance of clay supplement "A". Furthermore, clay sample "F" which had little if any growth-promoting activity was indistinguishable from clay sample "A" in appearance. Bentonite had significant growth-promoting activity although less than clay supplement "A". Silica and the ditch bank dirt, top soil and beach sand supplements were devoid of activity.

Discussion

Findings indicate that clay supplement "A" when incorporated at levels of 1%, 2% and 4% of the diet caused a highly significant increment in body weight and prevented the occurrence of pathological changes in the long bones of immature hats, hamsters and mice fed a low calcium, low protein, low fat, non-heat-processed, wheat flour containing ration similar to diet 256 of McClure with effects proportional to the level of clay supplement fed. The protective effect of clay supplement "A" was also observed on the microscopic and radiological appearance of the long bones of miniature pigs fed rations similar to the above although in this species no growth promoting effect was noted. Clay supplement "A" was also active in promoting growth and preventing pathological changes in the long bones of rats fed (a) a low calcium, low protein, low fat, rye flour-containing ration (b) a highly purified, calcium-deficient ration containing casein as the source of dietary protein, and (c) a highly purified, calcium-deficient ration containing methionine-supplemented soy protein as the source of dietary protein. Findings indicate that the protective effects of clay supplement "A" when fed with the wheat flour and rye flour-containing rations were due in large part to some factor or factors other than its calcium content. This is indicated by the fact that calcium when fed in the form of $CaCO_3$ at the same level of calcium as was provided by clay supplement "A" at a 4% level in the diet had no growth promoting activity and was far less active than the 4% clay supplement in preventing the pathological changes which occurred in the long bones of rats fed the unsupplemented wheat flour and rye flour-containing rations. The beneficial effects of clay supplement "A" when fed with the purified, casein-containing and soy protein-containing rations, however, were due in large part to its calcium content. This is indicated by the fact that calcium when fed in the form of $CaCO_3$ at the same level of calcium as was provided by clay supplement "A" at a 4% level in the diet was only slightly less active than the 4% clay supplement in promoting increment in body weight although it was substantially less active than the latter in promoting bone development in rats fed the purified casein-containing and soy-protein-containing rations. The latter findings suggest either that the calcium in clay supplement "A" is absorbed more efficiently than the calcium in $CaCO_3$ or that clay supplement "A" contains some factor or factors other than calcium which promotes improved calcium utilization and/or bone formation. Further studies are indicated to determine the factor or factors in clay supplement "A" responsible for its protective effects and the modus operandi involved. Although clay sample "A" was the most active of the various clay samples tested in promoting a weight increment in immature rats fed the low calcium, low protein, low fat, non-heat-processed wheat flour-containing ration other clay samples were also active in this regard although some were devoid of growth promoting activity. No correlation was observed between the color of the clay and its effect on increment in body weight.

Present findings indicate that clay supplement "A" was active in preventing rachitic changes and promoting bone development in several species of young growing animals. Further studies are indicated to determine whether this supplement would also be active in prevent osteoporosis in adult animals with normal skeletal development when placed on calcium-deficient and other osteoporosis-inducing diets. Studies are warranted to determine the effects of clay supplement "A" on calcium excretion and the occurrence and severity of osteoporosis in adult animals whose hind limbs are immobilized in bivalved body casts. Normal osteoblastic activity depends to a large measure upon the stresses of muscular contractions and weight-bearing compression forces (14-18). The loss of these stimuli results in insufficient formation of bone matrix, inadequate deposition of calcium salts and increased porosity of bone. The softened bone loses its strength and resiliency and is subject to fractures. It would be of interest to determine whether clay supplement "A" which had significant activity in promoting osteoblastic activity, formation of bone matrix and deposition of calcium salts in young animals fed calcium-deficient rations would also be active under conditions where the stresses of muscular contractions and weight-bearing compression forces are removed as would occur under plaster immobilization. Such studies might also be pertinent to conditions of prolonged exposure to a sub-gravity or weightless state where an increased calcium excretion is likely to occur. Since a high incidence of renal tract calculus formation might also be anticipated under the latter conditions, it would be of interest to determine whether clay supplement "A" would be active in preventing or minimizing the occurrence of renal calculi under experimental conditions where the latter occur.

Summary

Studies were conducted on the effects of clay supplementation on the weight increment and microscopic appearance of the long bones of immature male rats, hamsters, mice and miniature pigs fed a low calcium, low protein, low fat, non-heat-processed, wheat flour-containing ration similar to diet 256 of McClure. Findings indicate that the clay supplementation at levels of 1%, 2% and 4% in the above diet caused a highly significant increment in body weight and prevented the occurrence of pathological changes which were observed in the long bones of immature rats, hamsters and mice fed the unsupplemented diet. Effects were proportional to the level of clay supplement fed. The protective effect of the clay supplement was also observed on the microscopic and radiological appearance of the long bones of.miniature pigs although in this species no growth-promoting effect was noted. Clay supplementation at the above levels of feeding was also active in promoting growth and preventing pathological changes in the long bones of rats fed (a) a low calcium, low protein, low fat, rye flour-containing ration (b) a highly purified calcium-deficient ration containing casein as the source of dietary protein, and (c) a highly purified, calcium-deficient ration containing methionine-supplemented soy protein as the source of dietary protein. Findings indicate that the protective effects of the clay supplement when fed with the wheat flour and rye flour-containing rations were due in large part to some factor or factors other than its calcium content. The beneficial effects of clay supplementation when fed with the purified casein-containing and soy protein-containing rations, however, were due primarily to its serving as a source of dietary calcium although evidence was obtained that the clay supplement contained some factor or factors other than calcium which promoted improved calcium utilization and/or bone formation. A number of clays were tested and found to differ significantly in growth-promoting activity.

REFERENCES

Cooper, M,: Pica. Charles C. Thomas, Publisher, Springfield, Ill. 1957.

Christopherson, J.B.: Earth eating in the Egyptian Sudan. J. Trop. Med., xiii:3, 1910.

Mathieu, J.: Geophagy and intestinal parasitism in Morocco. Arch, de med. d. enf., 30:591, 1927.

Blair, M.D.: Native salts in Nigeria, C,R.(D),7,1926.

Lasch, R.: Ueber geophagie. Mitt. Anthropol. Gesellsch,, Wein 28:214, 1098.

French, M.H.: Geophagia in animals. E. African M.J., XXII: 103, 1945.

Foster, J.W.: Pica. Kenya and E. African M.J. , 63, 1927.

Dickens, D., and Ford, R.N.: Geophagy (diet eating) among Mississippi school children. Am. Soc. Rev., VII: 1,59,1942.

DeCastro, J.: The Geography of Hunger, Little, Brown & Co., Boston, 1952, p. 87.

Sydenstricker, V.: Personal communication, cited by Cooper (1), p. 86.

Cooper, M. (1), p. 87.

Ershoff, B.H. and Bajwa, G.S.: Unpublished Findings

McClure, F.J.: Wheat cereal diets, rat caries, lysine and minerals. J. Nutrition, 65:619, 1958-

Geiser, M. and Trueta, J.: Muscle action, bone rarefaction and bone formation: an experimental study. J. Bone and Joint Surg., 40-8:232,1958.

Grey, E. G., and Carr, J.L.: An experimental study of the factors responsible for noninfectious bone atrophy. Bull. Johns Hopkins Hosp., 26:331, 1915.

Stevenson, F.H.: The osteoporosis of immobilization in recumb' ency. J. of Bone and Joint Surg. 34-3:256, 1952.

Symposium on bone as a tissue. Lankenau Hospital Conference, Oct. 30-31, 1958, Blakiston Co., New York.

Urist, M.R.: The etiology of osteoporosis. J.A.M.A., 169: 710, 1959.

Dodds, M.L. and Lawe, R.: Mineralization of a cereal diet as it affects cariogenicity. J. Nutrition.84:272, 1964.

FOOTNOTES

1. Clay supplement "A" is a pinkish tan clay obtained from a deposit near Brawley, California. It is an impure mixture of clays (or interlayered clay) in which halloysite predominates. Some montmorillonite is also present. It contains no detectable organic matter or quartz sand. A chemical analysis of this material indicated it has the following composition:

Ingredient	% by weight
Moisture	4.38
Silica	50.66
Alumina	20.92
Iron Oxide	1.73
Calcium	3.00
Magnesium	4.30
Titanium	0.65
Sodium	1.13
Potassium	2.05
Phosphate	0.16
Carbonate	3.31
Nitrogen	0.00
Sulfate	0.00

Spectrographic analysis

Manganese	0.046
Barium	0.095
Strontium	0.016
Lead	0.013
Tin	0.009
Copper	0.088
Nickel	0.005
Vanadium	0.009
Cobalt	0.002
Chromium	0.009
Zirconium	0.018
Boron	0.004
Gallium	0.005

The authors are indebted to Mr. H. K. Hebbard of the Cal-Min Company, Brawley, California, for providing the clay supplement "A" employed in the present investigation.

Obtained from Tumblebrook Farm, Inc., Brant Lake, N.Y.

The miniature pigs (Black Barrows) were obtained from the Hormel Institute, Austin, Minn. They were approximately 10 weeks of age at the start of the experiment.
Obtained from General Biochemicals, Chagrin Falls, Ohio.

The calcium-free salt mixture had the following composition:

Ammonium phosphate, Monobasic	110.24 gm
Copper Sulfate	0.39 gm
Ferric Citrate	22.04 gm
Manganous Sulfate	0.20 gm
Magnesium Sulfate	90.00 gm
Potassium Aluminum Sulfate	0.09 gm
Potassium Chloride	120.00 gm
Potassium Dihydrogen Phosphate	310.00 gm
Potassium Iodide	0.05 gm
Sodium Chloride	105.00 gm
Sodium Fluoride	0.57 gm

Preliminary studies indicate that the protective effects of clay supplement "A" when fed with the wheat flour-containing ration were due in part to its sodium content. The addition of Na_2HPO_4 to the basal ration (diet Al) at a level of 1.4 gm. Per kg. of diet, an amount of Na_2HPO_4 which contained the same amount of sodium present in the 4% clay supplement per kg. of diet A4, resulted in a significant weight increment over that obtained on the unsupplemented basal ration (diet Al). After 8 weeks of feeding the average weight increment of immature rats fed the Na_2HPO_4-containing diet was 169.0 gm in contrast to an average weight increment of 81.4 gm in rats fed the basal ration (diet Al). This was less, however, than the average weight increment of 189.6 gm of rats fed the ration containing 4% clay supplement "A" (diet A4). The growth-promoting effect of Na_2HPO_4 is in agreement with the recent report of Dodds and Law (19) that diet 256 of McClure (which is similar to diet Al of the present investigation) is deficient in sodium. Preliminary studies also indicated that rats fed the above Na_2HPO_4 supplement exhibited a significant increase in the amount of hemotopoietic tissue and an improved appearance in respect to the modeling and growth of spongiosa bone over that of rats fed the basal ration (diet A1). The $Na2HPO4$ supplement had no effect, however on the thickness and mineralization of cortical or trebacular bone in contrast to the marked protective effect of 4% clay supplement "A".

Afterward

The author has written volume one to whet the appetite for those eager to explore effective alternatives to allopathic medicine. It has been written to help empower the individual's ability to make the transition from a place of medical powerlessness to a place of self-empowered exploration of vital health. It has been written to help open minds that might otherwise be closed to something as strange as healing with the living earth, and it has been written to bridge the lonely gap between the usually isolated worlds that exist among individual and small groups of "clay disciples".

However, more than anything, it has been written as a preamble to Volume II, which is still to come: A modernization of effective natural and alternative medicine put forth in an open-ended system for healing and supporting vital health. The next book will be a handbook of clay therapy and natural medicine, and will be designed to teach people exactly how to use healing clays.

The success of this project is largely up to you, the reader. As long as there is a growing interest in authentic research and information about using healing clays, I will endeavor to diligently work to make the information available. As long as there is support for the book project, I will work to serve this need, and I will work to be certain that the knowledge and experience uncovered is evermore available to the people who may need it—free of charge. If this book has impacted your life, please let the author know!

The place where an author must go to write a book is a very isolated place of being. As I write these final words, I'm pleased at the thought of regaining my life back. The mental landscapes that I've frequented during these last six months of writing have been fatiguing.

I would like to offer a personal thanks to my father for his willingness to proofread and edit, and to my exceedingly lovely wife Tanya for mentally and emotionally offering her support and guidance for the project. I would also like to thank my mother for her willingness to step into the unknown and explore healing clays.

I would like to thank my eleven year old son Nicholas, a true clay disciple, for not only tolerating his father slaving away at the computer during all hours of the day and night, but also for being living proof of the profound healing properties of therapeutic clays.

Finally, I would like to thank master composers Chris Hinze (Zen and The Art Of Dance and Meditation), Gerald Arend (Klangwelt's

Age of Numbers), Thomas Otten (Closer to the Silence) and Michael Hoppe (Afterglow, with Martin Tillmann and TimWheater) for providing much of the background music which helped keep me sane and focused during many long hours of writing.

And as the crisp coolness of autumn gives way to the serene, slumberous tidings of winter, I wish you only the best in your exploration and discovery of vital health and wellness with the help of....

….**Water, Earth and Sunshine!**

- Jason R. Eaton, October 08, 2009

CPSIA information can be obtained
at www.ICGtesting.com
Printed in the USA
BVOW11s0928240716
456589BV00011B/143/P